The Bicentennial of John James Audubon

THE BICENTENNIAL

 With chapters by
MARY DURANT • MICHAEL HARWOOD
FRANK LEVERING • ROBERT OWEN PETTY
SCOTT RUSSELL SANDERS

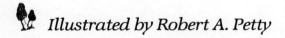 Illustrated by Robert A. Petty

INDIANA UNIVERSITY PRESS
BLOOMINGTON

OF *JOHN JAMES* AUDUBON

Alton A. Lindsey

Copyright © 1985 by Alton A. Lindsey
All rights reserved

No part of this book may be reproduced or utilized in any form or by any means, electronic or mechanical, including photocopying and recording, or by any information storage and retrieval system, without permission in writing from the publisher. The Association of American University Presses' Resolution on Permissions constitutes the only exception to this prohibition.

Manufactured in the United States of America

Library of Congress Cataloging in Publication Data
Lindsey, Alton A., 1907–
The bicentennial of John James Audubon.

Includes index.
1. Audubon, John James, 1785–1851. 2. Ornithologists—United States—Biography. 3. Artists—United States—Biography. I. Petty, Robert A. II. Durant, Mary B. III. Title.
QL31.A9L56   1985   598'.092'4 [B]   84-47791
ISBN 0-253-10650-8
1 2 3 4 5 89 88 87 86 85

To all those carrying Audubon's tradition forward

CONTENTS

Preface ix
Acknowledgments xiii

1. The Dream 1
2. The Compleat Naturalist 17
3. A Watershed for Ornithology, 31
   MICHAEL HARWOOD
4. Quill Pens, 48
   SCOTT RUSSELL SANDERS
5. Confronting the Wilderness, 66
   ROBERT OWEN PETTY
6. The Enchanted Forest, 78
   FRANK LEVERING
7. The Man Himself, 96
   MARY DURANT
8. Saving the Pieces 115
9. A Bird on the Hat 125
10. In His Name 136
11. Where to Look for Audubon 155

Epilogue 165
Audubon Biochronology 168
The Contributors 170
Index 172

Preface

April 26, 1985, marks the bicentennial of John James Audubon's birth in the town of Les Cayes in Santo Domingo, which is now Haiti, of French parents. We feel that this anniversary is highly noteworthy, and hope that our retrospective book by modern writers of diverse viewpoints is a suitable way of commemorating it.

The name Audubon is certainly distinctive. No other naturalist of note has borne that name, and no Audubon other than our partially self-named Jean Jacques Rabin Fougère Laforest Audubon is generally known. The combination of "Aud" with "bon" conjures up the *good sounds* of bird songs in the America of a bygone time. Today no individual with his surname is listed in either the Manhattan or the Greater Washington telephone directories. It is fortunate for Audubon's fame, and for the National Audubon Society which has disseminated it, that he was not christened John J. Smith instead.

Audubon's name is as distinguished as it is distinctive. Imagine a bird artist having had seven towns in as many states named for him! Mount Audubon is a 13,223-foot peak at the southern edge of Rocky Mountain National Park. Also bearing his name are a county in Iowa, a state park in Kentucky, and city parks or sections in New York, New Orleans, Louisville, and Memphis. Streets in cities and towns, including New Orleans and Montgomery, were named for him. The only naturalist who surpasses this record is Theodore Roosevelt, and he was not honored thus as a naturalist, although he was one. Literally as well as figuratively, Audubon put natural history on the map for the general public.

I wish to thank the writers who responded to my invitation to supplement my work with a new essay apiece. My intention in selecting these people was to show, without heavy-handed editing to eliminate all overlaps in coverage, the personal reactions of modern individuals representing a spectrum of backgrounds and viewpoints to a man whose varied talents and pervasive influence bestrode two hundred years of American life.

The writers include two widely recognized authorities on Audubon, one specialist in American studies, three college professors, four professional writers, three volunteer workers in conservation-preservation, two biological scientists, and six lovers of history both human and natural. This adds up to more than six writers because each of us wears more than one hat.

Many novelists have used the device of recapitulating the same event from different viewpoints, through the eyes of different narrators. The present book is not fiction, and each of us deals with a different facet of a multi-faceted subject, but there is still a slight element of that novelistic approach here. Each writer brings to his or her topic a unique perspective, but Audubon is only one person, and, despite all that has been written about him, a person who still seems to drift into and out of sharp focus.

All six of us are admirers of John James Audubon, though perhaps for different reasons, and are interested both in the real historic person and in how he has come to be seen in the interim between his time and ours. Any reader expecting uncritical adulation, in the vogue of much past writing about him, has come to the wrong book. Neither will a reader find here a "now it can be told" exposé. We are not out to prove either that Audubon was a hero or that he was not. We believe that present-day readers expect a balanced presentation of the facts of his life and career (which Audubon scholars have enunciated in stupendous detail elsewhere) and near-fetched interpretations of their significance to our time.

Audubon's was not the first published set of carefully done color plates and writings on North American birds. But he became more celebrated than any other artist-naturalist before or since. His first notable successor, Louis Agassiz Fuertes, and subsequent bird artists have depicted their subjects both more accurately and more artistically than Audubon did. Yet, two hundred years after his birth, his name is known to more people in the world than that of any other artist-naturalist, and this situation seems unlikely to change.

In other ways, too, Audubon captures our interest today. He epitomizes an era in our history when, it appears in hindsight, at least, an American, if not female or a black slave, could enjoy an individual freedom unusual in the span of human civilizations. Human life was not dominated by big business, big government, big labor, big media, big population, and big threats to its continued existence. His ideas were his own, not like modern organ transplants for the mind. Nothing he thought, did, or wrote was standardized. Such people are extremely rare. They usually are, as Audubon was, self-employed!

Definitely not a "genuine American primitive," Audubon was one of the most complex personalities in our nation's history. He was humble and arrogant, humorous and grave, gregarious and solitary, lazy and obsessively hard-working, versatile yet single-minded. He attracted incredibly devoted and helpful friends and was hounded by venomous and persistent enemies.

During his years of promoting subscriptions to *Birds of America* among wealthy potential patrons, Audubon saw the necessity for self-promotion, and he proved to be very good at it—nature had given him a superb start toward a glamorous personality. Putting his accomplishments in present-day terms, he not only created visual images of wild nature, but served also as writer, director, producer, narrator, advertising manager, and salesman. Who else could have put across, in the critical society of Britain and France, an apparently exorbitantly priced project based on one class of organisms in a distant country? It may have galled such a man to play the role of long-haired, wolfskin-clad American woodsman in the salons of Europe. Or perhaps, with his penchant for practical jokes, he enjoyed the irony. Although he did love wilderness and was quite at home there, Fate chose strangely when Audubon became a symbol for the mountain men, the *coureurs de bois*, the squawmen, trappers and fur traders, and homesteaders of the new continent. Contemporary countrymen regarded Daniel Boone as the quintessential American woodsman. Since legends acquire lives of their own, Audubon has come to symbolize both woodsman and conservationist, two somewhat antithetical types, in his adopted country. Both kinds of symbolism have always had a powerful grip on the American imagination, and today we realize that further loss of wilderness not only means the loss of a part of our past, but of a part of our future as well.

Not the least appeal of wood(s)craft today is the nostalgia associated with a lost art. The skills of "living off the land" as practiced by Audubon and Boone, and more recently by Nessmuk, Ernest Thompson Seton, and Dan Beard, are too exploitive and consumptive of nature for the population density of today. Hence, woodcraft has largely been abandoned in favor of using the lightweight gadgets and dehydrated foods one can carry into the back country. Although considerable tent-camping persists, probably to most people "camping" now connotes dragging out from urban life a figurative extension cord behind one's recreational trailer or mobile "camper."

The last example of old-time woodcraft that I saw was in the autumn of 1920, at a Scout pow-wow near the Ohio River, the stream which Audubon knew and loved best. The chief attraction was old Grizzly Smith with his long gray beard (he was then the Scout Executive of the Pittsburgh Council)—we were sure that he must have been a western mountain man. Every camper watched in fascination as he prepared his shelter for the night among the fallen leaves in that colorful grove of sugar maples near Sewickley. With his keen hunting knife he cut some low, slender branches from the trees, sharpened both ends of each, and thrust them arch-like into the ground about three feet apart and bowed upward to the same height. This formed a framework about seven feet long, into which he wove smaller branchlets still bearing green leaves, to form a cocoon-like wickiup open at one end. Grizzly and the boys then gathered armfuls of crisp dead leaves from the ground and crammed the shelter full of them. At bedtime, we watched the old woodsman remove his boots, loosen his clothing, and burrow full-length into the mass of bright leaves for the night. When the bemused young Scouts next looked around their firelit campground, their commonplace pup-tents had somehow been transformed into wickiups, buffalo-hide tepees, overturned voyageur canoes, log cabins, and sod huts. And, as they went about their own preparations for the night, "All lost, wild America was burning in their eyes."

ALTON A. LINDSEY
West Lafayette, Indiana

Acknowledgments

The quotation about Boone used on page 20 was taken from Aldo Leopold's book *A Sand County Almanac* (1949 and reprints) with the kind permission of the publisher, Oxford University Press.

Several sentences included in my Preface appeared earlier in the author's book *Naturalist on Watch*, reused by permission of the copyright-holder and publisher, Merry Lea Environmental Learning Center of Goshen College, Goshen, Indiana.

The idea for a bicentennial book on Audubon was suggested by Professor Scott R. Sanders of the Indiana University Department of English, who also provided one of the chapters. For various courtesies I am grateful to Elizabeth S. Lindsey, Olin Sewall Pettingill, George E. Watson of the Division of Birds of the National Museum of Natural History, and Director Edward W. Graham of the Audubon Wildlife Sanctuary at Audubon, Pennsylvania. Helpful comments on Chapter 1 were provided by Mr. Michael Harwood and Ms. Mary Durant, authors of *On the Road with John James Audubon*. Joseph Ewan answered several botanical questions. Douglas James supplied the list of Audubon's bird names that remain valid. Information about the current structure and operations of the National Audubon Society was kindly supplied by personnel in the Central Regional Office in Michigan City, Indiana, and in the national office, but these individuals hold no responsibility for the way I have summarized and reworked the voluminous material for Chapter 10 nor for any other portion of the book. Through the kind permission of the American Library Association in Chicago, the one and a half pages of Chapter 1 on the present status of *Birds of America* sets and copper engravings was winnowed from here and there in the remarkable book *The Double Elephant Folio: The Story of Audubon's Birds of America* (1973), by Waldemar Fries.

The Bicentennial of John James Audubon

The disappearance of John Jones's shadow

The Dream

1

> One of the most extraordinary things amongst all these adverse circumstances was that I never for a day gave up listening to the songs of our birds, or watching their peculiar habits, or delineating them in the best way I could; nay, during my deepest troubles I frequently would wrench myself from the persons around me, and retire to some secluded part of our noble forests. . . . Yet through these dark ways I was being led to the development of the talents I loved, and which have brought so much enjoyment to us all.
>
> —Audubon

John James Audubon was thirty-four when he made the first cent from his art (a portrait), and he was thirty-nine when he first had an art piece published. He had been preparing for and working on a great book for a quarter-century without knowing that that was what he was doing. He did not even know that it was work.

The boy Jean lived near Nantes, France, from age six to eighteen; there he happily roamed the fields and woodlands and started when very young to draw birds and small mammals. He received lessons in music, dancing, and fencing, and played the violin, flageolet, and flute, but little formal education came his way and the child did not learn to be industrious and responsible. In later life he sometimes bolstered his reputation by mentioning art lessons with the famous David in Paris, but there is doubt that they occurred. His unhappy experiences at an academy convinced him that he was not cut out for a military or naval career.

There was deep affection in the Audubon family, but his father worried about his son's future and decided it would be brighter in America. He owned a farm two miles north of Valley Forge, originally part of the large Penn grants. The stone house at Mill Grove estate had been built in 1762 and was later owned by John Penn, a nephew of William. John was the governor of Pennsylvania appointed by the British Crown. Young Audubon went there in 1803.

The house, now an Audubon museum within a bird sanctuary, stands on a hillside overlooking the Perkiomen, a delightful small river. The youth spent most of his time in fishing, hunting, speed skating, taxidermy, drawing, music, and dancing. Without effective supervision, he had a fairly free hand to follow his old interests in nature and visual art, with a workroom "studio" on the third floor of the spacious farmhouse. He invented a method of using stiff wires for posing birds in natural postures for his art work. Although Audubon lived at Mill Grove for three years, he did not attempt to make the acquaintance of the naturalists, artists, or museum people of nearby Philadelphia; while his interest in birds was serious in its own way, it was not yet scientific.

William Bakewell, a neighbor of substantial means, late from England, had children about Audubon's age. His daughter Lucy was sixteen when Audubon met her during a visit to the Bakewell estate, Fatland Ford, and he soon added portraiture to his artistic interests. In 1805 he visited his father and stepmother in France to discuss his marriage to Lucy and the affairs of Mill Grove, where lead mining was being attempted along with farming. Soon he was working in a New York countinghouse to obtain business experience. Then, with a partner, he took a shipment of goods to Louisville, the French settlement at the Falls of the Ohio, a scenic wonder since obliterated by the Army Corps of Engineers. In the spring of 1808, Audubon went back to Pennsylvania, disposed of his remaining interest in Mill Grove, and married Lucy. He was twenty-three and she was twenty, a daughter of wealth now married to a man without promising financial prospect.

The morning after their wedding the couple left by public coach on the arduous journey across the Alleghenies to Pittsburgh, en route to Louisville where John had decided to go into business. At Pittsburgh the newlyweds joined a party going down the Ohio by flatboat.

In Louisville, there were cultivated French people who had escaped the guillotine. Bird life was abundant on an important migration route. The settlement was backed by the near-wilderness of pioneer Kentucky. Audubon made long trips to buy and transport wares for the store he operated with a partner, Ferdinand Rozier. The latter and a clerk named Pope spent far more than their just share of time behind the counters, while Audubon was out collecting and painting birds and taking notes on their "manners." His art was crude, but improving, and he was building up a portfolio of what he then thought were finished pieces. Probably he could scarcely remember a time when he had not been following the same pleasant hobby, as satisfying as it was unsystematic and disorganized.

The "father of American ornithology," Alexander Wilson, was on one of his journeys to solicit subscribers to his book. He came to Audubon's store, and was flabbergasted when shown Audubon's portfolio. Audubon examined Wilson's work with equal interest.

> I felt surprised and gratified [wrote Audubon] at the sight of his volumes, turned over a few of the plates, and had already taken a pen to write my name in his favour, when my partner rather abruptly said to me in French, "My dear Audubon, what induces you to subscribe to this work? Your drawings are certainly far better, and again, you must know as much of the habits of American birds as this gentleman." Whether Mr. Wilson understood French or not, or if the suddenness with which I paused, disappointed him, I cannot tell; but I clearly perceived that he was not pleased. Vanity and the encomiums of my friend prevented me from subscribing. Mr. Wilson asked me if I had many drawings of birds. I rose, took down a large portfolio . . . and showed him . . . the whole of the contents, with the same patience with which he had shown me his own engravings.
>
> His surprise appeared great, as he told me he never had the most distant idea that any other individual than himself had been engaged in forming such a collection. He asked me if it was my intention to publish, and when I answered in the negative, his surprise seemed to increase. And, truly, such was not my intention; for, until long after, when I met the Prince of Musignano [Charles Bonaparte] in Philadelphia, I had not the least idea of presenting the fruits of my labours to the world.

Audubon writes that he lent Wilson several of his drawings while the latter was in Louisville. He presented him socially, took him on hunts during which they collected birds Wilson had never seen before, and even offered both to let Wilson use his drawings and observations for no reward other than credit for the artwork and to enter into correspondence about birds. "But I did not subscribe to his work, for, even at that time, my collection was greater than his." Wilson made no reply to Audubon's offers of help, and the latter was astonished much later to read, in the ninth volume of *American Ornithology*, Wilson's account of his Louisville stay: "I bade adieu to Louisville where I had neither received one act of civility . . . one subscriber, nor one new bird . . . Science or literature has not one friend in this place." Alexander Wilson and his friends in the Philadelphia establishment continued down the years to be both jealous of Audubon and hostile to him—they were to prevent his obtaining a publisher in America.

After two years in Louisville, the Audubons moved to Henderson, Kentucky, to operate a general store. (A superb wildland tract near Henderson is now Audubon State Park.) But Audubon's heart was not in his work as a merchant; his meeting with Wilson may have given him the idea of eventually making his hobby a profession. More and more of his energies were spent in finding and painting new birds. Times were hard; his assets became depleted by unsuccessful investments like a steamboat and a grist and lumber mill which functioned erratically. After years of ups and downs, the business failed and the partnership with Rozier was dissolved. Once, Audubon was arrested, and he escaped debtor's prison in Louisville only by declaring bankruptcy. He had lost all of Lucy's inheritance. Two young daughters had died, and his sons were eight and ten when he began trying to make some sort of living for his family as an itinerant portrait painter and teacher of art and music, studying and painting birds withal. His wife worked as a governess and teacher, commenting wryly, "If I were jealous I should have a bitter time of it, for every bird is my rival."

The artist stored two hundred of his drawings in a case while he visited Philadelphia; on his return he found that they had been destroyed by a family of Norway rats nesting in the box.

> I slept not for several nights, and the days passed like days of oblivion, until . . . I took up my gun, my note-book, and my pencil and went forth in the woods as gaily as if nothing had happened. I felt pleased that I might now make much better drawings than before; and, ere a period not exceeding three years had elapsed, I had my portfolio filled again.

Early in 1820 the Audubons moved to Cincinnati, where he worked as a taxidermist for the economically precarious Western Museum. Despite all discouragements, John and Lucy decided in 1820 that he should devote himself to the great goal of depicting all the birds of North America. He had already lived fifty-four percent of his eventual life-span before he made this leap of faith.

In order to increase his collection sufficiently to propose its publication as a more complete and better work than Wilson's, Audubon left in late 1820 with apprentice Joseph Mason on a flatboat heading downstream from Cincinnati, for an eight-month absence. During this first professional trip as an artist-naturalist, he supported himself and Mason by odd-job painting and tutoring. Was Fate trying to test the depth of his resolve when his pocket was picked irretrievably, and when he lost an important portfolio on his way to New Orleans? (Porters had mixed it in with a pile of luggage. Fortunately, it was eventually sent on to him, much later.)

Finding a meager market for his portraiture in and around New Orleans, the naturalist obtained a tutoring position at Oakley Plantation near St. Francisville. There he enjoyed much free time for finding and painting new birds, and spent the summer thus profitably, but left later after a falling out with his employers, the Pirries. Lucy met him in New Orleans in mid-December; she found congenial employment running a private school on a Louisiana plantation.

During this stay in New Orleans, Audubon seems to have received advice, from at least one person familiar with Britain, that he should look for a publisher in Europe. In 1824 Audubon sought for a publisher of his folios in Philadelphia and New York, and conferred with scientists and artists. Some of his writings on natural history were published as separate papers, but no publisher would take on his paintings. His failure to credit young Mason for the botanical additions turned some people against him, as well it might, and his brash tactlessness in lauding his own work while denigrating Wilson's proved a poor tactic in Philadelphia. That city was then the intellectual and scientific capital of North America, but even though Audubon had begun his study of natural history within twenty miles of there he could realize his goal only by playing the role of American backwoodsman on the other side of the Atlantic, where Wilson had not preceded him.

Leaving his family in Louisiana for Lucy to earn money, as was her essential custom, Audubon boarded a ship at New Orleans on May 17, 1826, bound for the British Isles. Risky as it undoubtedly was for a foreigner among a people he had long disliked on principle, this was a logical step after his definitive failure to find support in America. It amounted to a fresh start after learning some hard lessons, with a new degree of dependence on his basic personal resources—his artistic talent, unparalleled experiences, and attractive personality. Not the least satisfaction in succeeding would be the bolstering of his family's understandably dwindling faith in him. John James Audubon had finally grown up—it was a new and thoroughly realistic Audubon who wrote home from Europe, "It is not the naturalists that I wish to please altogether, I assure thee. It is the wealthy part of the community. The first can only speak well or ill of me, but the latter will fill my pockets."

Liverpool was the first European city Audubon touched, bearing his letters of introduction from prominent friends and well-wishers in America. New friends of wealth and influence, especially the Rathbones and Roscoes, started him off on a resounding social and scientific success over several weeks there; he even made some money from an exhibition at the Royal Institution. When a Liverpool lady, a relative by marriage, made bold to urge him to cut his flowing locks and change his manner of dress from that of an uncouth frontiersman to that of an English gentleman, Audubon ignored the well-meant counsel. Presumably, intuition told him that the woodsman image was a valuable part of his stock-in-trade in Europe where the American frontier was a place of "glamour." It certainly proved an asset during two visits with the famed writer Sir Walter Scott, who naively judged that his guest's predominant characteristic was his great simplicity.

On arrival at an English or Scottish city during the early part of his promotional years, Audubon would rent rooms, then take his letters to prominent people and invite them to come and inspect the bird paintings in his rooms. Once an individual, family, or a group had appeared there, the artist would go through part of his portfolio with them, holding up one picture at a time, answering questions, and listening to comments. When this succeeded (and visitors were very rarely rude but were often indifferent), he would be given the opportunity to meet others who could help him, and would often be entertained at houses of wealth and fashion. The ensuing social whirl was a means toward the end of enlisting suitable people as early as possible during his visit to each city and augmenting his reputation (the process was rather like interest compounding daily). In the larger cities, formal exhibitions would be set up in cultural or scientific institutions. He often lent his presence to these events; though he was reluctant to appear mercenary by charging admission, this was necessary to meet expenses. It was a killing pace Audubon had set for himself in his determination to succeed, and little time remained for rest and sleep.

After Liverpool Audubon went to Manchester. The indifference he encountered there made him fear that his taking Liverpool by storm had been a fluke. Deciding that he was not yet ready to dare London, he next went to Edinburgh, which, though smaller, was an important cultural center in its own right.

Scotland's capital was to prove a fortunate choice for promoting his work and himself, although his start there was disappointing. Soon he met the capable engraver W. H. Lizars. In the painter's apartment Lizars highly praised the spectacular, life-sized bird images, and proposed at once that he would like to engrave some of them for Audubon to sell separately. Lizars began lining up people who could not only appreciate their value but might also subscribe and help bring the work to public attention.

Audubon wanted them sold in a more aggregated and permanent form, but could not meet the expenses of going far in that direction. The two men agreed on a compromise plan. Lizars would issue the colored engravings in "numbers" or sets of five; Audubon would collect two guineas for each number, on delivery, so that payment by customers, and by Audubon to Lizars, would be on the installment plan. Customers who signed with Audubon for the whole eventual work would pay, not in advance, but piecemeal as they received the numbers, or volumes in the case of later subscribers. Probably few would have been willing to pay the whole expensive cost at once.

To reproduce the life-size paintings in the original spectacular size was a crucial decision, setting *Birds of America* apart from any other book on any subject. A glance would distinguish it from the work of Wilson or any other rival alive or dead, as the very first Double Elephant Folio. Each page was 39.5 by 26.5 inches!

Lizars had to duplicate Audubon's lines on large copper plates to form mirror-image copies of the originals. These plates were used to print black lines and outlines on fine-quality paper. (It is still fine after a century and a half. The prints will long outlast most books published today, for the acidic paper now commonly used has, according to the American Association for the Advancement of Science, a life of only twenty to thirty years.) After printing, artists at Lizars' shop added the colors to each copy by hand, using Audubon's painting as a guide. Because Audubon's technical skills were now much greater than they had been, Audubon set himself to redo many of the earlier paintings before allowing the engraving. Another problem was his frequent dissatisfaction over the careless work of one or another of the colorists, making it necessary to chide the manager about quality control.

Lizars was astute in public relations—he had Audubon sit for his publicity portrait garbed as the American woodsman in his wolf-skin coat, with hair falling over his shoulders. In Liverpool, the naturalist had enjoyed a sudden bright lightning-flash of acclaim; it showed him what the future *might* hold for him. In Edinburgh he learned the practicalities from Lizars, and settled into a round of demanding work and social responsibilities which could, if he survived the pace, eventually fulfill his long-held dream. He painted for many long hours day and night, often with an audience of potential customers; hostesses of the nobility and the wealthy happily exploited the Audubon vogue. It was as though a modern novelist, instead of merely making the rounds of retail outlets to autograph his book for buyers after publication, had first to write it in public also.

Looking ahead, the naturalist realized that the task would necessitate long stays in Europe. Besides painting and augmenting the list of names in his subscription book, it was necessary to deliver numbers as they came out, collect payments, insure continued high production quality, and hold up the business end in general. He could not accomplish all this alone. From Edinburgh he wrote to Lucy, "I am now better aware of the advantage of a family working in unison than ever, and am quite satisfied that by acting conjointly and by my advice we can realize a handsome fortune for each of us. It needs but industry and perseverance."

One of Audubon's triumphs in Edinburgh was his reception by the prestigious Wernerian Society. There he demonstrated, with dead pigeons, his method of posing birds, supported by wires, in a semblance of natural postures. An officer of the society intoned Audubon's written account of buzzard habits, and Audubon displayed his drawing of that species. At the following meeting, Audubon was elected to membership, thus collecting the first set of distinguished initials to place after his name on the folio pages.

Before leaving Edinburgh for London in early April of 1827 with his first printed prospectus, the woodsman submitted to a haircut. He enrolled a few subscribers in cities along the way. On this second try in Manchester he garnered eighteen signatures in his subscription book, more than anywhere else to that time. For the first week in London, Audubon was busy delivering his letters of introduction to pompous servants at impressive doors, and the results were gratifying. However, a letter from Lizars brought what seemed to be bad news—his colorists were on strike and Audubon would have to engage others in London. The upshot for Audubon was that, deprived of his main income, he was forced to make new arrangements, and he did so for the engraving as well as the coloring. Lizars had done the first ten plates (two numbers or Parts); the rest of the *Birds of America* was produced by the establishment of Robert Havell and his son of the same name, in London.

The Havells were slightly better than Lizars, the new agreement brought the naturalist financial and other advantages, and Lizars was not sorry to relinquish the growing responsibility, now that he had helped to usher Audubon into success. For success, in significant measure, had already touched Audubon—George IV, King of England, had subscribed even though he and Audubon had not met. Audubon did meet the extremely rich and notorious Marchioness of Hertford, who was then the King's mistress even though the wife of the living Marquess. She "promised to recommend my Work to her large and valuable Circle of acquaintances." One noble lady pasted the hundred plates from the first Volume on the walls of one of her mansions. George IV was succeeded by William IV, whose wife had subscribed earlier. On the other side of the ledger was the fact that Philadelphian George Ord, Audubon's most outspoken and persistent critic, had come to England and was stirring up trouble for the naturalist in the Royal Society.

After twenty-six months in England and Scotland, Audubon, with his naturalist friend William Swainson, crossed over to France for two months, but there he collected only a dozen signatures. He went to much trouble to enroll King Charles X, and finally succeeded through officials.

Back in England, in November of 1828 Audubon could count 144 subscribers, a moderate success only. Each had received fifty birds, or ten unbound Parts, delivered in installments, or, for the most recent buyers, all together; they were delivered in tin cases, with the two guineas per number payable on delivery. The first binding was done only after the initial hundred plates were ready, constituting Volume I; thus the earliest subscribers received unbound numbers of that volume. Some later subscribers also got unbound plates, since binding them cost extra.

For each few steps his subscription list took forward, it retreated one step through cancellations or deaths. In order to meet his expenses, Audubon had to paint, for immediate cash sales, subjects not necessarily related to birds. Many of the extra paintings were done in oils, not the artist's best medium. Despite all the celebrity accorded him in London, the high cost of his *Birds* discouraged potential subscribers. Only through nearly superhuman efforts during the years spent in Great Britain was enough money forthcoming, even with Lucy's earnings while she remained in Louisiana supporting herself and the boys. Little wonder that his moods swung between elation and long bouts with depressed feelings. Things were going well when he wrote the following in the modest third person and not for publication. Much writing home in this vein was with the hope of persuading Lucy to join him in Britain, an idea which she long resisted, even ignored.

> Who would believe that a lonely individual, who landed in England without a friend in the whole country, and with only sufficient pecuniary means to travel through it as a visitor, could have accomplished such a task as this publication? Who would believe that once in London Audubon had only one sovereign left in his pocket, and did not know of a single individual to whom he could apply to borrow another, when he was on the verge of failure in the very beginning of his undertaking; and above all, who would believe that he extricated himself from all his difficulties, not by borrowing money, but by rising at four o'clock in the morning, working hard all day, and disposing of his works at a price which a common laborer would have thought little better than sufficient remuneration for his work.

Having failed to persuade Lucy to come to England, and needing new species to paint for *Birds of America*, Audubon decided to return temporarily to America. The voyage began on April 1, 1829, and brought him to New York in early May. He staged an exhibition there and another in Baltimore, but, more important, he was in time for the spring migration along the Atlantic Flyway. He worked in New Jersey, especially along the coast, in Great Pine Swamp in Pennsylvania, and during a New Orleans trip. By spending far more time in field work than in drumming up subscriptions, Audubon was able to take back more than forty new paintings when he returned to England with his wife in April of 1830.

With completion of the folios of bird portraits seemingly assured even though some years away, Audubon decided to work up his copious notes, memoranda, and knowledge of bird life for publication. The new work would be titled *Ornithological Biography*; it was to be published in five octavo volumes, separate from but supplemental to the double elephant volumes. There was the naturalist, at age forty-five, starting another highly ambitious facet of his life work before the major enterprise was anything like finished.

He needed an editor with scientific qualifications superior to his own, who would also be able to turn Audubon's writing into standard good English. The choice fell on young Scottish zoologist William MacGillivray. His collaboration involved far more than "correcting" and polishing the master's writing; as the joint effort progressed from October, 1830, he found himself giving an intensive and not-so-short course in technical ornithology, including internal anatomy, to an eager and retentive pupil. Throughout the work with MacGillivray, Audubon, field man *par excellence*, had become a skilled and persevering dissector in detailed anatomical studies. It was well that Audubon had largely heeded the advice, given him by the Secretary of the Royal Society, to cease publishing scientific papers as too distracting, and save his material for such a work as was now being written. It was decided, too, that for every five bird biographies, Audubon would lighten the tome with one "episode" about backwoods America. Many years later, his granddaughter (son John's child) Maria R. Audubon was to include these in her two-volume work on his life and journals, and, still later, ornithologist F. H. Herrick assembled and edited them as a fascinating book, *Delineations of American Scenery and Character*.

In his introduction to the bird biography volumes, Audubon described how he proportioned the life-size drawings. "Of avoiding error in this respect I am particularly desirous. Not only is every object, as a whole, of the natural size, but also every portion of each object. . . . The bill, the feet, the legs, the claws, the very feathers as they project one beyond another, have been accurately measured."

So far, Audubon's collection was weak on oceanic, subtropical, and western species; in 1831 he brought Lucy back from England and began to augment the paintings of these groups and other birds new to him. Working his way southward in the winter of 1831-32, he enjoyed the gratis use of government vessels, and made many spectacular paintings as far down as Key West and the Dry Tortugas.

During the summer of 1833, he and his assistants in art and taxidermy cruised along the coasts of southeastern Canada and Labrador. The naturalist was in his prime throughout this period of productive travel in the early Thirties. From the professional standpoint, those were the relatively few really golden years for Audubon.

In 1834, after a good winter of painting in North Carolina, Audubon sailed with his wife back to England, where his affairs had suffered from his absence. The following year, when he was fifty, marked the issuance of the third volume of his *Ornithological Biography*, and near-completion of the third *Birds of America* volume. Lucy and son Victor were living in England and supervising the family business during Audubon's absences in America, where he returned in 1836 and again in 1837. The Audubons had an engraver but did not have a publisher, since they really constituted a private publishing group themselves. Often they had difficulty paying the Havell firm as the engraving and coloring progressed there. Victor might have garnered more subscriptions as his father expected him to do, but he did little more than collect for those numbers and volumes he delivered.

In 1836 between Audubon's last two stays in England, he was elated to be able to purchase ninety-three duplicate specimens taken in the Rockies and the Columbia River valley by Thomas Nuttall and John K. Townsend. From that material he painted eight species new to his folios. Then in the spring of 1837 he sailed along the Gulf Coast, visiting Galveston and Houston, and met Sam Houston in the latter new town. The prevailing economic depression prevented his obtaining the number of American subscribers that he needed for him to get out of the woods financially.

Back in England, he completed the "Large Work" on birds on June 16, 1838, "consisting of 435 plates including 497 species." "An immediate weight from off my shoulders, and a great relief to my ever fidgety and anxious mind respecting this immense undertaking." The subscribers were also glad to see the end of it, since many were wearied of the seemingly endless paintings and payments. Eleven more months were required before the publication date of the fifth and last volume of the *Biography* to accompany the *Birds*.

Despite herculean, long-drawn-out efforts for producing and marketing *Birds of America*, it had fallen short of real financial success abroad; in America many subscribers cancelled because of the 1837 panic. In the autumn of 1839, soon after finally returning to New York, the family engaged to publish the bird paintings in a form more practical for the buyer of moderate means. Young John, with an ambition now rivalling his father's industry, reduced the portraits by *camera lucida*. Sixty-five new ones were added, bringing the total to 500. They were lithographed instead of being engraved, and the edition was published in the manageable octavo size. The seven volumes, each including both plates and text of the biographies, appeared from 1840 through 1844. Audubon the elder again hit the road in America, and found that buyers were comfortable with the price of $100 per set. Income from this edition enabled the Audubons, including their sons Victor and John and their families, to live in their large place in New York City, Minniesland, in the comfort that Lucy had theretofore missed.

Rev. John Bachman, whom Audubon met in Charleston, South Carolina, while en route to Florida in late 1831, was to become his closest friend and collaborator. The Audubon boys were to marry two of Bachman's daughters; Maria became the wife of John Woodhouse Audubon, and Eliza that of Victor. In 1840 the two naturalists began a major work, with the forbidding title *The Viviparous Quadrupeds of North America*. The subject was simply the mammals! With much input of mostly raw material from Audubon, Bachman was responsible for the final text. Young Johnnie was the co-artist with his father, and the art, like that in the octavo *Birds*, was lithographed. The size was imperial folio, not the great double elephant, and resembled the original *Birds* in having separate volumes for the textual material. Few of the bird paintings (only those done under late pressure for completion of the big *Birds* volume IV) had depicted birds which Audubon had not seen alive, but it was simply not possible for him to adhere to that rule for the mammals work.

An expedition, Audubon's last, to the Upper Missouri and Yellowstone rivers was made in 1843. Paintings, observations, and scientific measurements were needed for the *Quadrupeds* volumes. Audubon was only fifty-eight, but he complained in his journal about feeling old. He allowed the dramatic and dangerous hunts for elk and obsessive searches for bighorn rams to distract him and his assistants from needed attention to smaller mammals. Even with four assistants with him on this trip, it did not yield scientific results to fulfill Bachman's expectations.

The first folio volume of the *Quadrupeds* was published in 1845. The next year, after the second book of mammal paintings was issued, Audubon's sight and health were so poor that he left the remaining work to the others involved. The third and last folio volume came out in 1848. John Woodhouse Audubon had blossomed into a capable artist; he painted 71 of the 155 plates in the three volumes. Bachman had been writing to his old friend, pressing him to continue supplying observations, reference books, and specimens, not understanding how things were with Audubon. After Bachman visited him in May of 1848 he wrote, "His noble mind is all in ruins." John James Audubon died at Minniesland on January 27, 1851.

The first prints of birds in double elephant size were published in late 1826, when Lizars' first engravings were released in a "number" of five prints, to the summer of 1838. The first three volumes contain a hundred plates each, and the fourth, which weighs fifty-six pounds, has 135. There are large, middle-sized, and small plates in the volumes. The last volume of *Birds* was followed eleven months later by the final volume of the bird biographies.

As one leafs through *Birds of America* or one of its several reduced reprintings, a drastic difference from later bird books becomes conspicuous. The sequence of plates follows no systematic plan, but is haphazard, apparently an artifact of the artist's convenience and the timing of the final paintings he used. The watermark of the excellent rag paper shows the Whatman name, usually, and the date the paper was made. Various types of bindings were offered; this factor and the proportion of numbers bound for a customer determined the total price. For each bound, complete set taken to America, Audubon charged $1,070. His records show that he spent a total of $115,640 on this project from 1827 through 1838, "not calculating any of my expense, or that of my family."

In 1983, one set of the 435 plates, unbound and unmounted, sold in lots at a New York auction for a total of $1,700,000. Audubon's Trumpeter Swan went for $45,100, the record for a single original Audubon engraving.

Waldemar H. Fries devoted many years to tracking down 131 extant sets and described them, their production and subsequent history, in full detail as a major portion of his 500-page book entitled *The Double Elephant Folio: The Story of Audubon's Birds of America*. Although the list of original subscribers shows 308 names, about eighty of them persons in America, less than two hundred complete sets were produced. The precise number is not known—subscribers fell away after signing, for various reasons, so that the number of copies produced fell far short of the full number of listed names. In addition to the complete sets, of which Fries located 134 and inspected 131, he found fourteen incomplete sets. Also in existence here and there are original prints as individual entities, and collections comprising a few loose prints.

The legends on the original plates include "Part" numeral (usually Roman), common name, scientific name (often obsolete now), an indication of which bird is which when more than one is shown, the names of plants, reptiles, or other kinds of species shown in the plate, the artist's name, the engraver's name, and the date engraved. There is considerable variation in the lettering engraved on the plates and in the descriptive legends, and all this is interesting to bibliophiles. Three different legends were used from time to time under the Wild Turkey, Plate 1.

The initials after Audubon's engraved name, (usually limited to two sets although he acquired more membership, fellowship, and award honors as time went on), represented the Wernerian Society, Linnean Society, Royal Society, etc. The three engravers credited were William H. Lizars, Robert Havell, and Robert Havell, Jr. The engravers worked from the artist's watercolors. The Havells worked together in making many plates beyond Lizars' ten; later they worked separately, the son doing the engraving while the father printed, colored, and supervised other colorists. From 1831 onward, the son handled everything under his own name, and from 1832, when his father died, he signed himself as merely Robert Havell.

The 435 heavy, bulky copper plates from which the prints were made were shipped from England to New York in 1839. Nearly all were stored in a warehouse and a few of these were damaged in the widespread city fire of 1845. After his father's death, young John constructed a small building on the Minniesland estate for storage of the remaining plates. In 1863 Lucy offered them to the Smithsonian Institution, but nothing was done.

Since the Audubons could find no buyer on the artistic merits, they sold 350 of them, more or less oxidized, in 1870 to the highest bidder for old copper. Most of these engravings were shipped to Ansonia, Connecticut, to be melted into copper bars. Charles A. Cowles, a boy of fourteen who was interested in birds and taxidermy, happened to be watching while workmen were loading the furnace, and noticed a bird's foot on a plate about to be thrown in. Frantic appeals to the workmen, the foreman, the superintendent, and his father the general manager brought no encouragement, even though Charles had washed the plate with acid and revealed the Black Vulture engraving, Plate 106. The boy's mother inspected the plate, recognized it as an Audubon, and directed her husband to save them.

A few were sent to the American Museum of Natural History and to the U.S. National Museum. Those which his family kept were later bought from the estate by Charles. He sent two of them gratis to Audubon's granddaughter Maria R. Audubon, who later donated them to the American Museum. These are the Snow Goose, Plate 381, and the Great White Heron, Plate 281. Seventy-eight of the engraved copper sheets, including the famed Wild Turkey, are now extant, according to Fries. The Metropolitan Museum of Art has Plate 11, the Bald Eagle, and seven others. The museum at Mill Grove has the Gyrfalcon, Plate 196.

As for the bound sets of *Birds of America*, it is surely appropriate that the National Audubon Society possesses one of them in its New York office. Another set is at the Mill Grove house in the Audubon Wildlife Sanctuary owned and operated by Montgomery County at Audubon, Pennsylvania. An 1827 set, one of the earliest produced, that was formerly to be seen at Audubon House in Key West, is now owned by the Historical Association of Southern Florida, which opened a new museum in 1984 in Miami where the Double Elephant set is on display.

A number of the larger museums in the United States and many university and college libraries, in the eastern states mainly, have one set apiece. The museum at Audubon State Park near Henderson, Kentucky, houses one set and many other valuable Audubon memorabilia. Some libraries of various levels of government in this and other nations have bound sets. Mr. Fries' book brought the story down nearly to its publication date, 1973.

The four Audubons, with much help from their extended family including Bachman, and some from apprentices and assistant artists, had eventually succeeded in fulfilling the father's original dream, and gone far beyond it. They had self-financed, privately published, and distributed expensive and highly acclaimed productions on birds and mammals—four major works of several to many volumes each, combining art with natural history, and deserving attention on both the popular and scientific levels. This stupendous tour-de-force resulted from a family enterprise the like of which had not been seen before. Anyone who had known John James Audubon only during the first half of his life would have been astounded!

The Compleat Naturalist

2

> Compare naturalists with any other sect, religious or irreligious, such as poets, philosophers, physicians, divines, admirals, generals, or worthies in general, civil or military, and you will acknowledge that they are, peculiarly, a peculiar people, zealous in good works. . . . Let us introduce you to Naturalists whom we are confident you will take to at once most kindly.
>
> —Blackwoods Magazine (Edinburgh) 1831, reviewing Audubon and Wilson

Many a field biologist will cough uncomfortably if introduced as a naturalist. His attitude may be based on the distinction between professionals and amateurs or on the differences between modern scientists and the naturalists of history. Less justifiably, scorn of naturalists is often a form of snobbery based on the misconception that whereas natural history was "descriptive," present-day science is not. Actually, all the physical and biological sciences are descriptive. Fundamental interpretation addressing the basic question "Why?" is the domain of philosophy, religion, and art (including literature), not science.

A naturalist is a generalist of Nature, whereas most research scientists prefer, or are forced by the proliferation of facts, principles, and techniques, to specialize. A professional ornithologist who works only in the laboratory and library, or only on the one class Aves, is not a naturalist. He studies aspects of the *science* of bird life, while the great majority of amateur birders see birds as the subjects of recreation (in a broad and wonderful sense) rather than subjects of scientific interest. To rate as a naturalist, amateur or professional, one must have a wide, but not necessarily deep, knowledge of the natural world, with some science in the mix but not necessarily predominant over visual or literary art. By outlining the four main kinds of naturalists recognizable today, we may see where LaForest Audubon, as he sometimes called himself, finds place in the professions that deal with outdoor Nature.

Teaching naturalists often consider themselves "interpretive naturalists" because they bring to the public the scientific material discovered by others. Naturalists in national and state parks, nature centers, museums, zoos, preserves, and wildlife sanctuaries speak and write simply and clearly, addressing themselves primarily to the laymen. The editors and staffs of natural history magazines belong here also. Teaching naturalists are not expected to perform and publish original research on natural phenomena; they are productive as educators rather than as scientists or litterateurs.

Artist-naturalists include painters and photographers of movies and stills. The late Ansel Adams is honored as an artist-naturalist and preservationist. Visual artists of nature are now coming to the fore at the expense of writing naturalists. In most current popular nature books, color pictures tend to overwhelm the text, as the visual influence of television carries over to the printed page. Looking at or watching pictures is easier than reading, and the shift in popularity from the Word to the Image has paralleled the general development of technology toward increased etherealization. Electromagnetic waves coming through directly, or bounced back to Earth from circling satellites, provide a far more ethereal and rapid medium of communication than paper, printer's ink, and the mails or bookstores. Outdoor pop science has attained splendid heights in some recent TV series; the better ones do not emphasize chase and capture. My one reservation about many of these programs (not applicable to Captain Cousteau's) is that the photographers and scientists are completely overshadowed by the narrators, who often are actors unable to pronounce crucial words.

The *literary-naturalist* profession includes, still, most of the naturalists whose names are familiar to the reading public, since their output merges the "two cultures," scientific and humanistic. Early literary-naturalists include familiar names—Henry David Thoreau, John Muir, John Burroughs, and Theodore Roosevelt. Nearly forgotten today, though they were very famous around the turn of the century, are Gene Stratton Porter and Ernest Thompson Seton. More recent natural history writings having literary merit are by Henry Beston, Joseph Wood Krutch, Sigurd Olson, Edwin Way Teale, Aldo Leopold, Rachel Carson, and Victor B. Scheffer. The most scientifically inclined of the above authors, with whom popular nature writing was a sideline, are Roosevelt, Leopold, and Scheffer. Conservation themes are most prominent in the works of Muir, Leopold, Krutch, and Carson.

The *scientific naturalist* group comprises workers in outdoor sciences if they are not too minutely specialized to rate as naturalists; most of them are found in ecology, behavior studies, evolution, and classification. Among physical scientists, the broad training enjoyed by many geographers places them among the naturalists. Historically, no one exemplified the scientific naturalist better than John Wesley Powell.

Present-day ecology is a synthesizing discipline in which the unit of study is not the molecule or cell but is at the opposite end of the scale of ascending integration, the ecosystem. Scientific ecology (there is no other kind in the original and still proper sense of the word, ecology being a biological science) is so broad and complex that ecologists must specialize in their research work. Yet they are the heirs of the old-fashioned observational naturalists like Audubon, and ecology developed as "*scientific* natural history." Many of the ecologists who have a philosophical bent are as close to being both specialists and generalists as anyone could be, for this is a difficult dilemma. A clearer focus on present-day ecology derives from the simple definition—ecology is the science of the structure and function of nature. In contrast with most kinds of scientists, many modern ecologists, though ever so theoretical, mathematical, and "sophisticated," are proud to regard themselves as naturalists.

In a book attempting to view two centuries from the perspective of the 1980s, when we see ecology and ethology (behavior study) as lineal descendents of the natural history of Audubon's day, it is important that the *difference* between these and the parent field be pointed out. Most obviously, early natural history was largely unaware of biology's guiding principle, organic evolution. Even more remote from anyone's mind was the conceptual basis for understanding how nature "works." It was a long and tortuous path from the time when most botanists were physicians, who needed to know plants for their medicinal value, and the naturalists on exploring expeditions were also medical men, to the ecosystem "naturalist" of today. The scientific naturalists of Audubon's day, being neither evolutionists nor ecologists, lacked the background necessary for perceiving the earth's interwoven tapestry of life. Audubon and his fellow naturalists saw the various kinds of pieces which make up the structure of the natural world, but they necessarily saw them only piecemeal. We may well read "Audubon" or the name of any naturalist contemporary with him at each place where Aldo Leopold wrote "Boone" in the following:

> Ecological science has wrought a change in the mental eye. It has disclosed origins for what to Boone were only facts. It has disclosed mechanisms for what to Boone were only attributes. . . . As compared with the competent ecologist of the present day, Boone saw only the surface of things. The incredible intricacies of the plant and animal community . . . were as invisible and incomprehensible to Daniel Boone as they are today to [the uninitiated].

Should we, then, pity John James Audubon because what science he knew had not progressed much beyond the stage of naming and cataloguing the parts? Decidedly not! Audubon was indeed fortunate in being a superlative observer and reporter in a time when a magnificent scene, little disturbed by human proliferation, was still out there to be seen. His genius lay in taking such full advantage of the glorious opportunities no longer available to his successors. We, in turn, are fortunate in being able to visualize that fresh continent through Audubon's eyes.

Various writers from Audubon's day to our own have extolled him as a virtual saint or condemned him as a charlatan and poseur. The latter accusations were based not on his paintings but on his natural history writings and tales of the frontier in his "Episodes." The authenticity dilemma, I believe, is best appreciated if one carefully and critically analyzes Audubon's accounts of his visits to Indian Key in Florida, comparing them with the log of the vessel *Marion* which was anchored off the key, and other sources. Instructive discrepancies appear in the date of arrival at Indian Key, the date he hunted Roseate Terns, the occurrence of a night rainstorm, and particularly in his dramatic account, told as sober fact, of his hazardous ordeal during a hurricane and its aftermath. All other evidence available—the spring non-hurricane season when he claims it took place, the entries of innocuous weather in the ship's log ten miles or so away, and Ludlum's 1963 book *Early American Hurricanes 1492-1870*, clearly indicates that the hurricane Audubon weathered was a second-hand one.

Does non-literal writing of this sort mean that Audubon's reports on bird life are generally untrustworthy? It most certainly does not! Audubon was thoroughly serious about birds and other life of nature. It merely shows that he applied a different standard of accuracy to his bird writing than to his Episode narratives. He faced commercial requirements besides artistic, literary, and scientific ones. He had lost two young daughters and survived desperate times in keeping body, soul, and family together. He was an artist, and art involves selection, rearrangement, and interpretation. Success in his quasi-commercial project required catching and holding the interest of wealthy patrons who liked romantic yarns. To his everlasting credit, the embellishments were handled in such a manner as to be ornithologically harmless. He himself admitted to Bachman, "My episodes are very so so indeed, but I think that the *information* connected with the *Birds* is pretty 'fair.'"

In the many Smithsonian volumes by Arthur Cleveland Bent, now the definitive source for life histories of North American birds, Audubon is one of the principal ornithologists quoted. Charles Darwin cited Audubon's observations on three widely separated topics, making him one of the few American naturalists (and I think the only American artist) whose work is included in the epoch-making *Origin of Species*. One of Darwin's refutations of special creations was that some beings display habits inconsistent with their relict structures. "No one except Audubon has seen the frigate-bird, which has all its four toes webbed, alight on the surface of the water." That is, it must happen *extremely* rarely!

In arguing that instincts, as well as structures, vary, and that such variations may be inherited, Darwin stated, "Audubon has given several remarkable cases of differences in the nests of the same species in the Northern and Southern United States." In discussing the dissemination of the propagules of freshwater organisms, Darwin wrote that he had thought the distribution of the water lotus "*Nelumbium*" quite inexplicable, "but Audubon states that he found the large, heavy seeds . . . in a heron's stomach."

The artist-naturalist took his place among the scientific-naturalists of his day by having a number of papers of his published in respectable technical journals. These included an account on alligators, another on bats, and several on birds. Later he decided to cut out further extraneous publishing and to concentrate his writing on his major works.

An analogy is found in today's excellent wildlife programs—the animal sequences, informative and credible, alternate with commercials which no adult, at least, takes for the literal truth. We habitually tolerate two standards of veracity and accuracy during an hour of watching commercial TV's nature presentations. Audubon's Episodes were his commercials.

On the principle "birds of a feather flock together," Audubon was clearly more than an artist, since he was welcomed into the naturalist fraternity by the best of them. This happened only belatedly on his home turf of Philadelphia, where he was dogged by the shade of his old rival Alexander Wilson, but in France it was no less a scientist than Baron Georges Cuvier who in 1828 introduced him to the French Royal Academy of Sciences. Charles Bonaparte was a friend (with lapses), in both America and France. In England, Audubon became an associate of zoologist William Swainson, and was befriended by Thomas Bewick, P. J. Selby, Thomas Traill, John Backhouse, and others. Among the American naturalists proud to call Audubon friend were John Leconte, Thomas Nuttall (chiefly a botanist), Spencer Baird, and Thomas Lesueur. By 1831, Audubon had formed a productive writing association with one of America's outstanding naturalists, the Rev. John Bachman of Charleston, South Carolina. That Audubon, once he had become known in Europe, was rapidly elected to prestigious scientific societies and honorary academies attests to the respect of his peers in science, though he did not himself press a claim to being primarily a scientist, and was hardly one in the modern sense.

In Audubon's journals, letters, and "episodes" are to be found many of the classic firsthand descriptions of early American landscapes, from the Great Plains to the Florida Keys, from the Mississippi delta to the coast of Labrador.

His account of the roaring muddy waters of the flooding Ohio River conveys the feelings encountered in seeing natural forces operating beyond any possibility of control by man. It also suggests, by the fact that the watershed was still well forested in that day, another point about flooding which has scarcely been appreciated until very recently. Whereas small floods may be controllable, which hardly matters since they do little damage, the great floods have not been and cannot be controlled. They are meteorological phenomena due to combinations of precipitation with frozen ground under protective snow, or other factors unfavorable to rapid infiltration of rainwaters or water from melting snow. These combinations occurred even under primeval conditions and nothing that man can do will affect the occurrence of such great floods, or significantly reduce their heights. He can do a much better job of keeping his buildings and installations out of their pathways.

Audubon's geological observations are less frequent and profound than those of botanist David Thomas of England who traveled our Midwest in 1816; Audubon's landscape records tend to be more general and geographical, but they are so vividly written as to make the reader feel that he is riding or striding through the countryside with the writer. The descriptions are sometimes very detailed. For example, he devoted six pages to one of several accounts of a badlands area where he hunted bighorn sheep for a couple of days. During the 1833 expedition to Labrador Audubon's writing became more perceptive in the fields of geology, landscape ecology, and the effects of climate on wildlife. The following is an interesting bit of coastal ecology north of latitude 50°.

> The waters of all the streams . . . are of a rusty color, probably on account of decomposed mosses. . . . The rivers appear to be formed by the drainage of swamps, fed apparently by rain and the melting snows, and in time of freshets the sand is sifted out, and carried to the mouth of every stream, where sandbars are consequently met with. Below the mouth of each stream proves to be the best station for codfishing, as there the fish accumulate to feed on the fry which runs into the river to deposit spawn, and which they follow to sea soon after this, as soon as the fry make off from the rivers to deep water.

No one then knew about the continental ice sheets of the recent-past Pleistocene epoch. Therefore, Audubon attributed to another icy cause the "stones" from ten to one hundred feet tall, "probably brought on shore in the masses of ice during the winter storms." The racing tides at the Bay of Fundy also interested him, and he measured the rise in height during a time interval.

The naturalist was amazed not only by the rapidity of the birds' breeding cycle in the subarctic and the brevity of the parent birds' stay in the north, but even more by the quickly greening sedges, the flowering and fruiting of plants, and the changes in vegetation over the thirty days from snowmelt in spring to the autumnal snows. In writing of these ecological (more specifically, phenological) observations, he calls the country there "wonderful" and "marvelous," words not used for the barren scenery, biting insects, sea fogs, or anchor-dragging gales.

The time for completing the breeding periods of insects was also seen as limited in the northern bioclimate, and he made the most of his opportunities for collecting a wide range of life forms. "We saw some rare plants, which we preserved, and butterflies and small bees among the flowers, which we gathered."

During the nineteenth century, the fashion, one might almost say craze, for displaying hunting trophies brought taxidermy into popularity. Early naturalists needed this skill for preservation of mammal and bird specimens, especially. Many naturalists, including Theodore Roosevelt, entered the field through an early hobby interest in hunting and taxidermy. Audubon, while a young merchant in New York in 1806, had worked nights making up museum skins and mounting bird specimens for a prominent naturalist-physician of the city. (Musuem skins look like dead creatures laid out in state, and are suitable for compact storage and handling in study.) Audubon was eventually to collect thousands of birds and mammals, and preserve many of them as study skins, and some as mounted or "stuffed" specimens. One of his scientific skins, a Passenger Pigeon, is on display at Mill Grove.

Collecting and using bird and mammal skins definitely contributed to the naturalist's ultimate success. Henry Ward was a taxidermist who traveled with Audubon, but the latter continued work himself along that line, including skinning a large alligator in Florida. For the 1843 expedition to the Upper Missouri River, his taxidermy assistant was John G. Bell. As an old man in New York City, Bell, still straight and vigorous, taught taxidermy to the boy Theodore Roosevelt.

Artwork, writing, and, to a markedly lesser extent, specimens were the ways in which Audubon left his legacy to posterity. Englishman Mark Catesby had pioneered such work in America a century before Audubon. Alexander Wilson slightly preceded Audubon in the painting and textual descriptions of birds, and in traveling widely in soliciting subscriptions. Both Thomas Nuttall of Harvard and Charles Bonaparte were publishing illustrated works on American birds in Audubon's time. Nuttall was better rounded as a naturalist than Audubon, for he was highly knowledgeable about both botany and birds. England had its own excellent bird painters in John Gould and Edward Lear (although the latter is better known today for his nonsense verse).

The celebrated literary man Oliver Goldsmith wrote four popular volumes on *The History of the Earth and Animated Nature*. The only publication dates given are for the 45 varied plates, nearly all of animal organisms, which range from 1822 through 1839 (though the original purchaser of my set signed all four volumes in 1838.) The artists were T. Dixon and three others. Volume I is illustrated only by the author's portrait, a volcano, and plates of a nude Man and Woman. Sixteen plates are of birds, usually including more than one species each. Despite the overall title, no plants are pictured or described. That group is mentioned only to distinguish it in a general way from animals. One long chapter is devoted to human monsters, another to "Mummies, Wax-works, Etc." The index takes up 123 pages. Apparently published in the same year as the engravings for *Birds of America* were completed (1838), Goldsmith's work made Audubon's appear a model of artistic and scientific achievement.

Thus, there was contemporary competition for Audubon in general popular nature writing, as well as in bird painting and bird life-history accounts.

From the flowers and other plant structures in Audubon's bird paintings, it might be concluded that he understood plants well and rendered them, for the most part, very accurately. But this cannot be our criterion for judging how good a naturalist he was on the botanical side. Although he drew and painted many plants, Joseph R. Mason (who was thirteen when he became Audubon's apprentice), George Lehman, and Maria Martin, sister-in-law of John Bachman, did a great many of the plants in the *Birds of America* plates.

With minor reservations, I believe that the best way to approach a judgment of Audubon's botanical interests and knowledge is to examine the selection of plant subjects shown with his birds, using modern data as to the natural habitats and ranges of both. It seems that this has not been done before. Do the plant-bird combinations which he selected (or permitted) make sense in the light of presently known facts?

The real test is when a single bird species occurs with a close-up, identifiable (or named in legend) plant or plants. Since the assistants who painted the plants and scenic backgrounds were usually with the master in the field, one should not expect to find many mismatched combinations. And there are indeed many successes, such as Plates 29, 33, 134, 174, 187, 193, and 251.

But there are a number of failures. They fall into several categories. The bird species is not always characteristic of the type of habitat or microhabitat indicated by the plant. Examples are Plates 64, 94, and 183. The Ruby-crowned Kinglet is shown with a plant of its northern breeding biome, but in an unusual stratum of the vegetation—presumably the artist (or his engraver, who made some of the choices) wished to include the attractive flowers of the low-growing narrow-leaved laurel (*Kalmia*).

A more serious type of error is lack of overlap between the geographic ranges occupied by the bird and plant. The range of the Gray (Canada) Jay scarcely extends far enough south to touch the northern edge of the white oak's natural occurrence. The Raven (Plate 101) only seems to be a case in point. Though its *modern* eastern range does not overlap with that of shagbark hickory, it was widespread earlier. There are other improbable combinations. Since the artist lived so long in the South, it is only natural that his plant backgrounds reveal a strong bias in that direction; southern plants are frequently shown with northern birds. The breeding range is more significant in the bird's ecology than the wintering range when the two differ, and is certainly far more significant than the areas covered in migration between the two, but birds that nest in southern or even northern Canada are often shown in the plates with plants of their winter ranges or even plants that the bird might see only briefly during migration. The Bay-breasted Warbler (Pl. 69) nests northward from the Great Lakes and winters in tropical forests, but it is shown with a flowering cotton plant, as is a Phoebe (Pl. 120). The Palm Warbler (Pl. 163), which breeds only north of the four southernmost Great Lakes, is shown in a wild orange tree in the southernmost part of its winter range. The Canada Warbler (Pl. 5), whose only southern nesting is in the high Appalachians, does not winter in the United States. It is depicted in a *Magnolia grandiflora* tree which bears dangling "berries" in summer condition. Another case of a bird associated with a plant which it could encounter only while in migration is a Blue-headed Warbler in a canebrake. Sometimes plant paintings were shipped separately to the engraver Havell in London, who used his own ideas of composition to match them with the bird pieces. Audubon either did not understand the ecological mix-ups which this practice could cause, or did not care.

That he did not take his bird-plant coordination very seriously is also shown by many of his later plates, those which have several bird species to a painting, usually on one plant. In Plate 393, a northwestern-breeding warbler and two western bluebird species are in a Carolina allspice bush. In Plate 395, three far-western kinds of warblers are perched in an eastern shrub, the wahoo. Other composite paintings are almost as meaningless ecologically.

These examples illustrate the point that the plants were not of interest to Audubon intrinsically nor as indicators of natural associations, but rather for furnishing a stage setting and giving an attractive composition. To his credit, he seems to have insisted that the plant structures should be well executed. And yet, Audubon's work does far more justice to the Plant Kingdom than other bird artists were achieving in his day. Hindsight confers no right to expect him to have done better than he did. It should be no surprise that he was an indifferent botanist, even though the oldest dated American art work he did is a July 15, 1806, drawing of a flowering plant, the false foxglove.

We have learned of no plants named validly for Audubon. He described and named one dogwood species (*Cornus nuttalli* Aud.) for his botanist friend at Harvard, and was probably author of no other plant name. Joseph Ewan, who supplied the latter fact, knows of but one specimen of Audubon's in an herbarium. Audubon took a plant press on his Labrador and Missouri trips, for botanists to identify the plants shown in bird paintings.

Bird watchers who have binoculars, field guides, funds, and modern travel amenities, can sympathize with a field naturalist who did not know such simple, recent tricks of the trade as "squeaking" up woodland birds. Such is the problem in being a pioneer, but the opportunities compensated for difficulties. By virtue of marking nestling Phoebes and finding them nearby in the following springtime (Chapter 11), Audubon is credited with initiating bird-banding in North America, and even with pioneering experimental ornithology.

During his earlier work, Audubon was not careful to insure that the skins of his purported record birds were saved in museums. The two most intriguing puzzles that resulted were his record of the Greenshank and description of Townsend's Bunting, as late as 1832 and 1833. Only one other record of the Greenshank in North America was ever reported; on May 29, 1962, W. J. L. Sladen saw four together in the Pribilofs, Alaska, and collected one of them, a male in breeding condition. The nearest point where the species is known to breed is on the Kamchatka Peninsula of Asia. There is no doubt that Audubon's bird(s) must have been the Greenshank *if* he did the painting and description from the Florida collection of 1832, based on individuals shot but not kept. On the other hand, the identification was made by his helper Henry Ward. Hence, Audubon could later have drawn the picture and described the bird from specimens he saw in European museums. Further confusion arises from the fact that the bill of his purported Greenshank in the painting is far too heavy and not upturned enough for a Greenshank. Yet, by 1832, Audubon was depicting bills and feet very accurately. In the Fifth Edition (1957) of the American Ornithologists Union Check List, Audubon's record is the only one given for Common Greenshank, but it is termed "unsatisfactory" and the species is placed in the hypothetical list. However, the next edition of the check list (1983) accepts the species, based on Sladen's record, as a full member of the North American avifauna. In a sense, Audubon is vindicated.

There is a still rarer species which Audubon pictured in *Birds of America* in color (Pl. 400); a different, black-and-white drawing of it which was never quite finished was reproduced as the frontispiece of Volume 2 of Maria R. Audubon's *Audubon and His Journals* (1883). This Townsend's Bunting (*Emberiza townsendi* Audubon), shot by naturalist J. K. Townsend on May 11, 1833, near New Garden, Chester County, Pennsylvania, must be the rarest known bird, since that is the only record of it. It was never recorded before that time, and it has never been recorded since. Audubon's depictions of the only specimen ever known are adequately diagnostic and the bird's traits are distinctive. The 1983 Check-List states: "Its peculiarities cannot be accounted for by hybridism or apparently by individual variation." Yet the AOU places the species in the hypothetical list, probably because it seems incredible that the first individual found could also be the last—the sole individual standing alone in the cosmos at the very end of its long evolutionary history, the last, lost generation.

When one reads now, "A Spotted Sandpiper dove under water repeatedly, thereby escaping a Pigeon Hawk . . ." one wonders how many modern birders can match that observation. Alertness is not enough—the observer has to be out where such things can happen. To see the unusual and to recognize it as such requires spending much time afield, and seeing much that is commonplace. Those who have not seen much in the class of the ordinary are unable to know what is extraordinary when they do see it.

We have noted that there were books on American birds before Audubon's. Nothing like his work on mammals, however, had been published on this continent before. These books were done in collaboration with his friend Bachman who was responsible for the text in its final form. The artist had been interested in mammals from his youth; the earliest of his extant mammal pictures, a groundhog, was made in 1805. That he absorbed a great deal about mammalian natural history is revealed by his paintings, the planning, and field observations that were put in more scientific costume by Bachman. Audubon knew mammals in the same fashion he knew birds, though not as intensively and not as a namer of many new species.

Little about mammals is to be found in his 1832 writings from his Florida trip, but a considerable amount on them came into his journals during the Labrador cruise of 1833, including an off-beat finding on the Canadian coast: "the most beautiful and softest hair imaginable—of Sables, Ermines, Martins, Hares . . ." used by a Hudsonian Chickadee to line its nesting cavity in a dead tree.

It was 1840 when he started doing paintings of mammals with a view to publication, but he had painted some of them much earlier; in 1826 he referred to an otter in a trap, which he painted over and over as a "potboiler" in Britain, as "my very favorite subject." And his field notes for 1833 include not only mammal observations which he made himself, but also what he was told by persons he trusted. In Labrador he noted, "In the early part of March the Caribou leave the hills and come to the sea-shore to feed on kelp and sea-grasses cut off by the ice cast on the shore. Groups of many hundreds may be seen thus feeding."

The notes taken on mammals along the Missouri again tie in what he saw with what others told him. "Our Captain tells us that the Black Bear is rarely seen swimming and that one or two of them are about all he observes on going up each trip. I have seen them swimming in great numbers on the lower part of the Ohio, and on the Mississippi." His mammal records from the 1843 Missouri River expedition, especially on the larger species, are profuse and detailed, including many sorts of body measurements and weights. The moult of buffalo was described, and their numbers and time of calving were noted.

The cold-bloods were also grist for his mill. He collected and sent them to the people most interested, after "spiriting" them in pickling fluid. Exchanges and gifts to naturalist friends, zoos, and museums were the order of the day, and Audubon was active in this work, so fundamental to systematic zoology. In 1829 Audubon had collected thousands of insect specimens and sent them to a friend in England. He correctly noted that "the honeybee was not found in this country twenty years ago and now they are abundant." Thomas Jefferson understood that this important insect is not native to America; the eastern Indians called honeybees "white men's flies."

It is clear that during his wide travels Audubon was deeply interested in recording the "manners" not of birds merely, but also of many other facets of nature that came to his curious attention. That he considered himself an all-round naturalist is shown by such jottings as "in search of birds, plants, shells, and all the usual *et cetera* attached to our vocations." Although a self-made naturalist, or perhaps because of that, he was a generalist of nature, which is an adequate definition of a naturalist in any time period. And, of the "new" species he found and described, twenty-one are still regarded as valid by modern ornithologists.

Audubon, not uniquely, had faults, for which he paid more severely than most of us do for ours. To recognize that he was human does not detract from his personal achievements in natural history nor from the later triumphs in conservation carried through in his name by others. Rather, we mortals of more common clay may take heart from such accomplishments by someone who shared some of the human foibles.

The Audubons constituted the First Family of American natural history, for the impossible dream of the *Birds of America* was not an individual one. Lucy, Victor, and Johnnie were indispensable in seeing it through— the family was a working unit in the various aspects of the work and the business. How much more human, in the best sense of that word, was the Audubon style than that of artist George Catlin, who permanently abandoned wife, children, and the practice of law for painting and writing his record of the Indians!

A Watershed for Ornithology

3   Michael Harwood

> My father . . . constantly impressed upon me that nothing in the world possessing life and animation was easy to imitate, and that as I grew older he hoped that I would become more and more alive to this. . . . As I wandered, mostly bent on the study of birds, and with a wish to represent all those found in our woods, to the best of my powers, I gradually became acquainted with their forms and habits. . . . The better I understood my subjects, the better I became able to represent them in what I hoped were natural positions.
>
> —Audubon

The French scientist Frederic Cuvier, in an 1832 review of Coenraad Jacob Temminck's colored plates of birds, remarked that so far Temminck had only provided the world an *introduction* to the birds he depicted. To convey "knowledge of them," said Cuvier, "he still must give us their natural history, properly speaking. For without the knowledge of living birds—active, realizing the designs of nature and their destiny on earth, fulfilling, in a word, the role that they have to play in the general economy of nature—ornithology is only an incomplete science, which leads us only to the entrance of the structure; we admire the outside, and we are left entirely ignorant of all the riches it contains."

But the ornithological establishment in that day was not much interested in digging up those riches. It was largely concerned with studying the bloodlines of birds—the relationships between different groups and species. That was the sort of investigation that could be carried on in the museum, using specimens, drawings, and books. Frederic Cuvier was then one of a mere handful of pioneers interested in bird behavior—study that had to be undertaken mostly out of doors, even sometimes in the wilderness. The available "information" about the life histories of most bird species, when it existed, was an exasperating mix of superstition, hearsay, and fact.

But at that very moment another pioneer, John James Audubon, was leading the way in popularizing the behaviorist aspect of the science. Frederic Cuvier noted a year later, as Audubon began publishing the text that accompanied the dramatic engravings of his double elephant folio, "Monsieur Audubon is . . . a skillful painter and an intelligent observer. Perhaps it is exactly because he is a stranger to the study of nature that he was led to create an original work of natural history that no professional naturalist would probably have the idea of attempting."

At the beginning of the 19th century few people studied or drew birds as a profession: there wasn't much financial support for such careers. Ornithology was not yet really a science on its own. It was merely a category in natural science, a discipline in which the heroes were extraordinarily eclectic. One thinks of Frederic Cuvier's famous brother—the baron, Georges, or before him the Comte de Buffon; such people were interested in *everything* in natural science, from fossils to geology to plants to reptiles.

But much bird discovery was going on around the world, many new species were being collected, and thousands of specimens were flowing into public and private collections, particularly in Europe. A number of sumptuous and expensive bird books had recently been or were being published. They contained beautifully finished engravings and almost no descriptions of anything about the birds other than their plumage and anatomy. The essence was evident in the engravings: virtually every bird was shown perched on the same anonymous stub of branch or standing in the same anonymous patch of turf or floating in the same anonymous puddle. These were mounted specimens, painted.

Onto this scene came Audubon. Until his mid-thirties he was only an amateur would-be gentleman naturalist who fitted his bird watching and bird painting into his business career, not unlike hundreds of thousands of serious birders today. To be sure, he was an exceptionally enthusiastic amateur. In fact, reading his letters and his reminiscences, not to mention the letters and reminiscences of people who knew him, some have received the distinct impression that it would be more accurate to say he fitted his business career into the gaps in his bird watching and bird painting.

One example will suffice to demonstrate the height and breadth of this amateur's passion. In Louisville, Kentucky, when he was in his early twenties and just getting started in the dry-goods business, he heard about a tree in the neighborhood that was said to be a roost for Chimney Swifts. That very July afternoon he went to look, and found the swifts using an old, hollow sycamore, sixty or seventy feet tall, seven or eight feet across at the roots and about five feet across in the trunk. At sunset Audubon watched the birds enter the trunk through the hollow stub of a broken branch about forty feet up. He put his ear to the tree to listen to "the roaring noise made within by the birds as they settled and arranged themselves. . . ."

He went home only when the evening was too dark for him to see well. "I thought of [them] almost the whole night, so anxious had I become to ascertain their number, before the time of their departure [on migration] should arrive." The next morning he was back at the sycamore before first light, his ear against the trunk again. He heard not a sound. "I remained in that posture probably twenty minutes, when suddenly I thought the great tree was giving way, and coming down upon me. Instinctively I sprung from it, but . . . it [was] standing as firm as ever. The [swifts] were now pouring out in a black continued stream. I ran back to my post, and listened in amazement to the noise within, which I could compare to nothing else than the sound of a large wheel revolving under a powerful stream. . . . I could hardly see the hour on my watch, but I estimated the time which they took in getting out at more than thirty minutes."

He wanted to see the inside of that roost. He rounded up one of his many hunting companions, and the two of them got a rope around the broken entrance stub in the sycamore so that Audubon, carrying a fifteen-foot cane plucked from a canebrake, could climb to the hole, peer in, and probe around inside. That experiment told him nothing. So he hired someone to cut a doorway in the base of the tree and dig a path into the matted bird excrement and feathers heaped up within. A few nights later he and his friend went back with a "dark lantern," which would give off no light until its doors were opened. They scrambled inside and up the pile of guano, and Audubon slowly opened the lantern. He noted that the swifts were clinging to the sides of the cavity and that as far as he could tell, although they were tightly packed, there was only one layer of them—no bird roosted on another bird's back. He later estimated that the tree then held about 9,000 swifts. Before leaving, he and his friend caught and killed 115 of the birds for examination at home, "stowing them away in our pockets and bosoms." The examination showed that 87 of the birds were adult males, 6 were females, and 22 were too young to be sexed.

It wasn't the end of his observations—not by a long shot. He went back to the tree on the evening of August 2, after many young swifts were on the wing from nests in Louisville chimneys. He found the numbers in the roost were the same, but the fifty-plus specimens he collected this time proved to be mostly young and females. "Day after day I watched the tree. On the 13th of August, not more than two or three hundred came there to roost. On the 18th of the same month, not one did I see near it, and only a few scattered individuals were passing, as if moving southward. In September I entered the tree at night, but not a bird was in it." It was commonly said in those days that swallows and swifts didn't migrate but hibernated. So: "Once more I went to it in February, when the weather was very cold; and perfectly satisfied that all . . . had left our country, I finally closed the entrance, and left off visiting it." He came back in the spring as the swifts were themselves returning, and about June 1 he tried another experiment, temporarily plugging the birds' access hole to see how they would react.

One can easily believe his later recollection that birds were then "the objects of my greatest delight," and that he "seldom passed a day without drawing a bird, or noting something respecting its habits. . . ." Much of this effort would eventually stand him in very good stead. But it wasn't formal *science*, in either intent or approach.

In fact, Audubon didn't really like what little "professional" natural science he was exposed to in the years he was an amateur birdman; he found it rather ridiculous. Years later he published an uproarious tale about a visit from a traveling naturalist at the Audubons' second Kentucky home, in Henderson. The visitor was the eccentric Constantine Samuel Rafinesque, who in 1818 explored the Ohio and Mississippi valleys, collecting data and specimens of plants, fish, and animals. He arrived in Henderson bearing a letter of introduction to Audubon from a mutual acquaintance. In his memoir of the visit Audubon hid the naturalist's identity behind a different name and probably exaggerated the truth somewhat for the sake of humor, but there is other evidence to verify the general picture he gives. Rafinesque was apparently *mad* for new genera and new species; Audubon portrayed him as literally dancing with delight when he was shown something that he believed had not yet been described and published in the scientific literature. Publishing such discoveries was a way of making a name for oneself. Audubon was highly amused by this excitement and used it to play practical jokes on Rafinesque. On one day's expedition, he said, he got Rafinesque so lost and tired and panicky that the guest threw away that day's plant specimens to lighten his load. Before the visit was over Audubon showed Rafinesque drawings of ten utterly imaginary species of fish and several of imaginary birds (e.g., "Devil-Jack Diamond-Fish," "Scarlet-headed Swallow"), about which he provided imaginary information—all of which Rafinesque soon published, giving Audubon due credit. From a scientist Audubon's behavior would have been disgraceful; from a Kentucky businessman who only made a hobby of watching and drawing birds and other creatures, it was a bit of frontier fun.

He still thought Rafinesque funny years later, but he had a higher opinion of Rafinesque, who had at least gone out looking for things, than he had of the traditional museum scientists of his day. He called them "closet naturalists." They spent most of their time with the skins of birds, constructing mathematically and philosophically tidy systems of relationships between species and groups of species—trying, as Audubon capsulized it, "to arrange our Fauna in Squares, Circles, or Triangles. . . ." His friend and patron Edward Harris once described him as "a terrible cutter-up of bookish systems and a thorough radical among dried specimen naturalists."

He was interested in what could be learned in the field—learned from the birds in life. That interest came naturally to him. He sat or lay quietly in hiding to watch birds in action; and he made practical experiments, such as his studies of the swifts. He kept notes on what he saw, and he collected the observations of others. Eventually he presented this material in five thick octavo volumes, called the *Ornithological Biography*. He remarked as he began to plan that text that though he was no scientist he knew he had a contribution to make to the study of North American birds:

"I am aware that no man living knows better than I do the habits of our birds, . . . and with the assistance of my old journals and memorandum books, which were written on the spot, I can at least put down plain truths, which may be useful."

He also looked for birds over a wide area in eastern North America, where he traveled extensively: he went as far to the northeast as Labrador, to the southeast as the Dry Tortugas off the Florida Keys, to the northwest as the junction of the Yellowstone and Missouri rivers, and to the southwest as the Texas coast. That in itself allowed him to make scientifically useful observations. At the end of the trip to Texas in 1837 he wrote to his friend Thomas M. Brewer,

> One thing that will interest you most, as it did me, is that we found west of the Mississippi many species of ducks breeding as contented as if [far to the northeast]. There is, after all, nothing like seeing things or countries to enable one to judge of their peculiarities, and I now feel satisfied that through the want of these means many erroneous notions remain in scientific works that cannot otherwise be eradicated. We have found not one new species [on the Texas expedition], but the mass of observations that we have gathered connected with the ornithology of our country has, I think, never been surpassed. I feel myself now tolerably competent to give an essay on the geographical distribution of the feathered tribes of our dear country, and I promise that I will do so, with naught but facts and notes made on the very spot.

This was all essentially trail-blazing. His successors tend to forget the circumstances surrounding Audubon's start in ornithology—the limited equipment, the limited literature on birds, the fact that at any moment in his travels he was likely to come upon a species or a plumage phase he had never seen or read about before—possibly one that *no one* had ever noted or drawn or written about.

When, having decided to produce a complete collection of paintings of North American birds, he went off down the Ohio and Mississippi rivers to New Orleans in the autumn of 1820, he took with him no binoculars. He had a "spy glass," but such optical equipment was rudimentary. If he wanted to scrutinize a bird he usually relied on his gun to deliver the bird to his hand.

He brought along on his 1820 journey no field guide to the birds; there was no such thing. The best he could do was carry a copy of the bird volume of Linnaeus's *Systema Naturae*, 13th edition, the English translation by William Turton—500 six-by-eight-inch pages listing and briefly describing all the known birds of the world. It had a single plate of illustrations. He might have brought along Alexander Wilson's *American Ornithology*, but he didn't own it. Even if he had owned a copy, it was unwieldy—nine volumes—and very expensive, not the sort of thing one stuffed in a duffle bag and risked losing overboard.

The absence of reference material could be frustrating in ways that we, who are swamped with reference works, can barely imagine. For example, that autumn Audubon noticed a strange bird that looked at long range like some member of the loon or pelican family. After several distant encounters with this "brown pelican" (as he thought it might be), he finally managed to get close enough to one to shoot it. "I took it up with great pleasure and anxiety—but I could not ascertain its Genus—for I could not Make it an Albatros the only Bird I can discover any relation to."

He drew it anyway. At Natchez, a few days down the Mississippi from where he collected the strange bird, he decided that he wanted as little more such puzzlement as possible during the remainder of the trip, so he managed to borrow a copy of the Wilson and spent a day "Writting the Name and Such Descriptions of the Watter Birds in Willson as would enable me to Judge whenever a New Specimen falls my [Prize]." But Wilson had not described or drawn the species that looked a bit like an albatross. Audubon's notes and drawing did not constitute quite the first notice any birdman had taken of the Double-crested Cormorant, for William Clark had reported it.

It is instructive to read his journal of this river trip to New Orleans—his first purposeful birding expedition—because his notes reveal a great deal about the state of ornithology and also about his approach to birds, which never wavered for as long as he painted and wrote. There were the new birds, of course, and the birds he thought *might* be new. He was hungry for new birds. In fact, he was as anxious to find what he called "nondescripts" as Rafinesque was. But he was not in a great hurry to publish them. A description of the Double-crested Cormorant was not published in the scientific literature for more than ten years after Audubon met up with it—and he didn't publish the first description. The presence of new species in his collection of drawings heightened its value, he knew very well. But *writing up* a new species for publication in a scientific journal may not have even occurred to him at the start, and later, after he understood the value others placed on such publication, he still didn't race into print but saved the paintings and descriptions of birds he had discovered for the folio of engravings and the *Ornithological Biography* and the octavo *Birds of America* with its small lithographed versions of the big engravings.

There were the observations about bird behavior: "Saw some [vultures] that were attracted by the scent?? of the Deer We had hung in the Woods??" Later he would conduct experiments to discover the answer to that question and would publish controversial papers in which he concluded that North American vultures depended on their eyes, not their noses, to locate their rotting food. (Further experiments by others showed that smell sometimes helps.)

He was delighted to see a pair of Bald Eagles copulating on December 1—"a scarce proof I have had the pleasure of witnessing of these and all of the *Falco Genus* breeding much Earlier than any Other Land Birds. . . ." That was the sort of original detail he provided in his life histories of species—details that other authors often failed to supply. Years later, in England, he wrote that he had read some new books about European birds, but "not a word could I find in them but what was compilation [from earlier works]—I could not even be told at what time the Golden Eagle laid her eggs in Europe!"

The journal of the 1820 river trip also includes observations about bird physiology and stomach contents: "found the Stomack of the Great footed [Duck] Hawk filled with Bones, feathers, and the Gizzard of a Teal, also the Eyes of a Fish and Many Scales—it was a femelle Egg numerous and 4 of them the size of Green Peas." That sort of information, too, found its way into his bird biographies—foundations of knowledge about food habits and breeding biology. When Audubon eventually decided to publish the *Ornithological Biography*, he hired a Scottish ornithologist, William MacGillivray, to help him. MacGillivray would edit Audubon's colorful, French-accented, badly spelled English prose; but more important, Audubon needed help with scientific aspects that interested him and in which he was not trained—the anatomical descriptions. MacGillivray became in effect tutor to a delighted student as together they produced detailed accounts of the structure and plumage and sometimes the internal organs of species.

We must look at his art from the same perspectives as we look at his science. Here, too, his emphasis was on behavior, action, the bird in life, the bird as living organism, rather than the specimen, the traditional formal pose. And here, too, he came to the craft as an amateur.

He was largely self-taught. True, he claimed that as a young man in France he had been a student of Jacques-Louis David, the French court painter. In general his biographers have not really seemed to know what to make of that assertion. There are no large slots of time in his life during which he was not doing something else we already know about—time when such study could have taken place. It may be significant that when he wrote an autobiographical sketch for his sons he didn't mention studying with David, and in all the millions of words in his surviving writings there is no description of David the personage or of David's atelier. We know he often made up things about himself, either to hide an unpleasant truth—e.g., his bastardy—or to gain some other personal advantage. Charles Lucien Bonaparte, a contemporary ornithologist often on the outs with Audubon, said that he had asked David about the claim and that David had said he had no recollection of Audubon's having studied with him.

On the other hand it is quite likely Audubon did take some art lessons as a boy. He wrote offhandedly of learning to draw the human figure using a wooden manikin, of drawing the figure in life classes, of being assigned to sketch statuary. Later, after he had committed himself to the *Birds of America* project and was trying to support himself as an itinerant artist, he picked up some tricks in oil painting from another itinerant artist with whom he happened to be traveling in the Lower Mississippi Valley. Eventually he had a few lessons in oils from the great American portraitist Thomas Sully. That is about the extent of the training we can document. In any case, passion, hard work, and doggedness, not formal lessons, were the major factors in his development.

When he began drawing birds as a boy he depicted them, as he put it, "*strictly ornithologically*, which means in stiff, unmeaning profiles." That didn't satisfy him. He wanted to show more about birds, not just the creatures with wings folded, at rest. So he tried hanging his specimens by the foot, which meant the wings and tail flopped open. He joked later that this allowed him to make "some pretty fair signs for poulterers." He really wanted to show the birds as they looked *alive*, in nature, but that wasn't easy. He could sketch free birds from a distance, if they cooperated by sitting still long enough, but he needed the details, too—the texture and flare of feathers, the scaling on the legs, the measurements of parts, the nuances of color. So he tried to lay out dead specimens in life-like poses next to his drawing paper, but that didn't work; the bird corpses had their own "natural" poses, and they lay every which way. He tried hanging his subjects like puppets, on threads. That was a bit better but far from ideal. At last a solution came to him—in a dream, he said. He could insert wires inside a freshly killed specimen and mount it on a wooden base—construct a sort of sculptor's armature, so that now when he posed the bird as he wished to show it, the armature would keep it there. Modern bird artists work from field sketches and photographs to get the poses they want, and use unposed skins for the fine points. Audubon's method was essentially one-step: the wired-up specimen was his stop-action photograph, his swiftly accomplished and completely detailed three-dimensional sketch.

After a while he learned to set this model against a sort of backdrop ruled off into squares, and he lightly ruled his drawing paper to match the graph of the backdrop. That approach helped him solve problems of perspective and foreshortening and also helped get the relative sizes of parts of the bird right.

That was not the only way he worked. Sometimes he drew from live specimens. Eventually his experience and growth as an artist made it possible for him to draw birds in action even when all he had to work from was a skin and maybe someone else's notes. All the engravings bear the legend, "Drawn from Nature by J. J. Audubon," but strictly speaking that was out of the question when it came, say, to species found on the Pacific coast or in the Rocky Mountains—parts of the continent he never saw. In such cases other people saw the birds in life and shot them and then gave or sold him the skins. Many of his later paintings began with such lifeless models. His later paintings have a poor reputation, because the limitations of the engraving project made it necessary that some of the later plates be filled with rafts of species, crowded into unrealistic gatherings, and the settings are often undistinguished. But as depictions of birds the original paintings that went into those plates are among his finest—as of course they should be, having been produced in the full maturity of his craft.

It is fair to assume that the style and character of his art was influenced—if negatively—by the lavish European productions that began appearing when he was still a young man. At the start, however, there was really no one working on birds who could have contributed much in a positive way to shaping the artist he became. In fact, the only such influence on his bird painting that I can detect was the work of his American predecessor Alexander Wilson, whom he knew only slightly and who died long before Audubon thought of himself as a serious professional. Furthermore, Wilson's influence seems to have been dreadfully snarled, wildly colored, by the competition Audubon felt from Wilson's work and by the hostility directed at him by Wilson's Philadelphia friends.

He displayed the influence in a way that seems to have been at first obvious, natural, and harmless but became blatant and a bit unworthy. A few of his paintings include figures that are strikingly like figures in Wilson's work; among them are two individuals in Audubon's drawing of Red-winged Blackbirds, one of his Northern Flickers, and his adult Bald Eagle posed on a dead catfish. These figures all appeared in relatively early drawings, and I suspect that he sometimes used Wilson's birds as teachers and models—copied outlines he liked and then filled them in and improved on them and redrew them and added nice settings. Years later, when he put together a painting to be engraved (sometimes pasting parts of old drawings into new compositions), he either forgot or ignored where the Wilsonian poses originally came from. There is other evidence that he liked to repeat something that Wilson had done and do it better; so, having improved on some model of a Wilson bird, perhaps he deliberately included it in the drawing for the plate—a way of thumbing his nose at Wilson's partisans.

Most of his work, however, was entirely original. A key mark of that originality was his settings. Even as early as 1806—fourteen years before he started on his great project—he was placing birds in pretty and realistic settings. This was a clear departure from almost all the previous bird painting in the western world. More than that, he combined birds and settings into dynamic units. "The more I examine Audubon's paintings," wrote bird artist Don Eckelberry twenty years ago, "the more I admire them. First and foremost he was a great designer. It is amazing how, in the precise execution of the part, he escaped the common tendency to lose control of the whole. We usually see the entire arrangement of an organized picture first and details later. He made the bird part of the picture and subservient to the design. Sometimes he became so interested in the design that he made the bird almost incidental. . . ." Fred Wetzel, another modern bird painter, neatly summarized this quality while looking across a room at an Audubon painting. The bird in the painting had been posed at the base of a plant from which sprung a long, graceful stem tipped by a berry. Said Wetzel in surprise: "My God, the painting is about that berry!" Audubon is seldom thought of or discussed as a serious *painter* rather than as an illustrator, but clearly his natural painterly qualities helped set him apart.

Settings take time, and Audubon very early realized that he would need help to finish his huge project. He often had another artist provide part or all of a setting, under his direction. So in about 125 of the bird paintings—less than one-third—the settings were not done by his hand, although there is reason to believe that he edited some or many of these settings. Occasionally an assistant even worked on or finished a bird. Audubon has been criticized for supposedly giving insufficient credit to these helping hands, but he was following an ancient tradition: established artists have often used anonymous assistants. Audubon's engraver, Robert Havell, Jr., improved and added to many settings, and his contribution to the finished product was more important than that of any of the five painters who worked with Audubon.

Audubon's bird paintings done before 1810 presented the subjects quite stiffly, perched or standing, usually in flat profile. He might show a crest flared or tail-feathers fanned or a head bent down to eat food, but (the settings aside) the birds were on the whole no great improvement over those done by other bird painters of the period. About 1810 we see him attempting to show a bird in flight and perhaps to turn it somewhat out of the plane of the drawing paper, giving it a third dimension. That is difficult to bring off well, presenting problems of perspective, foreshortening, and proportion, and it was about ten years before he began to master it. Although he also continued to paint many birds in profile, they were often doing interesting things—stretching the neck forward, or running, or reaching back and up to snatch an insect directly overhead. His best paintings began to show such action in three dimensions. There were sometimes also young birds in the scene, or a beautifully drawn snake, a spider, a small mammal, a fish, butterflies.

As Marshall Davidson tells us in his introduction to the excellent American Heritage two-volume publication, *The Original Water-color Paintings by John James Audubon for The Birds of America*, when Audubon started drawing birds, he worked with pencil and pastels or chalks. Then he added watercolors; a difficult medium, watercolors nonetheless began to replace his pastels in the early 1820s, but even when he was working mainly in watercolors—from about 1824 on, he also used pastels, oils, egg white, even gilt in his paintings to get the effects he wanted.

He drew these bird pictures life-size. Probably at first he felt most comfortable dealing with perspective and proportion when he did not have to reduce the subject as he transferred what he saw to paper. If the practice did begin because of such a "weakness" in craft, it became second nature and a trademark.

It was not easy, however, to present the larger species that way. An artist toting his portfolio wherever he went had to accept some limits on the largest size paper he could use. Audubon settled on sheets that were about thirty-by-forty inches. As soon as he did so he fixed limitations on how he could pose birds that were, in any dimension, too big for the space. The Whimbrel could be shown erect, with its neck stretching upward, but the Great Blue Heron could not, for example. The large birds had to be posed to fit the space—the long-legged wader head down, feeding or hunting, the swan on the water with its neck curved, reaching back toward the tail. As a result the big birds seem to be about to burst from the margins of his paintings; they convey a marvelous sense of unrestrainable life and energy. And they do not seem out of keeping with the rest of his work, because he painted to fill the space with action and color and beauty whatever the size of the bird. There are often two or more birds in a composition, usually *doing* something—fighting, courting, feeding young, defending the nest.

The size of the paper wasn't the only influence shaping his product. The audience, or market, played a part, too. Audubon had to attract to his engraving project professional scientists as well as the wealthy patrons of art and science. If he lacked the support of either one of those groups he would not succeed.

The scientists needed the sort of picture that would show them a great deal about a species—ideally, everything that could be learned by examining freshly killed specimens. The preservation of bird skins was not an advanced art, and skin collections were always in the process of being eaten by insects. Even when the skins were in good condition, specimens that truly represented birds as they looked in life were rare: colors faded within hours or days; tow stuffing did not shape the bird as flesh did. So good bird figures were extremely valuable, and the more information they contained, the better. Many of Audubon's plates suited science to a T. He showed males and females of a species, and sometimes immatures. He presented species fore and aft, or top and bottom, or one bird in profile and a second tipped, wing raised, revealing the underside. When, for example, he finished his painting of the one Crested Caracara specimen he obtained on his Florida expedition in 1831, he wrote, "I made a double drawing of this individual for the purpose of shewing all its feathers. . . ."

The patrons of art and science, on the other hand, were interested in the drama and romance of nature. Birds in the wild were looked upon as characters in a passion play. Their appearance and behavior contained moral lessons, lessons about nature and about "God's purpose." So it would not do just to present birds as if they were specimens; that "double drawing" of the Caracara had to be full of life and show something happening. And the reverse worked: in such activity the bird figures could provide the details the scientists wanted.

Furthermore, the patrons were also interested in display. According to Paul L. Farber in *The Emergence of Ornithology as a Scientific Discipline*, there was a long-standing European tradition in which well-to-do amateurs collected natural history items of all sorts—rocks and shells and stuffed animals; they arranged these tastefully with other kinds of "collectibles"—ancient bits of pottery and art and so on, to make a nice show for guests. Audubon's work fit this hobby very neatly.

"Fit" is the right word. I don't mean to imply that these things were mechanical influences—that Audubon responded to them simply because that was where the money was. He was very much a man of his times, and the information and approach that excited him was the sort of thing that interested many educated people, reinforcing his approach.

In considering the impact made by John James Audubon, we find that his reputation has always suffered from what might be called lingering disbelief.

Some contemporary critics, for example, charged that he had exaggerated or invented the poses he gave his birds and the situations he placed them in. Much modern commentary on Audubon's art has taken the same line. The great German ornithologist Erwin Streseman wrote, "Since he was unable to remember form and movement and render them artistically, he frequently attached dead birds to a board in theatrically distorted positions and so copied them 'after nature.'"

Audubon understood the limitations of his art. "[A]fter all, there is nothing perfect but *primitiveness*," he wrote in a letter after one successful expedition—during which he had produced some of his most beautiful work, "and my efforts at copying nature, like all other things attempted by us poor mortals, fall far short of the originals." But he answered the critics in his introduction to Volume I of the *Ornithological Biography*: "The positions may, perhaps, in some instances, appear outré; but such supposed exaggerations can afford subject of criticism only to persons unacquainted with the feathered tribe; for, believe me, nothing can be more transient or varied than the attitudes or positions of birds. The Heron, warming itself in the sun, will sometimes drop its wings several inches, as if they were dislocated; the Swan may often be seen floating with one foot extended from the body; and some Pigeons, you well know, turn over when playing in the air."

Every one of us who spends a lot of time in the field, watching birds, can recall moments of utter astonishment at bird positions and behavior. I shall never forget the first time I saw a Common Raven roll over on its back in midair—apparently just for fun. Peter Matthiessen wrote about seeing a long-legged Lesser Yellowlegs scratch its head in flight, making it look "like a sprung umbrella in a gale." Roger Pasquier, author of *Watching Birds*, tells me he has invented a long-playing game for his birding expeditions: he is trying to find all the species Audubon painted—in the positions shown in the plates. He is convinced that if he watches long enough he will see every one. The key to that proposition is *time*. It is fair to say that few of the critics of Audubon's work—including professional ornithologists—have spent even one-tenth of the time in the field, observing, that he did.

His written reports on birds have also been treated as unreliable. There are several justifications for this. For one thing, there are all the lies we know he told about himself. For another, there is his palming off fake species on Rafinesque, even though that was done before he had an interest in a reputation for scientific accuracy. For still another, he wrote "true" stories of adventures in America that appear to be partly or mostly fiction; this "food for the idle," as he called it, didn't have anything to do with birds, but he scattered many of the tales as literary interludes between the bird descriptions in the *Ornithological Biography*. He clearly kept copious records and notes about birds, but when he came to write up the birds for his text he did not always double-check all those notes carefully; some of his dates are clearly wrong, for example. Considering the scope of his project, perhaps such errors were normal, but they don't build confidence.

He also left behind him a raft of puzzles and unusual records of birds. He had a curious attachment, for instance, to some of his earliest "discoveries" of species—his "Cuvier's Kinglet," "Carbonated Warbler," "Rathbone's Warbler," "Small-headed Flycatcher," and the like—none of them since shown to be true species. Perhaps he wanted to demonstrate that he had been hard at work on birds concurrently with Wilson—that he was not a Johnny-come-lately. In any case, these birds were drawn for the first time many years before he began working on his project in earnest and before his skills were far advanced. Most of the drawings and paintings that he did before 1819 were ruined when rats got into the case they were stored in. But a few early works survived. About thirty had been sent to England as gifts to Euphemia Gifford, a relative of Lucy Audubon's. Audubon later saw at least one of those early drawings in England—the "Small-headed Flycatcher"—and repainted it for the folio. Perhaps most of the mystery birds in his collection sprang from a cabinet in Miss Gifford's house.

Those drawings were probably not in mint condition. The New York Historical Society has in its superb collection of Audubon drawings a crude little pastel effort that Audubon later copied for his plate of "Rathbone's Warbler," since identified as an immature Yellow Warbler. He said he discovered and drew it in 1808 at Louisville. The pastel is now so rubbed and faded that no useful field marks can be discerned, and the most that can be said about the shape is that it *is* a bird. Quite likely Audubon copied for the double elephant folio other relatively primitive efforts he found in Euphemia Gifford's possession—though they must already have been a bit worn and faded—believing the information they still transmitted.

If those mistakes were avoidable, many were not. Progress in science depends on the daring promulgation of new ideas, and some of those ideas have to be wrong—particularly when a science is young. If Audubon believed he had evidence that the "Washington Sea-Eagle" was a good species, not (as we now think) a large, female, immature, northern-bred Bald Eagle, or if he argued that the Sandhill Crane was just a young Whooping Crane, all later ornithologists have been similarly certain of facts that subsequently became un-facts. Many of his conclusions were good ones. He was the first to realize, for example, that the different color phases of the Reddish Egret represented only one species. He suggested that Snow Goose and "Blue Goose" were the same species, though he guessed wrongly that the latter was the immature form of the former. He discovered that there were two black-capped species of chickadee in the East, not just one. Of course, he found a number of new species for the North American list. And he made major contributions to the knowledge of bird behavior.

It has become fashionable to downgrade Audubon's science. Some writers set him up as a straw man: "Audubon used to believe such and so, but we know better." Others simply assert that his observations cannot be believed—that he lied, or forgot the facts, or repeated hearsay. A remark by one of his biographers, Stanley Clisby Arthur, is typical of this treatment. Arthur quoted a line from an Audubon journal: "Many of the Planters think that [the Chuck-will's-widow] has the Power and Judgment of removing its eggs when discovered, sometimes several yards. . . ." This entry proved, said Arthur, that Audubon's statement in the *Ornithological Biography* that the Chuck-will's-widow actually did this "was not founded upon personal observation, but upon hearsay. The declaration Audubon made that the bird picks up its own egg with its bill, and in this manner removes it a considerable distance away, has been thoughtlessly repeated and quoted by many writers." In making such a criticism, Arthur in effect called Audubon a truly formidable sort of liar, because the "declaration" in the essay on the Chuck-will's-widow is extremely detailed and includes personal observations. Moreover, Audubon was right. He had got his information by actually going into the field to watch how the nesting birds behaved after different sorts of disturbance. It is almost as if Arthur had not actually *read* the essay.

Many professional ornithologists do not read Audubon now, except as a curiosity. He is "out-dated," "unreliable." This can prove to be quite a mistake. Robert Cushman Murphy, for many years Lamont Curator of Birds at the American Museum of Natural History, wrote in the 1950s that though Audubon's writings about birds seemed to have been eclipsed somewhat in the twentieth century, they "are surely replete with information that compilers of later works have not yet used. Many ornithologists have had the experience of making some new discovery in bird behavior, which has proven unknown likewise to their most erudite colleagues, only to find that keen-eyed old Audubon had minutely described the same phenomenon a hundred years before! A case in point is the life history of the beautiful Roseate Spoonbill . . . which was exhaustively studied just before World War II by Robert P. Allen of the National Audubon Society. Mr. Allen found that of all the published accounts of this extraordinary bird Audubon's was the freshest and soundest, as well as one of the most exhaustive."

No individual ornithologist today deals with the size problem Audubon took on—portraying in detailed paintings and often lengthy essays all the known birds of a continent. He did a quantity of personal fieldwork unimaginable by modern standards and consequently left behind him a body of work that remains worthy of our careful and curious attention.

Quill Pens

4 Scott Russell Sanders

> I know that I am a poor writer, that I scarcely can manage to scribble a tolerable English letter, and not a much better one in French, though that is easier to me. I know I am not a scholar, but . . . no man living has studied our birds as much as I have done . . . so I shall set to at once.
>
> —Audubon

We are all familiar with him as a painter. Reproductions of his vivid birds and beasts hang in our courthouses, lie in slick books on our coffee tables, decorate our bedrooms and greeting cards. Say his name, and most listeners will at once see in the mind's eye a colored print. But Audubon was also a writer, and a notable one. During the years in which he was painting his famous illustrations, he was writing constantly as well—journals and letters, autobiographical essays, and many volumes of natural history. Taken together, these pages summon up for us the retreating wilderness and the boisterous frontier, and they display the appealing figure of Audubon himself, out in the fields and woods, observing it all with passion.

He did not *think* of himself as a writer. Although he was second to none of his contemporaries in field experience, he was lacking in book knowledge, in the formal armor of schooling, and this made him feel vulnerable. He also felt insecure in his grasp of English, which he did not use until he was eighteen. At the time he began learning to speak and write his adopted language, in the first decade of the nineteenth century, American English was in a state of ferment, stirred up by the break from the old country and by the revolutionary conditions in the new one. Vigorous, polyglot, rambunctious, America's newfangled speech deserved a dictionary of its own, and Noah Webster soon provided it with one. Audubon's use of this mercurial language was enthusiastic, expressive—and erratic. Like Thomas Jefferson and many another worthy, he was a phonetic speller, and the waywardness of his spelling was aggravated by the fact that he spoke English with a heavy French accent. He used punctuation in a carefree and bewildering fashion, or did without it altogether in his pell-mell rush of words. He wrote as he spoke and lived—impulsively, headlong—launching himself boldly into sentences before he had any clear notion of how to exit from them; and as a result his syntax was often as tangled as the Ohio River canebrakes he knew so well.

For these reasons, when it came time for him to publish his writings Audubon had the good sense to seek out collaborators. After his death, the letters and journals that he left unpublished were either "improved" or destroyed by his widow and a tidy-minded granddaughter. The initial problem one encounters in assessing his writing, therefore, is in identifying what, amid the several thousand pages appearing under his name, may actually be attributed to Audubon.

The text of the book on mammals, *The Viviparous Quadrupeds of North America* (1846-1854), although informed by Audubon's notes and bearing his name alongside that of John Bachman on the title page, was in fact largely written by the capable, long-suffering Bachman, and thus provides only indirect evidence of Audubon the writer. The nearly five hundred life histories of birds and the sixty "episodes" published in the five fat volumes of *Ornithological Biography* (1831-1839), on the other hand, are substantially the work of Audubon. In this case as well, he was fortunate in his choice of collaborator. The Scottish scientist William MacGillivray was responsible for most of the technical material in the bird biographies, and likewise for "smoothing down the asperities" of Audubon's style, as Audubon himself declared in the introduction.

By comparing the original text for "Pitting of Wolves" with the version published in *Ornithological Biography*, we can see that MacGillivray was generally faithful to the shape and texture of Audubon's writing, limiting himself for the most part to unsnarling the syntax and polishing up the diction. Thus, where Audubon wrote, "the mangled remains of his companion lay scattered around on the blooded snow," MacGillivray substituted, "the mangled remains of his comrade lay scattered around on the snow, which was stained with blood." "Winter once more had come dreary, sad, cold and forbidding," from the original, was reduced to, "Winter had commenced, cold, dark, and forbidding." Where Audubon indulged himself in romantic excess, writing that the "silence of night was as dismal as that of the tomb," MacGillivray wrote simply, "the silence of night was dismal." The colloquial "nag" was softened to the polite "horse"; "lugged" was transformed into "carried". Where Audubon, using a frontier expression, said that a cornered wolf fighting a pack of dogs "showed game," his editor wrote, "showed some spirit." Two men out on a courting expedition, described in the manuscript as "seminocturnal young sparks," in the published version were elevated into "ardent youths."

In the process of scrubbing Audubon's language and putting it through a wringer of Victorian prose, MacGillivray also washed out some of its color and idiosyncrasy. It became less American and more British, in part because of MacGillivray's background, but also in part because this was the language deemed proper at the time for an educated audience, on either side of the Atlantic. We may regret MacGillivray's scrubbing and ironing, yet we can at least be grateful that he did not distort the essential vision of the text. What we read in *Ornithological Biography* preserves Audubon's way of seeing, his quality of attention and turn of mind, which are the items of chief importance in any writer.

The journals were not so kindly treated. Audubon kept them almost continually from 1820 until the mid-1840s, writing next to campfires, in wayside inns, in the holds of ships. Serving the functions of diary, confessional, field notebook, and family epistle, they were the chief source for his bird biographies and his informal essays. With few exceptions, the only versions we now possess of these voluminous journals are those published by his granddaughter, Maria R. Audubon, in 1897. In her preface she says that from the mass of papers in her possession she used "perhaps one-fifth," but she does not specify how she chose what to include, and she makes no mention of altering what she *did* include. We gain an insight into her method, however, when she insists that contrary to published opinions, her grandfather was neither vain nor selfish and that in all of the writings she examined, "there is not one sentence, one expression, that is other than that of a refined and cultured gentleman. More than that, there is not one utterance of 'anger, hatred or malice.'" This is flatly untrue, as we can see from other sources. Audubon was a far more complicated, flawed, and intriguing figure than the one his wife and granddaughter wished for us to see. In the best Victorian tradition of scouring the icons of dead celebrities, Maria censored, prettified, and quietly rewrote the journals in such a way as to fit her image of Audubon as a "refined and cultured gentleman," immune to anger or jealousy or vanity. Having given her doctored portrait to the world, she burned most of the manuscripts.

Fortunately, some of the original journals have been preserved, including the extraordinarily interesting one from 1826, the pivotal year during which Audubon left Lucy and America behind and launched *The Birds of America* in England. We can judge the extent of Maria's surgery by comparing, say, her account of the ocean crossing with Audubon's. She did not content herself with correcting grammar, punctuation, and spelling. She also cut out references to anything she considered unseemly: mice, maggots, and cockroaches; cabins sour with sweat; stomachs growling with hunger. When Audubon wrote something as inoffensive as, "I smelt the putrid weeds on the shore" (a stench he subsequently traced to the on-deck latrine), Maria altered it to, "I smelt the 'land smell' "(and made no mention of the latrine). At one point he described a steward whose red flannel shirt stuck out of an open fly in a suggestive manner; Maria erased both shirt and sailor entirely. More than once, addressing Lucy, the lonely husband hinted at his sexual longings; but Maria would not let this pass her censor. In fact, whenever *any* feeling, any smell or sound or taste struck hard on Audubon's senses, Maria either expunged it or toned it down, as if strength of feeling, and anything to do with a man's rude flesh, were suspect.

Likewise, she moderated or avoided all passages that register Audubon's dizzy swings of mood, his swift slipping back and forth between elation and black despair. For instance, the following characteristic passage from the original journal never appears in her version:

> I know only the acuteness of the feeling that acts through my whole frame like an electric shock. I immediately feel chilled, and suddenly throw my body on my mattress and cast my eyes towards the azure canopy of heaven, scarce able to hold the tears from flowing.

There was ample precedent for such emotional gushing in the Romantics, especially Byron, whose poetry Audubon had been reading on this voyage. Whatever objections Maria might have had to these moody passages on stylistic grounds, she almost certainly excluded them because of what they revealed about the instability of her famous grandfather.

Since it would hardly do for a "cultured gentleman" to be revealed as a bastard, of course she omitted Audubon's few sly allusions to his illegitimate birth. In keeping with her image of the sober gentleman-artist, she cut out his numerous references to wine, "spiritous liquors," and porter, as well as the several maudlin, comical, semi-hysterical passages written while he was under the influence.

Borrowing a metaphor from the anthropologists, we can distinguish, therefore, between Audubon "raw" and Audubon "cooked"; between the private voice of the letters and unedited journals, on the one hand, and the public voice of the *Ornithological Biography* and the expurgated journals, on the other. In the raw, Audubon is more colorful, sensuous, and opinionated. He is more likely to lapse into backwoods slang—describe a crowded ship by saying "we will have to Pig together on the floor"; or proclaim his enthusiasm by saying that "with me it is *Neck or Nothing!*"; or advise a young woman "not to fritter herself with visionary fears"; or excuse himself at the end of a letter as "too dumpish to write any more"—and the unimproved Audubon is more vain and moody; more outrageous in ambition and self-doubts, more feisty, more complex. Yet even in his cooked form, he is a highly original observer both of nature and of humanity. He is large-hearted, driven by a passionate curiosity about everything, fond of gossip, vigorous in his storytelling, and filled with zest. Through his eyes we see the swirl and ferment of frontier America; we meet a huge cast of characters both wild and human, glimpsed during that once-on-a-continent moment when all wilderness east of the Rocky Mountains was on the point of disappearing.

Audubon was most candid in his letters, which were composed hastily, often late at night after a dozen hours of painting or exploring or canvassing for subscribers. Hundreds of letters have survived from the years 1826–1840—Audubon's great period, which included the creation of *The Birds of America* and *Ornithological Biography*. Because these letters have been published without alteration, they enable us to form an impression of the unedited, uninhibited writer. Filled with gossip and strong emotion, often confessional, by turns exuberant and despairing, they make lively reading, for their insight into the man and for their untamed language. Thus we overhear him confiding to Lucy:

> I dreamed a few nights ago that I was shooting Ducks with William in the Pond Settlement and that we had so many killed that our Horses

were scarcely able to walk under the load and that it was so pichy Dark when we returned that every tree came in contact with my own noble Nose!

We share his excitement upon glimpsing a strange bird: "I have not shot but have seen a Hawk of great size entirely *new*—may perhaps kill him tomorrow." We discover him fulminating against his detractors—"As to the rage of M*r* Waterton or the lucubrations of M*r* Neal . . . I really care not a fig—all such stuffs will soon evaporate being mere smoak from a Dung Hill"—or against a politician—"If I was not a good Man and a Christian I would have wished him under Way to the '*Sulphur Springs*,' and in the sulphur to have been *upset*, yes upset and up to his lips in burning Lava!"

The letters reveal more starkly than any of the other writings his stormy changes of mood. In one place we find him complaining about the "blue devils":

> I . . . have had the horrors all around me—Dreams of sinking & burning ships at night.—fears of lost Drawings & failures of subscribers by day have ever and anon been my companions—Not even the Bustle of this Large town can dissipate these unpleasant fancies—I walk the streets it is true, but neither hear nor see any thing but my fancies dancing about through the atmosphere like so many winged Imps resembling in shapes, colour, & capers all the *beau ideal* of the Infernal regions!

In another place we find him crowing:

> So you see or do not you see how lucky the "Old Man" is *yet!* and why all this Luck?—Simply because I have laboured like a cart Horse for the last thirty years on a Single Work, have been successful almost to a miracle in its publication thus far, and now am thought a—a—a— (I dislike to write it, but no matter here goes) a Great Naturalist!!!

The letters are peppered with exclamations. They are the record of an enthusiast, a man who lurches from boasting to dark self-doubts; a romantic, prey to the extreme weathers of emotion; a lady's man, fond of music and dancing; a showman; a salesman; a doting—if wandering—father and husband. The letters show us, more clearly even than the journals, the impulses that drove him through his long travels and sustained him through his grueling labors: the desire for fame, dread of failure, hunger for knowledge, yearning for approval, the sheer enjoyment of the hunt and the trek and the out-of-doors. The Audubon of the letters is a man obsessed, lured on by the gargantuan enterprise of his science and his art as powerfully as ever Ahab was lured on by the whale.

Written for the most part while Audubon was away from his family on birding expeditions and subscription tours, the journals are usually addressed to his wife, Lucy, or to his sons. They are reports about what he observes in the woods, where he sleeps, whom he meets, how he feels; but they are also apologies, justifying his long absences from home and chronicling his slow rise from obscurity to fame.

Even in Maria Audubon's expurgated version, the journals have an on-the-spot freshness about them, catching his impressions as they form. For example, here is a passage from the 1826 journal:

> my drawing finished, I caught four Dolphins; how much I have gazed at these beautiful creatures, watching their last moments of life, as they changed their hue in twenty varieties of richest arrangement of tints, from burnished gold to silver bright, mixed with touches of ultramarine, rose, green, bronze, royal purple, quivering to death on our hard broiling deck. As I stood and watched them, I longed to restore them to their native element in all their original strength and vitality, and yet I felt but a few moments before a peculiar sense of pleasure in catching them with a hook to which they were allured by false pretences.

This is an archetypal moment for Audubon. We see him delicately balanced among four identities—as hunter, exulting in the triumph over his prey; as artist, enjoying the play of colors; as scientist, observing behavior; and as nature-lover, regretting the death of something beautiful. In Audubon's own day, you could have found more accomplished hunters or scientists; in our time you could find more zealous conservationists and finer artists. What made Audubon extraordinary and what charges his writings with inner drama is the *combination* of these roles, the fierce interplay of identities.

The European journals, covering the period 1826-1829, show his transformation from backwoods shopkeeper to cosmopolitan artist. They are full of turmoil, because Audubon had been uprooted from the woods after more than two decades of tramping; and he had also been separated by an ocean from his family. In the learned and wealthy circles into which his work took him, he felt uneasy about his lack of formal schooling and the emptiness of his purse. Thus, upon meeting an Englishwoman, he wrote, "I knew that at one glance she had discovered my inferiority. . . . I must say the more I realized her intelligence the more stupid did I become."

London, where he was forced to spend most of his time while completing *The Birds of America*, never suited him. He was tormented by the size of the city and its crowds, and by "the constant evidence of the contrast between the rich and the poor."

> London is just like the mouth of an immense monster, guarded by millions of sharp-edged teeth, from which if I escape unhurt it must be called a miracle. I have many times longed to see London, and now I am here I feel a desire beyond words to be in my beloved woods.

Uprooted, lonely, and insecure, he alternated between giddy hope for his project and suffocating dread of failure:

> I unpacked my birds and looked at them with pleasure, and yet with a considerable degree of fear that they would never be published. I felt very much alone, and many dark thoughts came across my mind; I felt one of those terrible attacks of depression to which I so often fall a prey overtaking me, and I forced myself to go out to destroy the painful gloom that I dread at all times, and of which I am sometimes absolutely afraid.

No doubt there is a certain degree of romantic posturing here; but there is also a note of genuine anguish, which sounds repeatedly in the European journals.

The general theme of these early journals, however, is success—the swift, miraculous rise to celebrity:

> Now to me this is all truly wonderful; I came to this Europe fearful, humble, dreading all, scarce able to hold up my head and meet the glance of the learned, and I am praised so highly! It is quite unaccountable, and I still fear it will not last; these good people certainly give me more merit than I am entitled to; it can only be a glance of astonishment or surprise operating on them because my style is new, and somewhat different from those who have preceded me.

His style *was* new, both on the page and in person, and that had a great deal to do with his initial success. By luck and by shrewd performance he could play to perfection the role of the American woodsman, which at that moment the public on both sides of the Atlantic was eager to behold. In his Leatherstocking novels, James Fenimore Cooper was appealing to this same curiosity; he unveiled his noble frontiersman, Natty Bumppo, in 1823, three years before Audubon's arrival in England, and continued the enormously popular series through *The Deerslayer*, which appeared in 1841, two years after Audubon's return to America. Daniel Boone and Davy

Crockett had long since become folk heroes, and supplied models for both Cooper and Audubon. Andrew Jackson, a man of the western country and a symbol of the frontier, was elected president in 1828. Shortly thereafter, Sam Houston was presiding over the unruly republic of Texas.

The European journals show Audubon playing the woodsman's role in the drawing rooms of England with gusto and self-irony, imitating birdcalls and Indian yells, singing Ohio River songs, eating corn-on-the-cob and raw tomatoes (which his English hosts supposed to be poisonous), answering endless questions about the wilderness, the beasts, the "aborigines." In keeping with his image, he often sported fringed buckskins, brandished a walking stick, and wore his chestnut hair long, thereby inspiring the ladies to gaze at him with curiosity and provoking a servant boy to stare at him "like an ass at a fine thistle." To his way of seeing, by contrast, a judge's powdered wig—that utterly civilized headdress—"might make a capital bed for an Osage Indian during the whole of a cold winter on the Arkansas River."

Anticipating Mark Twain and, to a lesser extent, Henry James, Audubon also played the role of the innocent abroad, wondering at the wealth and decadence he found in Europe, comparing the manicured landscape of the Old World with America's grand wilderness. What the English called trees put him in mind of Louisiana saplings; their pears and apples were the size of green peas; beside the mighty Ohio, the Thames was a puny brook, across which "a Sand-hill Crane could easily wade . . . without damping its feathers." As for London's much-vaunted new zoological gardens, they contained fewer natural curiosities than one might find on a single morning in an American swamp.

Audubon was himself a natural curiosity, and made the most of it. But of course playacting alone did not enable him to sustain his enormous project of writing and painting and selling. In addition to artistic gifts and personal charm, it took dogged labor, as Audubon noted in a characteristic (and immodest) analogy: "If Napoleon by perseverance and energy rose from the ranks to be an emperor, why should not Audubon with perseverance and energy be able to leave the woods of America for a time and publish and sell a book?"

His later journals, recounting trips to Labrador (1833) and the Yellowstone country (1843), are less dramatic than those from the period in Europe, but they exhibit even more starkly his almost fanatical will. By the time he made those journeys, Audubon was no longer living in constant fear of failure; he knew what his mission was, and stuck to it with fierce determination. His official purpose was to observe the behavior of birds and beasts and to gather specimens. Unofficially, he was escaping into the open air, sleeping in ships and forts and tents, exploring the continent. Although lacking the inner tumult of the earlier journals, these later ones are still interesting for what they show about Audubon's powers as a reporter and about his growing ecological anxiety.

They provide keen observations on the Indians, on landscape and crops, on patterns of settlement, roads, and wild foods. Broiled dog, for example, struck him as surprisingly good—"no sooner had the taste touched my palate than I changed my dislike to liking, and found this victim of the canine order most excellent, and made a good meal, finding it fully equal to any meat I ever tasted"; hashed eider duck and heron's eggs proved to be tasty, as was raw buffalo liver in moderate portions; but he could not bring himself to try one hunter's favorite delicacy, steaming buffalo brains. What Audubon observed of the Indians was often at variance with the flowery records left by "poetical travellers." He wrote memorable accounts of once-powerful tribes fallen on hard times—the Seminoles of Florida, where the government was bent on a policy of extermination; the demoralized Indians of Maine; the horse warriors of the plains, reduced to begging, or jumping into the river to retrieve the rotting carcasses of buffaloes; entire western tribes wiped out by smallpox.

In passage after passage in these Labrador and Missouri journals Audubon captured the "wonderful dreariness" of the far north and the intoxicating desolation of the far west. He described flocks of gannets, their white bodies swirling in the air like blown snow; buffaloes pouring in a furious brown river across the plains. But amid this abundance of wildlife, where he hunted with as much gusto as ever, he also began to worry about how long nature would be able to support this slaughter. In the north, trappers were destroying the fur-bearing animals, and eggers were annihilating the birds. "In less than half a century," he predicted, "these wonderful nurseries will be entirely destroyed, unless some kind government will interfere to stop the shameful destruction." White men intent on profit had already driven away the Indians:

> Nature herself seems perishing. Labrador must shortly be depeopled, not only of aboriginal man, but of all else having life, owing to man's cupidity. When no more fish, no more game, no more birds exist on her hills, along her coasts, and in her rivers, then she will be abandoned and deserted like a worn-out field.

In the Yellowstone country, traveling as a celebrity, beginning to wear out after decades of tramping and laboring, he wrote obsessively about the "sport" and "frolic" of killing. He and his men shot everything with a skin around it—buffalo, rabbits, elk, deer, big horn sheep, all manner of birds. The aging Audubon would still perform antics to lure an antelope within gunshot:

> We determined to stop and try to bring him to us; I lay on my back and threw my legs up, kicking first one and then the other foot, and sure enough the Antelope walked towards us, slowly and carefully, however. In about twenty minutes he had come two or three hundred yards; he was a superb male, and I looked at him for some minutes; when about sixty yards off I could see his eyes, and being loaded with buck-shot pulled the trigger without rising from my awkward position.

Neither discomfort nor personal danger discouraged him from his zealous hunting. Yet he also protested against the mayhem. Surveying the prairies littered with the skulls of buffalo, most of them killed for sport, with perhaps no more than their tongues harvested, he complained in his journal, "What a terrible destruction of life"; if it kept up, he prophesied, the buffalo would go the way of the great auk to extinction.

In their capacity as field notebooks, the journals reveal another source of Audubon's enduring significance. No one before him in America had *looked* at the woods and wildlife so closely, or recorded in such exhaustive detail what they had seen. He paid attention to the behavior of birds, to habitats, mating rituals, the shape and placement of nests, the contents of crops and gizzards, patterns of migrations, and dozens of other matters. Audubon's field experience, faithfully recorded in the journals, distinguished both his paintings and his nature writings from those of the stay-at-homes, whom he dismissed as "crazed naturalists of the closet." When attacked by critics, as he frequently was, he appealed to the journals as proof of his truthfulness to nature:

> The World is well aware that it is not necessary for any one inclined to publish falsehoods or form tales of Wonder, to travel as I constantly do, at an (I am sorry to say) enormous expense, keeping a regular Journal of all my actions and the whole of *my* observations connected with the Science which I am studying, when on the contrary I might with ten fold ease settle myself in some corner of London and write nolens volens all such fables as might cross my brains and publish these without caring one Jot about the consequences.

With so many of his rivals busily publishing falsehoods and tales of wonder, he exclaimed, countless "niny tiny Works are in progress to assist in the mass of confusion already scattered over the World." Those who never left their studies might accuse him of extravagance, but Audubon insisted, "I write as I . . . see, and that is enough to render me contented with my words."

The transition from hastily jotted letters and informal journals to the publication of scientific studies was a difficult one, and Audubon undertook it with trepidation. When he resolved, during his first year in England, "to attempt the being an author," he confided to his journal: "It is a terrible thing to me; far better am I fitted to study and delineate in the forest, than to arrange phrases with suitable grammatical skill." When halfway through the composition of *Ornithological Biography*, he wrote to John Bachman:

> God preserve you, and save you the trouble of ever publishing Books on Natural Science! for my part I would rather go without a shirt or any inexpressibles through the whole of the florida swamps in musquito time than labour as I have hitherto done with the pen.— how glad I shall be when my labours of this latter nature are quite at an end.

Written over nearly a decade, from 1830 through 1839, running to five fat volumes and covering roughly 500 birds, the *Ornithological Biography* was an enormous undertaking. Despite Audubon's misgivings, it earned him a considerable reputation both as a writer and as a scientist. In all the works of Charles Darwin only two authorities are cited more often than Audubon. Spencer Fullerton Baird, a young friend in Audubon's later years and a future secretary of the Smithsonian Institution, declared that he found the essays about birds as dramatic as his favorite novels.

As we have seen already, *Ornithological Biography* owes its stylistic polish and a good deal of its technical information to its painstaking editor, William MacGillivray. But the energy, the wit, the sheer exuberance of detail, come straight from Audubon. He justly prided himself on working from field notes:

> *I* possess the knowledge that every word which I have published or shall publish is truth and nothing but the result of my own observations in fields and forests where neither of my enemies ever have or ever will tread with as firm a foot & step as I have done and still do.

More important than the accuracy of observation is the observer's fearless, passionate, indefatigable presence, which moves through all the pages of *Ornithological Biography*, offering us a personal encounter with nature:

> I still see the high rolling billows of the St. Lawrence breaking in foaming masses against the huge Labrador cliffs where the Cormorant places its nest on the shelves. I lay flat on the edge of a precipice, a hundred feet above the turbulent waters. By crawling along carefully I came within a few yards of the spot where the parent bird and her young, quite unconscious of my nearness, were fondling each other.

Or again: "I have approached trees whilst these Woodpeckers were thus busily employed in forming their nest, and by resting my head against the bark, could easily distinguish every blow given by the bird." Audubon takes us inside hollow trees to count chimney swifts, into caves to tie silver threads around the legs of phoebes, onto cliffs in search of eggs, through swamps and waist-high waters. He tells us how he nearly perished in quicksand while pursuing a great horned owl, how his fingers froze one December midnight while he awaited the arrival of Canada geese, how cactus spines scratched his feet when he hunted for the nests of white ibis, how he worked so feverishly on the painting of a golden eagle "that it nearly cost me my life," how he backpedaled furiously and leapt in the river to escape a wounded heron.

Ornithological Biography shows us the life of birds through the lens of a man's emotions. When fledgling water-turkeys are pushed from their nest prematurely, Audubon feels despondent; swans flying make him feel carefree and buoyant. Like Whitman, he might have claimed, "I am the man, I suffer'd, I was there." Many species he kept for pets, and he tells us about living with them for months or years as with intimate friends. A pet heron was suffered to stalk the family cat, and a trumpeter swan to chase the children. The birds are also granted the full range of human feeling. In Audubon's eyes, they betrayed courage and cowardice, innocence and guilt, hope and despair; when courting, they seemed to him coy or jealous, pompous or pugnacious. We are told, for instance, that after the turkey hens lay their eggs,

> the males become clumsy and slovenly, if one may say so, cease to fight with each other, give up gobbling or calling so frequently, and assume so careless a habit, that the hens are obliged to make all the advances themselves. They *yelp* loudly and almost continually for the cocks, run up to them, caress them, and employ various means to rekindle their expiring ardour.

When describing birdcalls, he searched high and low for analogy. The cry of the gannet is "wolfish," that of the bald eagle like "the laugh of a maniac"; that of the ivory-billed woodpecker like "the false high note of a clarionet"; the cormorant grunts like a pig, the golden eagle barks like a dog, and the great horned owl's call sounds "like the last gurglings of a murdered man." In describing the birds' behavior, he quite often appealed to human parallels. Atlantic puffins chase one another under water "with so much speed as to resemble the ricochets of a cannon ball"; and bluejays hammer "at a grain of corn like so many blacksmiths paid by the piece."

By comparison with modern scientific writing, this is all very messy, very subjective stuff. When Audubon chose, he could be as precise as any modern ornithologist. For example, he could provide an exact description of the ibis's eye, explaining, "I am thus particular in stating these matters, because it is doubtful if anyone else has paid attention to them." But it is Audubon's *personal* encounter with nature, more so than his science, that has kept his writing so pertinent and so fresh.

Probably the best known of Audubon's writings are the sixty informal essays, or "episodes," which he scattered through the first three volumes of *Ornithological Biography.* Dealing with his frontier experiences from the period 1818–1834, these interludes were designed, he told his readers, "to relieve the tedium which may be apt now and then to come upon you, by presenting you with occasional descriptions of the scenery and manners of the land which has furnished the objects that engage your attention." In his letters he was more forthright, saying that the episodes were "food for the Idle!" They were a literary analogue to his long hair and long beard, his fringed buckskins and drawing-room high jinks, a way of satisfying his readers' appetite for a taste of the wilderness.

Audubon knew those first readers very well. He had met nearly all his subscribers, his scientific rivals, his patrons and judges; they made up the audience he imagined as he wrote. For the most part they were not themselves outdoor types. They were rich and well-read, the denizens of high society. To defend himself against the skepticism of those who would peruse his "episodes" in the comfort of their parlors, Audubon insisted on the truthfulness of his accounts. "I shall not lead you into the region of romance," he assured his readers. And elsewhere: "This is no tale of fiction, but the relation of an actual occurrence, which might be embellished, no doubt, but which is better in the plain garb of truth."

Tales of fiction were, however, among the patterns he bore in mind for his writing, as this journal entry about Sir Walter Scott would suggest:

> How many times have I longed for him to come to my beloved country, that he might describe, as no one else ever can, the stream, the swamp, the river, the mountain, for the sake of future ages. A century hence they will not be here as I see them, Nature will have been robbed of many brilliant charms, the rivers will be tormented and turned astray from their primitive courses, the hills will be levelled with the swamps, and perhaps the swamps will have become a mound surmounted by a fortress of a thousand guns.

The most influential literary models at this time in America were—aside from the novels of Scott—the works of Washington Irving and James Fenimore Cooper. Irving's *The Sketch Book* (1819–1820) included American lore amid its genteel essays on England; and his *Tours on the Prairies* (1835) and *Astoria* (1836) set an example for writing about the West. Cooper's Leatherstocking novels established the pattern for writing about wilderness landscapes, Indians, and pioneer exploits. The influence of fictional romance can be seen in Audubon's portraits of frontier characters, the drunken trappers and renegades, the charlatans and eccentrics. Likewise, the landscapes of Scott and Cooper and Irving appear to have influenced his descriptions of the Kentucky forests, the Atlantic coast, the Florida Keys, the wastes of Labrador, the Ohio canebrakes, and the Mississipi River with "its mighty mass of waters rolling sullenly along, like the flood of eternity." By contrast with these literary masters, who were merely armchair explorers, Audubon knew the ground and the frontier types very well. He was not as refined a writer; but he was a better-informed observer.

Like all the Romantic writers, both novelists and poets, Audubon was attracted by the picturesque and the dramatic in nature—earthquake and hurricane, fox fire and forest fire, floods and cataracts; and he had a soft spot for melodrama and tear-jerking sentimentality. He was also fascinated by the workaday lives of those who settled along the frontier. Thus in the "episodes" he memorialized the festivals, the cornhuskings and July Fourth picnics, the ox-plowing contests, the fancy-dress balls. True to the practical outlook of his adopted homeland—as symbolized by his hero, Benjamin Franklin—Audubon paid close attention to the way people *did* things. He reports in detail how to trap beaver, how to set a trotline for catfish, how to dry cod, how to butcher a buffalo, how to make maple sugar, how to build a boat of hide; he instructs us in the firing of a flintlock, the poling of a keelboat, the locating of turtle eggs.

Although the "episodes" contain some of his finest writing, Audubon himself thought of them as "very so so indeed." Much of the material came straight from his journals, or from recollection; but much of it was also a recounting of stories that had been told to him. Thus he could ask of John Bachman, "Can you send me some good stories for Episodes? Send quickly and often." All the while he was traveling, Audubon was collecting lore about frontier toughs, about Indians and beasts, along the same heartland rivers where Samuel Clemens and William Faulkner would later gather material of their own. He heard an unending chorus of stories—on riverboats, around campfires, inside forts, on cross-country horseback rides, on hunts, in wayside inns. He gathered tales about the hunting of moose in Maine, buffalo in the Yellowstone country, and alligators in Florida; about desperadoes and vigilantes, pirates and runaway slaves; and he retold these tales in his "episodes." In a few cases, such as the essay about his shooting expedition with Daniel Boone or the one about his near-murder in a settler's cabin on the Illinois prairie, he placed himself at the center of stories which he had most likely heard other people tell.

As in the life histories of the birds, so in these "episodes" Audubon created a persona for himself. We see him penniless and downcast at the falls of Niagara, paying for his meals with quick portraits; and we see him, years later, grown so famous that settlers in the wilds of Labrador learned of his arrival from the newspapers. Through it all he preserved "a heart as true to Nature as ever." This public Audubon is fond of music and dancing, abstemious about food and drink; he is industrious, cheerful, as honest as the day is long; he rivals the Indians in his woodland skills; and he is driven by an "irrepressible desire of acquiring knowledge." He is a patient, keen-eyed messenger, bringing us news from nature.

As a writer, Audubon belongs to a distinguished American band of roving nature reporters. The earliest representatives were the Jesuit missionaries of the seventeenth century. They were followed, in the eighteenth century, by a host of vagabond naturalists, including Mark Catesby and the famous Bartrams, father John and son William; and in the early nineteenth century by those intrepid explorers, Meriwether Lewis and William Clark, and by the first great artist of American birds, Alexander Wilson. These men scoured the land, curious about everything, recording their observations in journals and letters, often publishing their findings in travel narratives. In the earliest days there was little distinction between rumor and fact; but gradually the more scientific observations of nature were separated from the background of anecdote and folklore. William Bartram's *Travels* (1791) influenced the next generation of poets, including Wordsworth and Shelley. Alexander Wilson's *American Ornithology* (1808–1814) was the standard against which Audubon measured his own achievement. Those who followed Audubon in this tradition of nature reporting include Thoreau, John Muir, John Burroughs, Aldo Leopold, and Rachel Carson. More recently, the essays of Loren Eiseley, Annie Dillard, Edward Hoagland, and Peter Matthiessen show how vital this literary form continues to be. All these writers confront nature not as aloof observers, seeking facts; but as human participants in nature, seeking meaning. This was Audubon's strength as a writer, not system-building, but reporting and collecting, bearing his keen sensibility through uncharted territory.

Audubon should also be read within the context of that burst of literary creativity which Van Wyck Brooks aptly called the "flowering of New England." While Audubon was reluctantly pushing his quills and his iron-tipped pens, in the East a remarkable cluster of young men was rapidly growing to maturity, including Emerson, Thoreau, Whitman, and Melville. By mid-century, they would supply America with its first great literature. One feature common to their masterworks—*Walden* (1854), *Moby Dick* (1851), *Leaves of Grass* (1855), and Emerson's *Nature* (1836)—was a preoccupation with the encounter between the human and the nonhuman, between society and nature. Their obsession was also Audubon's: to see, to question, to understand the wild milieu. In fact, this has been one of the central themes of our literature, from the very beginnings up to the present century. All along, what has distinguished America from the Old World has been the juxtaposition of civilization and wilderness.

Like the great figures of the American Renaissance, Audubon was encyclopedic, in ambition and method—as if, by spanning the continent, seeing and reporting it all, he could somehow make sense of it, take on its grand scale. The following passage, an ecstatic aside from his biography of the raven, may be taken as a typical specimen of the American sublime:

> Who is the stranger to my own dear country that can adequately conceive of the extent of its primeval woods, the glory of its solemn forests that for centuries have waved before breeze and tempest, of its vast Atlantic bays, of its thousands of streams, vast lakes and magnificent rivers? There is the diversity of our Western plains, our sandy Southern shores with their reedy swamps; protecting cliffs; rapid Mexican Gulf currents; rushing tides of the Bay of Fundy; majestic mountains; and thundering cataracts. Would I might delineate it all. . . .

When an English sea captain proposed to him, at the outset of his writing career, that he record his knowledge in a "little book," Audubon protested, "I cannot write at all, but if I could how could I make a *little* book, when I have seen enough to make a dozen *large* books?"

Although he registered a sympathy for the displaced Indians and he worried about the destruction of the wilderness and its creatures, this did not prevent him from identifying enthusiastically with the energies of settlement. He embodied, in his life and his work, the sheer joy of exploration, traversing the continent, testing himself against the wilds, the beasts, the border people. His ambition, he declared, was "to search out things hidden since the creation of this wondrous world," and in this he succeeded admirably. The emphasis here belongs on *wonder*, which was the keynote of his writing as of his painting. If he lacked the powerful sense of evil that would characterize the next generation of writers—especially Melville, Poe, and Hawthorne; if he ignored the wounds of slavery that were festering all around him; if he painted human emotions too freely onto nature, Audubon nonetheless provided us with the most comprehensive view of our continent anyone had ever achieved. His writings preserve for us glimpses of a pristine America, a landscape and a way of life that were altering even as he observed them.

Confronting the Wilderness

5 *Robert Owen Petty*

... Observe his leather hunting shirt, and a pair of trousers of the same material. His feet are well moccasined; he wears a belt . . . his heavy rifle resting on his brawny shoulder; on one side hangs his ball pouch, surrmounted by the horn of an ancient buffalo . . . containing a pound of the best gunpowder; his butcher knife in scabbard . . . a tomahawk, the handle thrust through his girdle. . . . He stops, looks to the flint of his gun, its priming, and the leather cover of the lock, then glances his eye toward the sky to judge of the course most likely to lead him to game.

—Audubon

In 1803 the United States of America received from France two phenomenal acquisitions: the Louisiana Territory and John James Audubon. The immense value of the first was apparent. It would be many years before the value of the second would be appreciated, but Audubon was destined to immortalize in his paintings an important part of our natural heritage.

And in his writings, particularly the letters and journals and the "Episodes" in the *Ornithological Biography*, he captured the flavor of American life in the wilderness and on the frontier in a remarkable time.

The years of Audubon's life in America, 1803 to his death in 1851, spanned a period of closure in the wilderness years of America. When Audubon first arrived here, the frontier of settlement still lay somewhere between the Appalachians and the Mississippi. In that region most of the settlements were along the rivers—the vast forests between the rivers were still mostly the domain of Indians. The trans-Mississippi West was largely an unknown quantity. In 1804 Meriwether Lewis and William Clark set out from St. Louis to find a route through it and over the Rockies to the Pacific. By the time of Audubon's death, less than fifty years later, the psychology of a wild "out there" for lands west of the Appalachians and east of the Rockies was coming to an end. Audubon's life connected the glory days of Daniel Boone and George Rogers Clark in then-living memory with the twilight period of the western mountain men, themselves aging men, who as young men had followed Lewis and Clark—men like William Sublette, Jim Bridger, Pierre Chouteau, Andrew Dripps, Kit Carson, and Owen McKenzie.

Few such men, however, left accounts of their experiences that are as vivid and as voluminous as Audubon's. From his writings no less than from his paintings, we can learn much about a vanished wilderness and a vanished way of life, that of the American woodsman.

Audubon first experienced the richness of the American environment near his father's property at Mill Grove, Pennsylvania. There were deep woods near the house at Mill Grove, but the creature comforts of civilization were not far to seek. After a long day in the forest, Audubon could be sure of a good dinner beside either his own fireplace or a neighbor's and the luxury of a dry, comfortable attic workshop to paint in. After he married Lucy and they moved west to Kentucky, it was still possible to find wilderness and wildlife close to home. But as time went on and his desire for new subjects and new experiences led him farther afield, he began to learn at first hand what every frontiersman needed to know to survive long periods utterly removed from civilization. Audubon, with his lively curiosity and high spirits, was an eager pupil and an apt one.

The chief prerequisite for success as a nineteenth-century woodsman was vitality of body and mind, physical endurance, good health, better than good if possible, and perhaps an inexplicable belief in one's own durability. In 1803, when newly arrived in America, Audubon was laid low with illness for many weeks. Again, in the summer of 1823, he was ill with fever and ague at Beechwoods Plantation near Bayou Sara, Louisiana. But from that time until the last year of his life, he was a man of uncommon physical vigor. As a young man and into middle age, Audubon considered a day's journey of twenty or thirty miles on foot to leave one agreeably tired, ready for a good night's rest. He had a well-practiced endurance from journeying in all sorts of weather.

It is tempting to suppose that during the years of his boyhood Audubon acquired a certain nobility of spirit and character borne of his father's affection for him and the example of his father's own ambitious self-confidence. In America Audubon's resilient temperament and genial wit would be tested by the scorn and the wiles of shrewd, and sometimes dishonest, frontier businessmen, and after that, by the arduous demands of the American wilderness. In time, he would prove equal to both.

Early nineteenth-century frontier life is necessarily unevenly documented. With some outstanding exceptions, the earliest settlers, those who braved the rigors of the wilderness to make new homes there, were, for the most part, unschooled men and women all of whose energies were consumed by the tasks of survival. The leisure for detailed observations and for writing them up, indeed the degree of literacy needed to do so, were possessed by few, only those rich enough or, if they were not rich, determined enough, to make time for such things. Those in the latter category were often dismissed as dreamers and wastrels. For the virtues most highly prized on the frontier were practicality, frugality, and hard work. The settlers, traders, merchants, lawyers, and doctors who were building frontier communities and their personal fortunes in places like Louisville had little patience with the ambitions of artists or, for that matter, chroniclers of natural history. Men who practiced seemingly unproductive pursuits were often viewed as pathetic oddities if not outcasts. A man like Audubon presented the fascinating spectacle of a curiously interesting but wasted life; the idea of a grown man practicing the pursuits of a child was somehow charmingly sad. Dabbling in art and deriving happiness from watching birds or studying nature were acceptable avocations, but no way to make a living. His poor family! How often Audubon sensed patronizing contempt in a look, or a casual remark that carried the unspoken message: Poor lunatic, poor boob. Insouciant as he was outwardly, he was inwardly sensitive to such criticism, as his long emotional letters show—many appeal to Almighty God to give him strength and patience. He did so want to succeed. But in his beloved wilderness there were no carping tongues. Nature did not judge or question conditions of birth or origin, creed, or ambition. Nature "was itself" and in it, he could be himself. He had been where the many had not. Only a few would ever know the keen high wonder and satisfaction of observing, of surviving this wild country the way he had. The common man had precious little time for romantic transcending of his daily round. In that sense Audubon was luckier than most men, and during most of his dark times he was able to remember that.

Besides physical strength, self-confidence, and emotional resilience, Audubon had other gifts that served him well. One was his generosity of spirit. From his accounts of his fellow human beings it is clear that he was the sort of man who "never met a stranger." He had a kind of naive trust in others and in his own innate amiability. His forthrightness, informality, and ebullience made a powerful impression on even the slightest acquaintance, arousing either a strong liking for him or an equally strong dislike, even sometimes both at once. Meeting Audubon must have been rather like meeting a force of nature.

One may wonder whether Audubon in his physical ordeals in the wilderness was sustained by his religious faith (as have been so many others in that situation) or, conversely, whether in the wilderness he found religion. His life and writings, on close examination, seem quite uncluttered by metaphysical speculations or sectarian or doctrinaire concerns. Most of his references to religion show a simple, unquestioning faith in the "the Good Creator of us all," a faith rather like his trust in his fellow men, which was undemanding and tolerant of differences in habits and mores. Baptized a Roman Catholic, Audubon married into the Quaker faith and assimilated easily the Quaker usage of "thee" and "thy." His tolerance, adaptability, and general freedom from narrow-mindedness were lifelong advantages.

Yet another, and not the least, of his gifts was his sense of humor. Life on the frontier was often grim and sometimes terrifying. Laughter was the psychological antidote for worry, fear, tears, and frustration. The tall tale, the cock-and-bull story, the waggish yarn, all flourished; indeed, they reached their grandest heights in nineteenth-century America. A teller would announce, "I come from one of the outlying areas, and I can outlie anyone in the house." One of Audubon's favorite stories was a lengthy tale of how poisonous the snakes were in Kentucky. He would tell the "sad but true story" of the man who was snakebit on his leather boot. He killed the snake, but, unbeknownst to him, a fang had broken off in his boot. He didn't even notice the scratch. He died the next day. A week later, his eldest son tried on the dead father's boots. Again, he hardly noticed the minute scratch and died mysteriously. And so it goes with the other sons, until finally the boots are discarded. The family dog chews on them and dies straight away. The cause of all these deaths was never discovered. Neighbors left the area thinking these folk died of fever. No one ever figured out, Audubon would say, that it was the broken tooth of a Kentucky rattler that was the killer.

Another traveler would earnestly report on the fertility of his farmlands, telling how he planted corn and bean seeds dipped in axle grease to keep the seedlings from burning up as they came whizzing up through the soil. One of Audubon's stories told how raccoons caught crayfish by dipping their own tails as bait. He'd watched 'em do it. Audubon's sons quickly assumed their father's sense of joking. Failing to bag so much as a single duck on a hunting trip, the boys explained, straight-faced, that a hawk had flown off with their father's gun just as they were about to fire it at a huge flock of mallards.

Any account of Audubon confronting the wilderness must include his first great adventure in the wild, which took place in the Tawapatee Bottoms of southern Illinois in the winter of 1809-10. Certainly Audubon himself remembered, talked, and wrote about this time well into his old age. At Christmastime he, his partner Rozier, and his friend Nat Pope left Louisville on a riverboat with a French patroon. They were making for Ste. Genevieve, on the Mississippi south of St. Louis, where they planned to trade merchandise from their store. At the confluence of the Ohio and the big river, they encountered ice floes and a terrible snowstorm which finally stopped their ascent of the river some twenty miles south of Cape Girardeau. Having pulled the boat to shore, the men set about making themselves and it safe for the duration of the bad weather. Some cut trees and lashed logs to the hull of the keelboat to protect it from drifting ice, while others built a three-sided structure of logs and packed snow, what the settlers called a "half-faced" cabin. The crew took the boat's large sail to roof the structure. Meanwhile, great logs of white ash as large as three feet through and sixty feet long were rolled together before the open side of the "half-faced." All frontiersmen knew that white ash is the only tree whose wood burns well when "green" (freshly cut). The storm and ice lasted six weeks. The huge fire attracted Osage and Shawnee Indians from a considerable distance. The company survived on wild turkey, swans, bear meat, opossum, and fish caught through the ice. Audubon and Pope played duets on violin and flute, and the French boatmen sang—all to the astonished pleasure of the Indians, who stayed on helping to hunt game. After six weeks the men were able to obtain provisions from Cape Girardeau. For a month-and-a-half, in snow and freezing weather, the great fire had roared, flames towering into the sky.

The know-how crucial for survival is learned first and fast. After that, what matters most is the kind of know-how that increases one's comfort: ordinary make-do's, matters of convenience. Audubon, who was already a skilled hunter when he came to Kentucky, quickly assimilated the folk wisdom of the frontiersmen there. All his life he was as fascinated with such human lore as he was with birds and their behavior. Evidence of his fascination abounds in his writings, which record many such bits of wisdom. "Trail your guns," George Rogers Clark used to call to his men, "Windfall thicket ahead, fallen timber!" A gun or a fishing rod goes best through the woods when pointing behind you, else you soon find a bush or branch between you and it. Approach game or enemy from downwind so your scent and noise is carried away from them. Walk Indian fashion, toe first, ready to lift off a twig that might crack, then heel. If you spook a squirrel to the far side of the tree, throw a chunk of wood past the tree and he'll be spooked back to the near side. Or if a squirrel is peeking but won't show his head, shake a piece of red flannel so he'll raise his head out of curiosity. Bang! Hunting antelope or buffalo on the plains, hobble your horse in a swale downwind of the herd and crawl a few hundred yards toward the animals. Then roll on your back and kick your feet in the air. This unusual activity will often pique the curiosity of the prey. Two men behaving thus strangely seem to interest them even more than one, and some may come over for a look, right into range of your rifle. Audubon used this trick on his 1843 expedition to the upper Missouri. When a bison is killed and you are very hungry, you cut off the tongue and salt it with gunpowder to flavor. As the butchering proceeds, a cut from the hump sprinkled with gall for the bile salts, is a mountain man's delight. In later years, Audubon would say of an ignorant man, "He wouldn't know to salt his meat with gunpowder." Smearing rancid bear grease on your face and neck will protect you against blackflies, deer flies, and mosquitos. Indeed, "It keeps most everything away," some said. Twirling or switching a leafy branch before your face clears spider webs or insect swarms from your path. Dense smoky fires keep both insects and wolves at bay. A coon or fox skin cap or heavy wool hat with a trailer of oilcloth keeps rain from running inside your collar. In Labrador Audubon wore such headgear, as well as boots whose soles were spiked with nails, to keep him from slipping on seaweeds and tidal rocks when wading, hunting for water birds, or fishing. Beaver and otter shot by moonlight will sink for an hour or so, then rise to the surface where they are easily collected at dawn. Dense grass or reeds wrapped tightly in bundles, then lashed together and covered with a buffalo hide makes an adequate raft for transporting trappers and their furs and hides downriver or for pulling behind a swimming horse. A black bear provides not only good meat and a skin for bedding or a robe, but also several gallons of grease, a good general lubricant, useful in cooking and good for greasing gun patches. Audubon used it for all of the above and also dressed his long hair with it, as the Indians did.

The American woodsman survived with relatively few tools; those needed to get fire and food were the most important: a gun, an ax, and a knife; a pouch of lead bullets or shot; a flask or horn of blackpowder; a "possible bag" with patches, wads, and bear grease; flint and steel for camp fires; and sometimes a magnetic compass (though nature gave signs enough).

Nearly every woodsman carried dry tinder for fires. Tinder often was shredded cedar bark or the abandoned nest of a field sparrow or a prairie warbler or "some such." He carried with it a fire starter kit. This included a chunk of rough flint and a steel striker (the shape of a flattened "C"). A lucky few had one of the kind of tobacco tins whose lid contained a "burning glass." One surefire method was to use the flintlock of a discharged gun (ideally a pistol). A hunter would pour priming powder into the pan, close the frizzen, leaving it wedged open a bit with a piece of leather. He would cock the flint hammer, then tilt the gun as he fired it so that the flash-in-the-pan dropped sparks onto a bird's nest, at the center of which was a greased patch sprinkled with gunpowder. The nest would usually erupt in a ball of fire when the burning patch and tinder was fanned by hand or hat. Small twigs and branches were quickly added, then the larger sticks and logs.

A reliable gun was absolutely indispensable equipment for the woodsman. Audubon, like most other frontiersmen, had a connoisseur's eye, and a special love, for fine firearms. In Audubon's case, his gun was not only a tool for providing game, but, more important, his specimen harvester. Audubon's choice, the long double-barreled fowler or shotgun, was more popular among European sportsmen than with American hunters. The quintessential arm of the latter was the now renowned Pennsylvania or Kentucky rifle. There is no record of Audubon ever having owned the famed long rifle; indeed, it was not suited to his needs. However, he wrote with considerable admiration about the rifle frolics where marksmen set themselves such tasks as driving a nail by plumb-center shooting and snuffing out a candle by shooting off the wick. Audubon claimed to have witnessed such marksmanship by none other than Daniel Boone himself at a Frankfort, Kentucky, tavern in 1810. The Boone references in his sketches are thought by some to be apocryphal, but true or not, Audubon knew and admired the value of such marksmanship, and he reports in detail his introduction to the then newly invented percussion lock which was replacing the flintlock ignition system.

In his lifetime Audubon owned many fine guns, both flintlock and percussion—all were long double-barreled shotguns. During his time in New Orleans he bought a shotgun of high craftsmanship for $125.00, a substantial sum for a struggling artist to pay. The gun was, in effect, a gift from a Madame André, who had sat, and paid, for a portrait. Audubon had an older shotgun from Mill Grove days which he then gave to his young art assistant, Joseph Mason. On the ramrod of his new gun, Audubon carved his name as Laforest Audubon and the date February 22, 1821. Unfortunately, this and other guns of his were destroyed in the great New York City fire of 1835. After the fire, he ordered a fine new weapon from the Manchester gunsmith, Conway. A description of this gun and Audubon's fondness for it is found in Stanley C. Arthur's book, *Intimate Life of the American Woodsman* (a biography of Audubon).

> Audubon was spending all his spare time in the woods and fields with the new gun he brought back from London. It was a handsome expensive weapon, with mountings of gold and silver. The fowling-piece was double-barreled, of 18-gauge bore, and was fired by means of a percussion cap, a remarkable advance over the old flint lock. The length was extraordinary, measuring 63 inches, and it weighed twelve pounds. Deeply engraved between the barrels was the inscription, 'John J. Audubon, Citizen of the United States, F.L.S.L.' the initials evidence of his fellowship in the Linnean Society of London. The gun carried a concealed trap door in the butt-plate, greatly exciting the curiosity of Doctor Pope and Augustin Bourgeat when they fondled and fired the beautiful weapon.

At that time English firearms were considered, properly so, the finest in the world. This is the weapon that appears in most later portraits of Audubon in which he is holding a gun.

It is impossible to categorize the Audubon of the years before 1820 by any one term: he was an artist, a lover of nature, a wilderness traveler, an entrepreneur, a woodsman, and so on. But from about 1820 onward, these various identities began to coalesce. Audubon's love affair with the American wilderness was gradually transforming itself from a pre-empting interest to something grander—a mission.

In 1819, after a series of business reverses culminating in his declaring bankruptcy, Audubon obtained a position through Dr. Daniel Drake at the Western Museum of Cincinnati (it was attached to the Lancaster Seminary, which later became the University of Cincinnati). Here he was associated with Drake and other naturalists. As resident taxidermist, he was offered the substantial salary (at that time) of $125 per month. His immediate superior, Robert Best, was a man with wide and informed interests in all matters of natural history. It would be difficult to overestimate the importance of this brief period in Audubon's life and what it meant to his future. While the museum soon proved to be a financial failure and was disbanded, it was here that Audubon consolidated his strengths as a naturalist and saw new purpose as a painter. Here he discovered a focus. It ended his haphazard, random painting of birds, and his portfolio took on new meaning. From that time on he would seek to obtain specimen skins, to identify birds with greater diligence, and to properly delineate them on paper. He began to think as a systematist and in a larger sense to see nature as a vast puzzle to be solved. A complete accurate portrayal of birds in natural poses now appeared to him as a worthy career. He could rival the great Mark Catesby or Alexander Wilson.

He would paint the birds of North America and publish a book of his paintings. For the next two decades he devoted his many considerable skills to accomplishing his mission. All that he had previously learned—about birds, about painting, about taxidermy, about natural history, about survival in the wilderness, about people, about America—came into play. The hours, days, weeks, months, years, spent in the woods with gun and sketchbook were translated ultimately into the magnificent plates of the double elephant folio. His lifelong curiosity about birds and their habits and all that time spent in satisfying it became the *Ornithological Biography*. And the adventures he had had along the way, the eccentric characters he had met, the tall tales he had heard as well as the true stories about the remarkable New World, provided a wealth of material for the "Episodes." Even his skills as a woodsman were useful now in more than one way, not only on his expeditions but also in the salons and drawing rooms of Europe, where his exotic appearance and his fund of stories caused a sensation and helped sell subscriptions among the fashionable world to his great work, while his merits as artist and naturalist won over the world of science and learning.

By the end of the 1830s, the *Birds of America* and *Ornithological Biography* had been published. Republication of them in smaller format, which was done in the early 1840s, made the Audubon family financially comfortable for the first time. They were able to buy the Minniesland estate on the Hudson, which was Audubon's home for the rest of his life.

In 1843 Audubon undertook a new project, one that would once again take him into the wilderness. For his first great work he had traveled downriver as far as New Orleans, gone southwest to Houston and the Texas shore, sailed southeast to the Florida Keys, and traveled north to Maine, Newfoundland, and Labrador. He had seen the Eastern wilderness when he was young and tireless and when the wilderness itself seemed invincible and inexhaustible, so vast and so rich was it. He had walked the banks of the Mississippi when the land belonged to Osage warriors; he had piped his flute and played his violin by Indian campfires. He had felt the great earthquake of 1811 that formed Reelfoot Lake. He was filled with memories, but now he had a new ambition and he wanted to go where he had not been before, to the trans-Mississippi West. He wanted to paint the mammals of North America, the "viviparous quadrupeds."

He and his party booked passage on an upriver steamboat, the *Omega*, which took them up the Missouri past Council Bluffs, past Fort Pierre, past the Mandan villages and on to Fort Union on the Yellowstone, fourteen hundred miles from St. Louis. He would, as he said, "ransack the west" in search of the mammals.

There is no doubt that Audubon enjoyed the expedition, but during it he wrote in his journal of feeling old. The first folio volume of the *Quadrupeds* came out in 1845, the second in 1846. By then Audubon's health had so far declined that he was unable to do any more work on the project, which was finished by others. His remaining years were spent in peaceful retirement at Minniesland.

Audubon would gaze across the Hudson with eyes too tired for painting, and remember . . . and remember. Among those long-fading memories were the bits and traces of how, as a younger man, he had survived alone or with other men, white and red, in a vanishing wilderness. Men who knew. As he gazed, he would be somewhere "out there," eating parched corn or cornpone and jerky, talking to Osage hunters in their own language; or he would be in a frontier tavern or cabin, then sleeping on calico sheets spread over cornhusks, or sleeping outside on bearskin robes. Or he would be threading lines through the bull-hide loops to *cordelle* a keelboat up the Mississippi. A while later he might be tying a smoked venison ham to a small sapling of a size he knew no marauding bear could climb. Next he might be setting trotlines on the Ohio to catch catfish, sturgeon, or buffalo fish. How the days had flown by. One moment, in his mind, he was in England smiling at the Scotch engraver, Lizars, who was insisting that he wear his wolfskin coat so as to not be mistaken for some one of the English gentry. He was, after all, "The American Woodsman." Then he would be sleeping on a buffalo hide under the wagon off from Fort Union with Culbertson and Harris, or shooting at wolves, elk, and beaver, killing all sorts of quadrupeds, and feeling now remorse or sadness for their dwindling numbers. He remembered when venison hams sold for 25 cents apiece, when a deerhide brought a dollar, when prime buffalo meat was a penny a pound.

There had been desperate times. There had been close calls. He remembered the summer day in 1843 when Culbertson's gun blew up, lock, stock, and breech but killing no one. Another time and place, the breech plug cone of another gun had exploded, and the cone whizzed past his head. He had been lucky. Where had the years gone? Where was that wilderness now, he thought. Was it ever really there as he saw it? Had the best of it come to ruin as he then felt his body had? Were all of the bird and animal species that he had painted still out there?

In his mind he retraced his travels—Mill Grove overland to Pittsburgh, Pittsburgh to Cincinnati and Louisville, Shippingport to Henderson, on the Mississippi from Cape Girardeau to St. Louis, Natchez to New Orleans, on and on, up the Missouri, St. Louis to Ft. Union and home. He moved along them all, his dream drifting in the flow of time. He stirred, watched the casual errand of a kingfisher as the western light fell across the Hudson. He felt the cool air drifting toward the valley.

It has been said that a genius is a man whose profession dies with him. Such a person invents a way of life. Audubon, in his perennial search for new species to paint, original forms and variations to be noted, folios to sell, did live an original life. He invented his own profession. Artist, author, natural historian, entrepreneur—that was an original hybrid. As he sought for new species, society was eventually to discover him. He was the new species on the wilderness frontier. History honors original lives. A name endures. In a commemorative labeling of all sorts, he endures. In the names of living species, streets and towns, societies and wildlife sanctuaries—"Audubon" has become synonymous with wild birds, wild America, around the world.

When thinking of Audubon, an image endures. It is the figure of a man crouching in wolf-skin coat, his auburn hair dark with bear grease, his boots firmly placed in the alluvium. He is raising a long flintlock fowler, cocking the flint hammers, click, click. Straining to level the gun, he blinks through sweat to draw the bead, steadies, his pet dog tense and waiting. Then, a thundering staccato of lead-shot rips the highest tree crowns. Above the drift of blackpowder smoke, the scream of wild birds echoes everywhere. A form, soft feathers folded, slips branch to branch, into the underbrush—one more bird to be transformed into an immortal image, its wings in flight again—this fragment of America to be known to millions. The man rises, moves on to some new difficult place, drawn and drawing across the wilderness.

The Enchanted Forest

6 *Frank Levering*

> How amply are the labours of the naturalist compensated, when, after observing the wildest and most distrustful birds, in their remote and almost inaccessible breeding places, he returns from his journeys, and relates his adventures to an interested and friendly audience.
>
> —Audubon

One cold day in winter, in a century not our own, a certain American was traveling with a visitor from a foreign country through a Kentucky forest. They spied a small black animal with pale yellow markings, and the foreigner was told that he beheld a squirrel. Indeed, remarked his companion, this was no ordinary squirrel, but a kind that would allow itself to be caressed. Having no reason to doubt the word of a woodsman as experienced as his host, the foreigner approached the creature. His long cloak flapping in the breeze, the bold fellow laid a stick across the animal's back, and leaned down to catch it. Woe be to unwary foreigners! The "squirrel" raised its tail and bathed the poor fellow in a memorable perfume.

Nor was this the end of the tale. Continuing their journey—the foreigner riding downwind from his host—the companions rode at nightfall into a heavy snowstorm. Gaining permission to spend the night at a cabin, the two men approached the hearth. The cold air had suppressed the scent of skunk; now, the heat of the fire fanned it pungently alive. All nostrils quivered in the uncommodious Kentucky cabin. "What a shock to the whole party!" wrote the prankster American host, none other than John James Audubon. "Although the cloak was put out of the house," he continues wryly, "its owner could not very well be treated in such a way." With corn-shucking to be done, the cabin-dwellers quickly "took to their heels."

Like Audubon's visitor after the encounter with the skunk, we now have good reason, at times, to doubt the word of John James Audubon. A born storyteller, Audubon would have made a dreadfully unreliable journalist. The brilliant painter of birds painted in words a remarkably broad canvas of the America of his era, but some of it must stand as wonderfully entertaining fiction. A chronicler of his life and times, Audubon in voluminous journals and in various books wrote for an intriguing diversity of reasons and readers, but above all he wrote, wrote, wrote.

Over the years Audubon compiled a small mountain of American lore and folklore. Curious about the ways of wild animals, he brought an equal curiosity to bear on the ways of humans. Audubon was fascinated by American know-how—how Americans hunted, fished, and forested, how they braced themselves for frontier perils, how they picked up the pieces after natural disasters. A cultural historian of sorts, Audubon amassed an impressive record of popular American wisdom—what Americans had learned, or believed they had learned, in their encounters with the wilderness, the native Americans, and their own diversity of folkways handed down from the various parts of Europe they or their parents or grandparents had come from.

As "cultural historian," Audubon often painted in broad strokes, describing heroic American types—lumberjacks, deer hunters, Kentucky marksmen—in generalized, highly idealized terms. Yarns, anecdotes, horror stories, his own brand of tall tales—Audubon the storyteller told them all. Like most raconteurs, Audubon seldom documented his sources. He begged, borrowed, stole, and invented his stories, embellishing them as he saw fit.

In the end, as storytellers sometimes do, Audubon created his own legend. A consummate self-dramatist, Audubon emerges in his own stories as a wandering folk hero, overcoming all obstacles, defying suspicion and numerous brushes with death in his never-ending quest to bring the birds of America before the eyes of the civilized world. Whether that version of his life is true, false, or somewhere in between, Audubon's unique story was in capable hands.

In *How to Tell a Story*, Mark Twain observed that "The humorous story is American, the comic story is English, the witty story is French. The humorous story depends for its effect upon the *manner* of telling; the comic story and the witty story upon the matter."

Like Twain, but years before him, Audubon drew from a substantial oral tradition of rough-and-ready frontier humor. And, as Twain might have, Audubon the humorous storyteller, in recounting the practical joke he played on the foreigner, relied much on the *manner* of telling—the wry understatement of the cloak—not the man—put out of the cabin. Though the matter of the joke is humorous in itself, Audubon's tale is more artfully told—more humorously, in Twain's sense—as a series of similarly wry understatements in the face of frontier necessities. Riding downwind from Audubon, staying in the cabin, sharing Audubon's bed that night—the scented foreigner must make adjustments while steering a course of necessity. Skillfully, Audubon exploits the story's humorous potential, doesn't spoil it with overkill.

Audubon was a young man at the time of the skunk episode, but he did not lose his relish of practical jokes as he grew older. When he was in his fifties, on an expedition to the upper reaches of the Missouri River, Audubon tried a joke on his earnest friend John Bachman. He claimed to have received word of an animal called the "Ke-ko-ká-ki," or "Jumper," a peculiar yet formidable beast, stretching nine feet and four inches from head to tail, weighing six hundred pounds, and possessing antlers and a pouchless belly. Carrying out the joke, Audubon assumed credit as the official discoverer of this North American reply to the kangaroo. Once a joker, always a joker, it seems. In a more celebrated incident of his younger years, Audubon, hosting the naturalist Constantine Rafinesque, persuaded his eccentric guest of the existence of horrendous fishes of the Ohio, as well as some herons, all sketched by Audubon. Unluckily for the gullible guest who included these discoveries in his book, they existed only in Audubon's mischievous imagination.

It is perhaps not coincidental that yet again the butt of Audubon's joke was a foreigner. On first encountering Audubon, his acquaintance Vincent Nolte described the Caribbean-born, French-reared American as "an odd fish." Here was a man wearing a Madras handkerchief around his head, in the manner of a French seaman, and claiming, in English spoken with a thick French accent, to be English. Later, Audubon described himself as "cosmopolitan," insisting that he belonged to all countries. Whatever his claim to an American identity, Audubon stuck out in his adopted country like a French cathedral. In the manhood proving grounds of frontier society, Audubon had much to prove. Not as complacent as Rafinesque, Audubon surely had paid a price for his own brand of picturesque individuality. His joke on Rafinesque was perhaps as much on the foreigner in himself—one of the forms of release from the frequent ordeal of difference.

Just as he delighted in pulling a foreigner's leg, Audubon in his stories describes eccentric characters with an added measure of comic relish. His lively portrait of Rafinesque fairly prances when he recalls how the naturalist one night, completely naked, went crashing around his bedroom swinging Audubon's violin at flying bats. A "war," Audubon described the scene—this time not resorting to understatement.

One of Audubon's most charming comic sketches was about a painter he encountered in New Orleans. He noticed a man dressed in a green coat, yellow trousers, and a pink waistcoat, who was carrying a silk umbrella in one hand and a cage of birds in the other and singing pompously. As Audubon got closer, he saw that a young alligator was peering out from a bunch of magnolias tucked into the pink waistcoat. Audubon asked if he could examine the birds. In the exchange that followed, Audubon learned the dandy's name—John Wesley Jarvis—Jarvis expressed his doubt that Audubon knew anything about birds, Audubon claimed to be "a student of nature," and the encounter was off to an auspicious start.

What came next, in Audubon's account, reads as broad farce bordering on the bizarre. Accompanying the painter to his studio, Audubon found paintings—and live birds—galore. Jarvis took up a gun and was using it as a walking stick; suddenly he asked the helpless Audubon if he had ever seen a percussion lock. Audubon had not. To Audubon's alarm, Jarvis was determined to prove that the lock was effective underwater. Placing it in a basin of water, he caused a deafening report—terrifying the caged birds, not to mention Audubon. Next intent on displaying his marksmanship, Jarvis fired at one of his easels, splintering a supporting pin. After firing off a second shot for good measure, Jarvis then ordered an assistant to bring forth a lighted candle, and with one shot snuffed its flame. Trying to remain calm, Audubon drew attention to the "uneasiness" of the alligator, forgotten in the artist's waistcoat, struggling to escape. Jarvis replied that his pet should "have a dram." He promptly dumped the poor beast in the basin of water. Audubon wished desperately to escape, but his fellow painter would not hear of it. Jarvis insisted on demonstrating his painting technique, and followed that up with a story. Audubon's final comment is a gem of self-deprecating, self-recognizing humor: "No doubt Jarvis looked on me, as I did on him, as an 'original,' a cracked man."

Audubon retained his sense of humor—and thus perhaps his sanity—through long periods of professional failure or uncertainty, separation from his wife and family, and genuine poverty. He peppered his letters and journals—often his solace during these times—with comic observations. In a letter describing conditions on board the steamer *Gallant*, en route to St. Louis, Audubon writes of a "state room" which, he observes, "was evidently better fitted for the smoking of hams than the smoking of Christians." In his journals of the Missouri River expedition, Audubon notes wryly how a bullet, fired by a Santee Indian from the riverbank, passed through the pantaloons of a sleeping Scot on board the boat. In his Episode, "The Ohio," a generally earnest account of travel through the Ohio Valley, Audubon describes how, traveling with his wife and infant son by skiff, he one evening heard savage yells, increasing in volume as his rowers pulled toward the opposite shore in alarm. Remembering recent Indian "depredations" in the area, Audubon was extremely apprehensive, until the source was revealed: "an enthusiastic set of Methodists," at a camp meeting in full swing.

If Audubon had a flair for humor, he possessed nothing less than a gargantuan gift for hyperbole and, on occasion, outright lies. A steady diet of Audubon's prose convinces a reader that here was a man congenitally incapable of telling merely the unvarnished, unembellished truth. Seldom could he resist the temptation to make a good story better. And some details of his own biography he made out of whole cloth. For if Audubon had much to prove, he also had much to hide. His birth was illegitimate and as a painter he was essentially self-taught. About those facts he not merely invented—no euphemisms here—he lied. Audubon in the face of criticism of himself or his work was capable of uninhibited flights of fancy—suddenly making his father an "admiral," and making himself one who had studied painting under the great French master David. He knew the truth about himself—that he was an untutored, Caribbean-born bastard—yet he was not anxious to disabuse those who thought him Louisiana-born, a red-blooded American, when it was the legend, the mythology, that would further the ends of his magnificent quest.

It remains difficult, however, to distinguish in Audubon the end point of hyperbole and the beginning of belief. What he knew to be false, what he wanted to believe, what he ultimately did believe—in all the smoke, where is the man? What we have is the writing itself, and what we know about the Episodes is that, here, Audubon among other things had to be a kind of salesman. To some extent, the vastly entertaining hype of the Episodes was the fine art of salesmanship. The Episodes were in effect "advertisements" for potential subscribers to the paintings, and in them America—and thus by extension America's birds—was sold as a kind of Olympus, a legendary land on a grand scale.

Audubon's America! What a land! Even in what would seem its more pedestrian pursuits, Audubon's America is no ordinary place. No fewer than eight bears chase a group of ax-carrying lumbermen in Pennsylvania—a tale told to Audubon which he retold with his own added touches. Audubon's description of Maine's Penobscot River conjures the image of Indian-filled canoes gliding in all directions, seemingly covering the river's surface, while "majestic" mountains loom in the background. The road to Bangor "teemed" with Penobscot Indians returning from market. In his account of a ride in the pine barrens of Florida, Audubon, while fearing for his neck every time his horse stumbles, regales the reader with his companion's tale of a horse whose lips were bitten off by an alligator.

Though characteristic of Audubon's legendary American landscape, these descriptions seem modest indeed when compared with his account of an event near the Maine village of Dennysville. Audubon describes how the "lumberers" unclog a creek full of milled logs, sending the timber rushing downstream to fill the miller's empty dam. The effect is a kind of damburst, the logs having dammed the creek a mile upstream. Two men knock out the abutment to the log dam with axes. Then:

> They had no more than escaped danger, by leaping from one crosslog to another and onto shore, than the mass of waters—frightful peril—burst forth with a horrible roar. All eyes turned toward the huge heap of logs in the gorge below. The tumultuous burst of water instantly swept away every obstacle and rushed in foaming waves through the timber. There was a slow heaving motion in the mass of logs, as if some monster lay writhing convulsively beneath, struggling with fearful energy to extricate itself from the crushing weight. The movement increased as the waters rose. The mass of timber reached in all directions and became more and more entangled. Logs bounced and clashed, submerged, rose in the air upon sharp collision. It was like the waging of a war of destruction which the ancients describe in

accounts of the Titans. To the eye of the painter the wrothy foaming, the angry curling of the water, might suggest such a scene. The tremulous, rapid motion of the logs that shot into the air must have inspired the poet to describe them as the conflict of giants.

Not the Columbia River, this was a creek in Maine dammed with logs. Yet what Audubon saw was "like the waging of a war of destruction which the ancients describe in accounts of the Titans." Here is a job for no local Dennysville reporter to describe, but some latter-day Homer. Here is a "conflict of giants." While the damburst at Dennysville was no doubt an impressive sight, Audubon's description leaves little room in the Audubon bag of analogies for some truly catastrophic event. Beyond the Titans, who could be summoned from epic mythology to do justice to catastrophe? Yet there is no denying that Audubon's hyperbole is exciting reading. And he continues:

> ... The mingled wreck swept along until the current reached such a pitch that the logs were dashed against the rocky shores. The report was like that of distant artillery or the rumbling of thunder. Onward it rolled, the emblem of wrack and ruin, destruction and chaotic strife. It was to me like watching the rout of a vast army that had been surprised and overthrown. The roar of the cannon, the groans of the dying, the shouts of the avengers, thundered through my brain. But from out the frightful confusion of the scene came a melancholy feeling that did not entirely leave me for many days ...

Whatever else might be added, a flow of logs, like beauty, is in the eye of the beholder, and Audubon's was a vivid eye. For his own version of the tall tale, Audubon was well-equipped to compete with the highly developed native tradition of his adopted land.

Cultivating, as he did, the image of "the American woodsman," it was perhaps only natural that Audubon would tell a tall tale or two, for tall tales, in their most striking native form, were the pride of the backwoodsman. Tall tales had been told in early New England, but it was after the War of 1812 and among the backwoodsmen on the Western frontier that they flourished. Confronted always with perils, some real, some perhaps imaginary, the backwoodsman developed the narration of his feats into a credibility-defying art form. He could wade the Mississippi, he could run like a horse and swim like an alligator. He could split bullets at a hundred paces, see a bee a mile away. By the early 1830s, the tall tale was in its prime. The story was told of the British Revolutionary officer, found buried in Rocky Mountain snows, who recounted his life story when the backwoodsman thawed him out. Tall tales about Davy Crockett started modestly enough—he could whip a wildcat or lead a buffalo to a drink of water—but after his death, storytellers had Crockett escaping a tornado by riding a streak of lightning, escaping up Niagara Falls on the back of an alligator, and, tallest of all, unjamming creation, which had frozen fast when earth and sun had become jammed on their axes, and couldn't move.

In its truest form, the tall tale blended in elements of the supernatural, and it was told deadpan, as if defying the listener to disbelieve. Toward danger, the teller of the tall tale preserved a characteristic attitude: it doesn't perturb the hero. Either he is oblivious, or he laughs in its face. In Audubon's tales, the supernatural is not stressed, at least in its most overt forms. But like the tall-tale tellers and their tales he seems to have admired, Audubon did want to preserve a heroic posture toward danger, and in the telling itself he sought to achieve a kind of gale force on his readers, knocking them down with the remarkable feats. Among the tellers of tall tales, in backwoods gatherings, there had long been a competitive tradition—which tale was best?—and the winner, like a champion wrestler, was the man with knockdown force.

Audubon himself figures prominently in one of his tall tales, though the hero is not the author, but his horse. No ordinary steed, Barro first made his future owner's acquaintance in Kentucky. Barro was fresh in from the headwaters of the Arkansas River, where his owner, also named Barro, had purchased him from Osage Indians. According to Barro (the man) the Indians had taken the horse from the wild, from one of the herds descended from the horses brought to the Southwest by the conquistadors.

In looks, Barro the horse, according to Audubon, was ungainly, a kind of Walter Matthau among horses, with a bulge in front of his large head, an unkempt mane, and a scanty tail that almost dragged the ground. But to Audubon's imaginative eye, he was a horse with spirit, and his chest was broad, his legs muscular. He was a four-year-old bay that had never been shod.

Audubon, whose hope nor imagination had also never been shod, upon learning the horse was for sale asked to give him a tryout. A tryout it was.

Barro soared over huge logs in the woods, "as lightly as an elk," until Audubon was persuaded that on a deer or bear hunt his mount could hurdle any obstacle. Barro was next put to a test of strength. Audubon plunged him into a muddy swamp, and Barro went through it as if it were butter, taking any and every direction in his stride, keeping his nose close to the water as if able to sense the depth underfoot. So far, so good. Next, Audubon launched his homely but game horse into the Ohio River. Immediately, Barro swam against the current, head held high above the surface, breathing effortlessly and without, as Audubon notes proudly, the grunting noises most horses make when swimming. Well satisfied that the mighty Ohio was no match for Barro, Audubon finally galloped him home, shooting a turkey along the way from the saddle. "The wild horse"—as if born for turkey-hunting—carried Audubon directly to the bird, where Audubon picked it up without having to dismount. Needing no further demonstrations, Audubon promptly paid Barro's owner fifty dollars.

Shortly after the purchase, Audubon tells us, he set out on Barro at a four miles an hour clip to Philadelphia. This journey, on a wild or semi-wild horse, carried Audubon through Nashville, Knoxville; Abington, Natural Bridge, and Winchester, Virginia; Harpers Ferry; Fredericksburg, Maryland; Lancaster, Pennsylvania; and on to Philadelphia. A distance that most motorists, traveling by Interstate, would be proud to have under their belts, this little excursion was apparently no sweat—literally—to Barro, with his one-horsepower engine. At fuel stops, Audubon pumped corn blades, oats, hen eggs, and even pumpkins into his American Pegasus. As Audubon has it, Barro would not drink water if instructed to desist.

On the return trip, Barro, now presumably an educated horse having been to the intellectual center, Philadelphia, virtually understood a conversation between Audubon and Vincent Nolte. Nolte rode an expensive horse of which he was inordinately proud, and Audubon could not resist a race. Or rather, Barro could not resist, for it was his horse, in Audubon's tale, who responded to Nolte's challenge by pricking his ears and lengthening his pace. Naturally, Barro won. Audubon arrived at the inn which was the terminus of the race so far ahead of Nolte that he was able to put Barro away for the evening, order trout for Nolte and himself, and be standing at the door waiting to welcome Nolte upon his arrival. In Nolte's account of this first meeting with Audubon—they were to meet again on other occasions—no mention is made of the race to the inn. In Nolte's version, it was at the inn that he first saw Audubon.

As Audubon ends the tale, Barro on the return trip from Philadelphia covered two thousand effortless miles. Then as horse and rider approached Henderson, Barro, more prescient than Audubon, suddenly stopped in his tracks, groaned, hung his head, and spread his legs, utterly refusing to advance. Audubon wondered if his horse was dying. All at once, trees swayed, the ground rose and fell, and Barro's horse sense was no longer in doubt. Luckily for both legends—man and horse were equally destined for legendary status—the earthquake subsided, and they were spared.

The story of Barro is Audubon's brand of tall tale, a mix of truth and outright fiction, credible or close to it in many details, yet straining credulity at every turn. It portrays the frontier tall tale's cavalier attitude towards danger, the risks of Barro's tryout being a mere trifle. The tale of Barro, however, was little more than a stretching exercise for what Audubon was capable of in his prime, for instance, his tale of the dying pirate.

Audubon had this story from a ship's officer he met on one of his expeditions. In a secluded cove on the Gulf Coast, the officer had come upon a drifting yawl that held two blood-bathed bodies. From the shore came awful groans and a plea for help. There he found a pirate *in extremis*. A protracted, wildly incredible deathbed scene follows, one that is distinctly a tall tale in its contrivances. The pirate of course does not die until he has finished telling his story. And a singular story it is.

With pride and an utter lack of repentance the pirate recounts his many villainous deeds. Not only has he "sent many rascals to the devil," he killed his mother. Finally, as the reader knows it must, comes the disclosure that he knows where there is buried treasure. He refuses to name the spot, and as his throat fills with blood, chokes out, "I am a dying man. Farewell!"

As entertaining and as unsubtle as any pirate movie, Audubon's tale asks us to believe not only that a mortally wounded pirate conveniently keeps death at bay, but that the elements of his story—a murdered mother, deadly battles, a gory career—are as real as Kansas. A pirate himself— having pirated the familiar elements from pirate mythology—Audubon gets away with murder. That's show biz.

Beyond stylized entertainment, in the childhood of a nation there was perpetually, it would seem, the child in Audubon. Written for a practical reason, Audubon's tall tales, yarns, and anecdotes make up in boyish ebullience what they lack in adult credibility. In Audubon's yarns and anecdotes, there is a winning spontaneity, an uncensored childlike exhilaration in mere adventure.

Audubon tells the story, related to him, of a family in Maine haunted by the trauma of having once fled for their lives from a forest fire. Spending the night in a cabin, Audubon is detained the next day by heavy rains, and hears the father's account of the event, while his wife sits nervously at a spinning wheel, convinced that the cat's behavior foretells another forest fire. In the middle of the man's story, as he describes how neighbors had not escaped the flames, Audubon shamelessly—but with exuberance and perfect timing—has a gust of wind blow sparks from the chimney around the room, scaring the man's wife and daughter. Calming his family, the man tells Audubon how the three of them had fled.

Late one night the man was awakened by the snorting of horses. Throwing open his cabin door, he saw a wall of flames above the forest. In an account worthy of Irwin Allen, the Hollywood producer of "Towering Inferno," "Earthquake," and similar disaster films, Audubon has the man recall the vividly perilous details of escaping through the flames on horseback, the man holding his child in one arm, as behind them the cabin exploded into flames. Lifting the horn at his belt, the man had raised it to his lips as he rode, sounding a blast to bid his livestock and dogs to follow him. But his cattle had been consumed in the inferno, and his dogs had chased the herds of deer that had appeared before the riders, dogs never to be seen again. Jumping fire-streaked logs and singed by the flames, the man and his wife urged their horses on, fearing the animals would collapse as the flames overtook them. At last they reached a lake, letting their horses go as smoke billowed over them and blasts of heat drove them to their knees. Dipping themselves in the water, they watched, their child crying in fear, as the fire roared into the woods on the opposite shore of the lake, and rushed on. Wild animals came crashing into the lake beside them. Passing a hellish night, they breathed the smoke, tasted the ashes. Again, Audubon interrupts the narrative, having the man pause for breath and his wife bring him a bowl of milk before the story can be concluded. With morning came fresher air, but no diminishment of the heat. Dragging themselves from the lake, the man and his family warmed themselves beside a burning log, then ate a deer the man had shot in the lake. Strengthened, the family marched across miles of scorched earth. After two days, they came to forest the fire had not touched. Safe, they came to a cabin and were welcomed as heroic survivors.

A good story evocatively told, this adventure of escape from death tells us, again, about the teller. In a story, what the teller emphasizes, we can be sure, generally reflects what he admires or values. In this story of escape from fire, Audubon admires not only the family's courage, but also the man's qualities of leadership—his stamina, resourcefulness, even the calm he displays to his family when, in the present, the sparks frighten mother and daughter. However skeptically we may regard nineteenth-century portraits of male American heroism, the handling of the story reveals a dimension of Audubon. A good yarn could make a wounded Indian or the leader of a family embody Audubon's own values, but so could one of his numerous anecdotes, perhaps even more pointedly, for anecdotes, traditionally, have a point to make.

In describing the habits of the black bear, Audubon told what is essentially an anecdote in its ultimate conclusion. Awakened one night, he was asked by a farmer to join a bear hunt, organized to exterminate marauding bears in the farmer's corn crop. Gamely, Audubon participated in a surprise charge on the cornfield, driving the startled bears up dead trees surrounding the field. By the light of blazing fires, the crowd of hunters shot two cubs, while dogs, than a slave named Scipio, battled and finally killed the mother. Near dawn, the hunters put the torch to another tree, bringing down two more cubs, which were killed by the dogs. The hunt was a triumph—for the hunters. Exciting in its action and physical details, the story bears Audubon's vivid signature. Tellingly, however, he concludes his account: "before we left the field, the horses, dogs and Bears, together with the fires, had destroyed more corn inside of a few hours than had the poor Bear and her cubs during all their visits."

Similarly, other Audubon anecdotes have what we now might call an environmental point to make, while still others express what seems to have been his native sympathy for the underdog, whether man or beast. Though not explicitly partial to the wolf, the effect of Audubon's descriptions in "Pitting of the Wolves" is to draw sympathy to wolves trapped and butchered by human beings in the name of animal husbandry and agriculture. In his story of his encounter with a runaway slave and his family who live hidden in the woods, Audubon's basic point is that "generosity exists everywhere," thus justifying his friendly treatment of the runaways. In Audubon's portrayal, they are underdogs, with a just cause: not freedom itself, but the right not to have their family divided by selling the children to other slaveowners. Only because he intervened (Audubon seems to be saying), treating the fugitives as human beings, then pleading their case to their owner, did Audubon win their trust, save them from ruin, and secure their rights. No modest player in this little drama, Audubon probably exaggerated his role to make a point. A slaveowner himself, and no critic of slavery per se, he was himself a slave to the conventional wisdom of his era, and frequently to the popular stereotypes of blacks. But to make a point about why even runaways should be well treated, Audubon could reach into a huge bag of anecdotes.

Entertaining and instructive as we find his pranks, tall tales, yarns and anecdotes, Audubon's collection of American lore is equally impressive. Relying primarily on his narrative skills, Audubon drew heroic portraits of folk heroes and American types, telling their stories and idealizing them at the same time he chronicled their work and play, their wisdom and wit. In a sense truer of him than most of us, Audubon the man became what he saw, and where he wandered. A master of many environments, intensely curious, he met many kinds of Americans, found out what they did and how they did it. Thus the man with the thick French accent became—if anything—more American than the Americans.

It will surprise no one that Audubon, an acquaintance of Daniel Boone, described the folk hero as a "broad-chested, muscular giant of the western forests," when Boone, for the record, stood less than six feet tall, and was quite slender. According to Audubon, "the very motion of his lips" created the sensation that Boone—unlike Audubon—would always tell the truth.

Nevertheless, Audubon's portrait of Boone, based on a night together, explains Boone's alleged technique in escaping certain death at the hands of Indians when captured. Guarded by squaws when the warriors went off to investigate a gunshot, Boone watched the women drink from his flask of whiskey—and get drunk. When the squaws began to snore, Boone rolled to the fire, burned the cords that bound him, and escaped. In what may pass to a modern reader as unintentional humor—or, worse, the arrogant contempt of Boone for Indian weakness—Audubon's heroic portrait combines a story with his characteristic fascination with how something is done. When captured by Indians, the heroic American will do well to have a flask of whiskey on hand if he wishes to escape with his life.

Audubon's own view of the native Americans he encountered during his career is generally much more admiring than Boone's, taking into account the kind of integrity he described in the Indian wounded by his own arrow, and finding much courage, wisdom, and skill in the Indians' adaptation to their outdoor life. Where Audubon went, there, usually, would be the native Americans—from the Shawnees of the Mississippi Valley, to the Penobscots of Maine, to the various tribes of the upper Missouri. What Indians did for their livelihood—whether hunt alligators in the lower Mississippi, green turtles in the Florida Keys, or harvest pecans and hunt swans—was always of particular interest to Audubon, who took the attitude that he had something to learn from them, as well as something to prove when he went with them into the woods.

At Cash Creek, near the confluence of the Ohio and Mississippi, Audubon wintered with fifty Shawnee families, his journey northward on the Mississippi thwarted by ice. The Shawnees spoke a little French, Audubon a little of their tongue, but the common language between them was the great outdoors itself. Waiting out the thaw, Audubon learned Shawnee lore first hand. On his first swan hunt, Audubon learned what the Shawnees knew—that swans at a nearby lake kept free of ice by swimming night and day. Riding with the hunters in one of their canoes (the squaws, he notes wryly, did the paddling, while the warriors slept) Audubon observed a hunter's ballet. Dividing into two bands, one group startled the swans, sending them airborne, while another group waited in ambush in the direction they flew. Fifty swans fell, were gathered up and taken back to camp, where the squaws removed the feathers, bound for the fashion market of Europe. Hunting bear, Audubon saw how the Shawnees approached one specimen hiding in a hollow log. Brandishing a knife, one warrior entered, while the others guarded the entrance. What the Shawnees knew was that the bear, so confined, would not resist, but retreat until it was trapped and could be easily killed.

When the ice broke, Audubon left the Shawnees, parting, he writes, "like brethren." That was his longest sojourn with Indians, but there would be many more encounters with what was increasingly a culture, or cultures, subservient to the new Americans. On a trip to Niagara Falls, Audubon found the village of Buffalo flooded with Indians, "come to receive their annuity." To Audubon, the chief Red Jacket still had the look of nobility, while an Indian named Devil's Ramrod still projected the proper effect of savagery. But these were hardly the unfettered Indians of fable and lore. Nor were the impoverished, disease-plagued tribes along his route to the upper Missouri—the Iowa, Potawatomi, Omaha, Mandan, and others—the net effect of which was only repulsive to Audubon.

In 1843, his upper Missouri party admired the courageous way the Indians hunted the depleted bison; the Mandans charged headlong into the herd and fired their arrows, but the Gros Ventres, Blackfeet and Assiniboins drove unsuspecting herds into an elaborate, camouflaged pen after they had ceremoniously smoked their calumet pipes. Audubon was only an observer, on a few buffalo hunts, but his friend Edward Harris risked his life in them. Moderns are led to believe that Audubon engaged in these hunts because Harris's journal was "borrowed" on this matter nearly word for word and inserted into Audubon's journal by editor Maria Audubon. Sadly, the image of trapped buffalo, herded into an inescapable enclosure, stands as an apt metaphor for the Indians themselves at the close of the naturalist's lifetime. A vanishing act of both hunter and hunted was in performance all around the chroniclers Audubon and his companions on the high plains.

If the Indian trails were vanishing, new and broader trails with new footprints were taking their place. The tracks of Kentucky marksmen, Mississippi Valley squatters, hunters, fishermen, Florida live-oak and Maine and Pennsylvania lumberjacks—a litany of new American heroes—crossed and recrossed Audubon's landscape of prairies, seashores, swamps and forests. "I hear America singing," another chronicler, Walt Whitman, was to write. Audubon heard America plowing land, chopping trees, shooting game. Though there were moments of doubt, a few, even, of dark environmental prophecy, the young nation's exuberant voices were music to his ears.

Ever wondered about the early navigation of the Mississippi? Audubon will detail it for you, from the days of the keelboats, manned primarily by French Canadians, to the steamboat era, and how much it cost ($25 in 1829) for a steamboat ride from Shippingport, Kentucky to Natchez, Mississippi. How was a nine foot tall moose hunted in the snows of Maine? What's the best method for hunting deer at night? Ever wondered how to cut down a Florida live oak? Audubon will explain how the nineteenth century pros—the live-oakers—did it. How old would a twelve-foot long alligator probably be?

A teenage refugee from European war, Audubon found the answers to these questions—and a million more tidbits of American lore—with a particular affinity for the "second chance" dimension of many Americans—for those, like himself, actively pursuing a new life. "Much of the American population," he observed, "came from the unwanted of other countries." Not exactly a reject, Audubon had come to America "a stranger in a strange land," had entered manhood with a double-edge of exile and opportunity. Perhaps it was this personal history, a native tolerance and empathy, that enabled him not only to listen to a wide spectrum of American opinion and experience, but also to look favorably on pariahs, as the squatters in the Mississippi Valley were, by some, held to be.

In some ways, the squatters—those who lived along the Mississippi without owning land or paying taxes—embodied, for Audubon, the worthiest qualities of the young nation. Kentucky, with its cultural elegance and legendary riflemen, was a land of charm and plenty, of unquestioned heroism. But anxious to defend them from those European travelers and others who thought them "miserable beings," Audubon was himself closer to the squatters, living marginally, having a long period of struggle to earn respect. To him, this prototypical American was the most tenacious, at the same time the most adaptable of American breeds. Having endured an arduous journey from the worn-out land of the East, the squatter had occupied and cleared swamps and bogs, raised his cabin, survived his first winter, and with tremendous industry expanded his assets, raised sons of good character, and vastly increased the value of the land he had settled, richly deserving the eventual ownership granted him by the government. By such people, suggests Audubon, is the nation settled, and by such will it prosper, eventually to be a land of opulent farms and great cities. Gathering the lore of an American type struggling for respect, Audubon places the future of the nation in the hands of the lowly squatter.

Knowing many of the facts, if not necessarily the "why's," of Audubon's life, we find much of Audubon's appeal in such idiosyncratic viewpoints. In part, he remained the outsider, reposing his fantasies for success in surrogate heroes like the squatter. Yet much of Audubon was fully caught up in the American experience. He must have been; a man so enraptured by the primal call of hunting can surely call himself American in spirit.

Audubon chronicled the lore of fishing in formidable detail. The angler's companion, he is nothing less than the patron saint of hunters, so voluminously did he write on the art of hunting. Besides that of Florida sea turtles, Audubon chronicles the hunting lore of bear, deer, cougar, squirrel, moose, buffalo, wolf, raccoon, and various birds such as swan and duck. Chronicling, as well, what he knew about wildlife, he often paired this knowledge with the lore of hunters, including himself—or with robust accounts of memorable hunts. Bear-hunting lore, we saw, Audubon learned both from Indians and settlers. In his discussion of deer-hunting, Audubon distinguishes a wide variety of techniques, including nocturnal hunting, and offers a description of the deerhunter romantically comparable to that of James Fenimore Cooper, who was to die in the same year as Audubon, and whom he greatly admired. Audubon had hunted squirrel with no less a deadeye than Daniel Boone himself. For his moose-hunting lore, uncharacteristically, he had to rely on second-hand accounts, but made up in color what he lacked in experience. Audubon himself participated in a rousing, all-night cougar hunt in Mississippi as the guest of a squatter. The raccoon, the bighorn and the wolf had all known the determined pursuit of the American woodsman. Audubon's description of a coon hunt captures the laconic flavor of the coonhunters as well as gives an entertaining summation of raccoon habits. "For my part," he concludes, "I prefer a living Raccoon to a dead one, and find more pleasure in hunting than in eating this quadruped."

Anyone who had lived through them might be expected to develop an interest in natural disasters—as did Audubon and many of the Americans he knew. In his stories of the forest fire and of the earthquake, Audubon chronicled much of the popular wisdom on these phenomena. Though he created a fictitious hurricane in Florida to embellish one of his stories, he did chronicle a wind in Kentucky that overturned houses. And, in a fascinating, quasi-historical overview of flooding on the Mississippi, he described how settlers put their livestock and supplies on rafts, then tied them to sturdy trees; how levees were repaired; how the Mississippi rises, and falls, at a consistently slow rate. To this discussion of floods, as to nearly all his chronicling, Audubon brought much color of detail, narrative flair, and a sense of grand adventure.

Like the squatter who told Audubon that he had "heard of men like myself and the existence of naturalists," we have a stranger from the nineteenth century in our cabin, an elusive character, a man who often loved and was certainly adept at masquerade, a man who perhaps disguised as much as he revealed. A season in the woods with Audubon has its days of clear weather, when, following in his footsteps, we think we see the man clearly. But on other days we lose him in the mist, a psyche with roots in a childhood about which we know too little; a man of transparent artistry but often opaque emotional undercurrents.

Yet the chronicles, the stories, remain. About Audubon's childhood we know enough to imagine a link between his solitude and his hyperactive imagination—yet the stories remain. About his life we know enough to imagine a link, a creative interplay, between an evolving sense of himself as an American, and his perceptions of America. Yet the stories remain.

Seemingly far removed from Audubon's America, as moderns it is fair to ask the question, why should we care? If Audubon took a great stride across a good hunk of the continent, so what? If the stories are good stories, even if (a big if) they are true—why should it matter?

Audubon's stories matter for a few compelling reasons. Stories are the primary way we get a handle on what has happened to us. They help give us perspective on where we've come from, and where we want to go. Stories bridge generations, transmitting values, refusing to let dreams die with the mortality of individuals. Unlike many of the things that divide us as Americans, stories can be shared. We are all of us, like Audubon, the stories we hear, and the stories we dare tell.

In Audubon's stories, in Audubon's personal story, we trace our own path through the wilderness. We see how it became a road, a highway, an Interstate. We see the way we have come, the shape we are in, and many of the values and dreams we would do well to embrace and follow. We see a vision of a life shared with other living things, of a habitable world. We see qualities of heroism. We see, as well, a faith in progress, in the broad sweep of the American ax, the sharp report of the American rifle, that had its element of blindness.

A man of his time, Audubon as a prophet fares no better than many of us will after we have gone. In a bounteous land, his were but sporadic moments of foreboding—for deer, for buffalo, for certain birds—that the land would not always be a horn of plenty. Yet Audubon had a dream, a dream carried to our generation by his stories, by the strokes of his brush and his pen. Audubon's was a vision of unity in diversity. America was not Europe; America was a new hope, a place where race and national origin were not the measure of the human being; a place where the human being and the great diversity of American wildlife could live together without fear of extinction.

Reading Audubon today, it is hard for us to find in our own experience an equivalent sense of continental adventure, of unfolding American wonders, of the unknown land. The land is ours; it has been mapped, settled, and plundered. We read Audubon with envy, and with stirrings of nostalgia for a place we have never known. Yet our need for stories goes on—stories we can call our own. Audubon told stories to help support his family, to help sell his paintings, to entertain, and, yes, often probably to help him overcome self-doubt, and to hide the truth. But his stories helped him find what his life meant to him, the kind of world he wanted. We are telling our own story now, trying to tell it, and it is leaner, unexpansive, between the rock and the hard place of the land we have inherited, and made. We need images of hope, chronicles of ingenuity, pathways out of the wilderness we have created. The story of Audubon is exemplary. He loved the country, felt an equality with its peoples and its wildlife, without intruding a sense of his own superiority, without surrendering, whether by hostility or paralysis, to the evil that men do. The good that Audubon did, the good that he beheld, lives after him. There are no true "American woodsmen" anymore. We must find our own trail—across the lakes of acid rain, through the disenchanted forest.

The Man Himself

7 Mary Durant
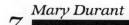

> As a man he [Audubon] is far more interesting than aught he accomplished.
>
> —Stanley C. Arthur

In 1826, when he was forty-two, John James Audubon wrote in his journal: "A curious event this life of mine." He expanded his thoughts in a later letter to his wife, Lucy, in which he commented on what an interesting and curious book could be written by a biographer acquainted with his life. This century and a half later, if Audubon could see a card catalogue—say, in the Library of Congress—he would be dumfounded at the mountain of biography, commentary, and poetry, too, that has been written about him—with more to come. There is no end in sight. But his was not merely a "curious" life. It was an extraordinary life—his career took him from riches to rags to fame, complete with high adventure and dark family secrets.

Audubon was a man possessed of manic vitality. He had drive and stamina enough for ten and went at life full tilt. He would be up and away before first light, into the woods, the marshes, and the hills, not only in search of his beloved birds, but also for the pure joy of being out and about. From childhood on, it was the ruling passion in his life, and as he stepped into old age, Audubon once asked, "Can this longing for the woods ever leave me?"

His hours in the woods were followed by long, intense hours devoted to painting, and with the publication of *The Birds of America*, a maelstrom of business details also demanded his attention, at a time when he was hard at work writing the *Ornithological Biography*. But still he found time, with that driving vitality of his, to leave an almost complete documentation of himself—his travels and rambles, the people and places along the way. In thousands of letters (he was an indefatigable correspondent) and in his journals he poured out his heart, the jubilations of his successes and the "blue devils" of his despairs. At the top of his form he was a man of enormous wit and awareness with an enviable gift for catching the essence of the world around him. One must never trust to memory, said Audubon. A man who keeps a journal should write down *"all he sees, all he thinks*, or all—yes, out with it—*all he does."*

Audubon never lost his French accent, and it is reflected in the phonetic spellings he so often used in English, such as *sheep* for ship, *Alifax* for Halifax, *head hake* for headache. He also, quite naturally, used many French spellings—*compted* for counted, *compagnion* for companion, *longue* for long, and *geay* for the blue jay. In his early journals and letters, Audubon's command of English was erratic and his spelling even more so, such as *smoake* for smoke, *wissle* for whistle, *stomack* for stomach, and so on. One must bear this in mind when reading Audubon. Immaculate English usually indicates the hand of an editor, but as the years went by, Audubon's command of his adopted language grew and errors appeared less and less often.

Also in reading Audubon, one must be alert to his cavalier disregard of facts—not in his ornithological writings, but in his adventure tales and accounts of his personal life. Sometimes these flights of fancy were used as a cover-up, sometimes because he saw no harm in making a good story better. However, even in those personal papers that were edited for publication, the evidence of a complex and contradictory personality shines through. He had an implacable craving for attention and reassurance from those he loved and was obsessed with himself, his own doings, and his appearance. It was as though he stood to one side carefully observing John James Audubon, sometimes in panic and alarm, sometimes with unabashed delight at what a fine fellow he really was.

He was riddled with inconsistencies. A bawdy roughneck one minute, a drawing-room charmer the next. A frontier rouser slapping his knee at a practical joke on some forlorn, unwitting victim, yet on the other hand as tender-hearted as one could wish. He adored children. They were always in his arms, in his lap, tagging at his heels. In Edinburgh, for example, he was distressed at the plight of small children begging in the streets and gave them money; to one child, whom he found barefoot on a December day, he gave a bundle of clothing and five shillings.

When he and Lucy lived in the southern states, they owned slaves, and he accepted slavery as the natural order of things. Yet in Mobile, Alabama, in 1837, one of the most moving passages Audubon ever put on paper dealt with the plight of the American Indian.

> 100 Creek Warriors were confined in irons, preparatory to leaving forever the Land of their births!—Some miles onward we overtook about two thousands of these once free owners of the Forest, marching towards this place under an escort of Rangers, and militia mounted Men, destined for distant lands, unknown to them, and where alas, their future and latter days must be spent in the deepest of Sorrows, afliction and perhaps even phisical want—this view produced on my mind an aflicting series of reflections more powerfully felt than easy of description—the numerous groups of Warriors, of half clad females and of naked babes, trudging through the mire under the residue of their ever scanty stock of Camp furniture, and household utensils— The evident regret expressed in the masked countenances of some and the tears of others—the howlings of their numerous dogs; and the cool demeanour of the chiefs—all formed such a picture as I hope I never will again witness. . . .

When it came to shooting and hunting, he was a man of his time, those careless days in which marksmanship with living targets was an admired sport in itself—a bitter pill for us to swallow, and all of his more thoughtful, twentieth-century biographers have commented on Audubon's insatiable passion for killing birds.

From his account of shooting adventures on the Florida coast: "You will doubtless be surprised when I tell you that our first fire among a crowd of Great Godwits laid prostrate 65 of these birds." On a sheltered pond near the Ohio, where hundreds of trumpeter swans floated and basked in the sun: "What a feast for a sportsman. . . . I saw these beautiful birds . . . their heads under the surface and their legs in the air, struggling in the last agonies of life, to the number of at least fifty." His essay on clapper rails in the *Ornithological Biography* leaves today's reader staggered by the minute account of birds in their death throes. There is a full page of fine print. And then, "The cruel sportsman, covered with mud and mire, drenched to the skin by the splashing of the paddles, his face and hands besmeared with powder, stands among the wreck which he has made, exultingly surveys his slaughtered heaps, and with joyous feelings returns home with a cargo of game more than enough for a family thrice as numerous as his own."

Yet when Audubon was away from the woodlands and his sweet companions, his sweet songsters, the thought of them could bring tears to his eyes. He had an unbounded love for birds—an anthropomorphic identification. As the mourning dove on her nest receives food from the bill of her mate, she listens "with delight to his assurances of devoted affection." The mockingbird "approaches his beloved one, his eyes gleaming with delight, for she has already promised to be his and his only." He writes of the "innocent vivacity" of the eastern bluebird, the "lively spirit . . . mirth and gaiety" of the flicker, the dour aspect of the brown pelicans which he fondly nicknamed, "The Reverend Sirs," and the "cool courage of the bald eagle, a "Noble Fellow" that looks upon his enemies with contemptuous eye.

But the very act of loading a rifle was described by Audubon with equally loving detail. The paragraph closes with the butt of the rifle braced on the ground, and as the powder and ball were tamped down into the chamber with a hickory rod: "Once, twice, thrice, has it rebounded. The rifle leaps as it were into the hunter's arms . . . Now I am ready, cries the woodsman."

Audubon himself explains the bond between huntsman and quarry—the thrill of having the bird in hand, the physical and emotional experience of *knowing* a bird, feeling its weight, studying the details of its plumage, the legs that still flex, the bill that can still be opened, the unfeathered parts still unfaded. In his essay on the Mississippi kite, he describes seeing what he thought was a chuck-will's-widow sitting lengthwise on a branch, took a shot, and discovered it was a young kite. "At the report of the gun, the old bird came, holding food in her claws. She perceived me, but alighted and fed her young with great kindness. I shot at both, and again missed. . . . The mother flew in silence over my head just long enough to afford me time to reload, returned, and to my great surprise gently lifted her young, and sailing with it to another tree, about thirty yards distant, depositing it there. My feelings at that moment I cannot express. I wished I had not discovered the poor bird; for who could have witnessed, without emotion, so striking an example of that affection which none but a mother can feel; so daring an act, performed in the midst of smoke, in the presence of a dreaded and dangerous enemy. I followed, however, and brought both to the ground at one shot, so keen is the desire of possession!"

Not only is it a question of Audubon's prevarications and contradictory ways that must be reckoned with, but the picture was further clouded by his widow and later by a granddaughter. After his death in 1851, both ladies wrote biographies drawn from his unpublished journals and letters. They expurgated and bowdlerized at will, deleting objectionable facts here, inserting suitable "facts" there, and presented Audubon to the world as a near flawless figure, a proper Victorian gentleman, a Sir Galahad of the Forest.

It was not really until the early 1900s that Audubon was released, so to speak, from the bosom of his family. Scholars and historians were at last free to challenge the tangled web of fact and fiction and begin research into original sources to give us a picture of the whole man, the flesh and blood Audubon. Unfortunately, some of the original journals, and who knows what other documents, did not survive his granddaughter and editor, Miss Maria Audubon. Many had been lost, she said. Others, she herself burned after copying "all I ever meant to give to the public . . . fire was our only surety that many family details could be put beyond the reach of vandal hands."

Two family details successfully kept from the public until shortly before World War I were Audubon's illegitimate birth, and, for some inexplicable reason, the true date of his birth. Mrs. Audubon gave the date as May 4, 1780. Miss Maria Audubon said that "the date usually given was May 5, 1780."

The true date, discovered among family papers in France shortly before World War I, is April 26, 1785. Audubon was born at his father's plantation on the island of Santo Domingo, in the part now known to us as Haiti. The senior Audubon was a seafaring man who started out as a cabin boy in the French merchant marine and worked his way up to become an officer in the French navy during the wars with England. He retired with the rank of *lieutenant de vaisseau*, the equivalent of lieutenant commander in the U. S. Navy. In peacetime, Lt. Audubon pursued a lucrative trade in slaves, coffee, and sugar with Santo Domingo as his base of operations. His wife, a woman of surprising complaisance, accepted his long absences from her household in Nantes, France, and make no complaints about her husband's second home, where Lt. Audubon lived with a succession of mistresses over the years and may have sired as many as five illegitimate children.

John James's mother, Mlle. Jeanne Rabin, was one of these lady loves. She apparently came to Santo Domingo from France to work as a chambermaid for a colonial family, but instead took up residence on Lt. Audubon's plantation. She died at the age of twenty-seven, six months after John James's birth, and her place was taken by a former mistress, who later gave birth to a daughter. In 1791, on the brink of the Negro revolution in Santo Domingo, Lt. Audubon whisked his two little love children to safe haven in France, where he officially claimed them as his own and filed formal adoption papers.

The stigma of bastardy, of course, was indeed a fact of life to be hidden. When it came to public pronouncements, Audubon himself chose to sidestep the issue altogether. In his introduction to the *Ornithological Biography* he said: "I received light and life in the New World." No date, no birthplace. Nothing. His alternate evasion: "The precise period of my birth is yet an enigma to me." But when it came to official documents, such as naturalization papers, Audubon correctly gave his birthplace as Santo Domingo. He also spoke of it freely to several friends that we know of. Nor was his age a mystery whether to himself or those close to him, as we know from his collected correspondence.

After Audubon's death, the story of his birth as published by his widow and his granddaughter, in their respective biographies, told the romantic tale of a lady of Spanish extraction, "as beautiful as she was wealthy," who met and married Lt. Audubon in Louisiana. There, her son John James was born, and shortly afterwards the family went to live on the Santo Domingo plantation, where the beautiful Spanish mother was massacred during the slave rebellion.

From that point on, Audubon's story is back on track—he had a petted childhood with a doting stepmother who granted his every whim and told John James again and again that he was the handsomest boy in France. He served a brief term as a midshipman—"Much against my inclinations," said he some twenty years later. Shortly before his eighteenth birthday, as the Napoleonic wars got under way, "the conscription determined my father on sending me to *America*." Said his father, "He is my only son and I am old."

At Mill Grove, the Pennsylvania farm his father had bought earlier as an investment, John James took up the life of a country gentleman. "I spent much Money . . . as Happy as the Young Bird; that having Left the Parents sight carolls Merily." He describes himself as having been "ridiculously fond" of fine clothes and going hunting in satin knee breeches, silk stockings, and ruffled shirts. "Not a ball, a skating-match, a house or riding party took place without me." He evidently cut quite a figure among the local gentry. From a contemporary, who met Audubon when he was twenty: "Today I saw the swiftest skater I ever beheld; backwards and forwards he went like the wind, even leaping over large air-holes fifteen or more feet across, and continuing to skate without an instant's delay. I was told he was a young Frenchman, and this evening I met him at a ball, where I found his dancing exceeded his skating; all the ladies wished him as a partner; moreover, a more handsome man I never saw, his eyes alone command attention."

In Audubon's own descriptions of himself as a young man, he speaks of his large, dark eyes, aquiline nose, fine set of teeth, and hair of "fine texture and luxuriant, divided and passing down behind each ear in luxuriant ringlets." He compared himself to his father, citing the same "erect stature" and "muscles of steel" and the same irascible temper that would suddenly erupt like a storm and as quickly pass into calm of a sunny day.

Meanwhile, he still devoted himself to nature studies and his drawings of birds. And he had fallen in love. Lucy Bakewell was a young woman of gentle breeding and good education, whose family had recently come from England and lived on the farm-estate next door. It was an uncle of Lucy's, incidentally, who was probably the first to describe John James as "volatile"—a favorite adjective among Audubon scholars. Said Benjamin Bakewell in a letter: "Mr. Audubon, Lucy's beau . . . is a very agreeable young man, but volatile as almost all Frenchmen are." Lucy's father, William Bakewell, found John James to be "aimless" and his parties "noisyish."

It was at some point during these Mill Grove years that we have firsthand testimony of Audubon's compulsion to re-invent himself, as it were. To embroider, to dramatize, to win attention. From a letter by William Bakewell, it seems that John James spun a riproaring yarn about himself and his family having been imprisoned by Robespierre during the French Revolution.

But with the prospect of marriage came the question of money. By his own admission, he was fit for nothing. How would John James support a wife? His father could be of no appreciable help. Lt. Audubon's holdings in Santo Domingo had been wiped out by the slave rebellion, and the Mill Grove property was tied up, and soon to be lost, in an imbroglio of partnerships, mortgages, and an ill-advised investment in a lead mine at the farm.

John James went to France to seek his father's help and advice, and it was decided that he should enter the mercantile trade. Lt. Audubon gave his son his blessings and supplied him with a partner—one Ferdinand Rozier, a steady, level-headed young Frenchman also anxious to avoid conscription. The two slipped out of France with forged passports, also supplied by Lt. Audubon—John James was listed as Louisiana-born and Rozier as a Dutchman.

Rozier and Audubon eventually headed west to make their fortunes, John James with his new bride under his wing. They went first to Louisville, then downriver to Henderson, Kentucky, and in 1809 Audubon and Rozier took off for Ste. Genevieve, Missouri, to the north on the Mississippi, to size up commercial possiblities. They left by barge in a December snowstorm with a cargo of three hundred barrels of whiskey, some dry goods, and gunpowder.

In April of 1810 the team of Audubon and Rozier split up. The two remained friends, but they did not mince words about their reasons for splitting up. Said Rozier: "Audubon had no taste for commerce, and was continually in the forest." Said Audubon: "Rozier cared only for money . . . I could relate many curious anecdotes about him, but never mind them; he made out to grow rich, and what more could *he* wish for." Rozier stayed in Ste. Genevieve, prospered and founded a dynasty. A Rozier department store still stands in the heart of town. The owner, Joseph Jules Rozier, Jr., a great-great-great-grandson, tells a family legend that's been handed down. As the story goes, Ferdinand Rozier went East on a buying trip, leaving Audubon in charge of their new store. "But you know how Audubon was, off in the woods, never behind the counter. When Ferdinand got back, he found the store locked and door covered with cobwebs. Perhaps *that* was the last straw."

Audubon never troubled to conceal his disinterest in a mercantile career: "I could not bear to give the attention required by my business . . . and therefore my business abandoned me." Several of his letters to Rozier would seem to corroborate this inattention. In one, for instance, Audubon wrote in bewilderment: "The famous bill for the indigo has at last arrived, but I don't understand it." In retrospect, however, Audubon quite enjoyed the image of his younger self as the scatter-brained merchant, head in the clouds, and thoughts on the birds. He often repeated the story of having absent-mindedly mailed an $8000 bank deposit in an unsealed envelope (in some tellings the sum was $10,000). He also wrote a bemused account of chasing down birds during his business trips "through the beautiful, the darling forests of Ohio, Kentucky, and Pennsylvania," while his pack horses laden with goods and dollars plodded on without him.

On one such journey, he made friends—a friendship that would last for life—with a German merchant, Vincent Nolte, who described their first meeting in his autobiography. On this occasion, said Nolte, Audubon was wearing a madras kerchief tied around his head in the style of French mariners and laborers in seaport towns, and in a thick French accent he announced: "Hi emm an Heenglishman." When Nolte expressed his considerable disbelief, Audubon replied: "Hi emm an Heenglishman becas Hi got a Heenglish wife." He then told Nolte that he actually was a Frenchman by birth, a native of Rochelle, had come in his early youth to Louisiana, "and had grown up in the sea service." Again, Audubon had re-invented himself. It is an enormously revealing anecdote. It should also be noted here that John James not only re-invented himself, but always spoke of his father, Lt. Audubon, as "my father the admiral," who had met General Washington at the "battle" of Valley Forge, and who died at a great age well beyond ninety, leaving behind him much wealth in land and money. He also gave his father's height as five feet ten and a half inches.

In truth, Lt. Audubon was five feet five inches tall, was not in America during the winter of 1777-78 when Washington and his men camped at Valley Forge, and when he died in his mid-seventies, Lt. Audubon left a very meager estate. The aggrandizement of one's forebears is a common psychological phenomenon that somehow helps to assuage a sense of inadequacy, though we continue to be startled that Audubon—John James Audubon!—was so uncertain and uneasy about himself. This explains, of course, his elaborate hints of royal descent, of being the son of Marie Antoinette and Louis XVI—the lost dauphin who died tragically in prison at the age of ten. After the French Revolution "lost dauphins" popped up all over Europe—there were even a few in North America. Audubon might very well have heard some of these tales as a boy, but fantasies of noble birth are not uncommon. Beethoven, for example, claimed to be the illegitimate son of the King of Prussia.

In the real world, among the bitterest blows to Audubon's self-image were his business failures: first, the collapse of his business ventures in Henderson, and then, the failure of the New Orleans store which he owned in partnership with Lucy's older brother, Thomas Bakewell, "Audubon & Bakewell, commission merchants." In the 1869 biography of her husband, Lucy wrote accusingly: "In this speculation he embarked all the fortune at his disposal; but instead of attending to his interests he remained hunting in Kentucky, and soon afterwards . . . his money was swept away."

And it had all been going so well. He had been a man of property, living in comfort with Lucy and their young sons, Victor and John, with a family of slaves in attendance. Lucy's younger brother, William, who stayed with them for two years, spoke of these golden days in a memoir, of "doing little else but hunting, fishing, and exploring the country with Audubon in pursuit of new birds to add to his collection of paintings." But everything was lost, including Lucy's dowry—her wedding silver, china, furniture, her piano—in the attempt to meet the demands of creditors. Nonetheless, Audubon was jailed for debt. He pleaded bankruptcy, and was released. The family was reduced to living on the charity of Lucy's relatives in Louisville. To what extent this disaster was Audubon's fault has never been fairly determined. A depression hit the western states after the War of 1812: many banks and businesses failed, and bankruptcy was the order of the day. But he was not popular with Lucy's side of the family. One member of the Bakewell clan wrote: "He . . . is forever wasting his time, hunting, drawing, and stuffing birds, and playing the fiddle. We fear he will never be fit for any practical purpose on the face of the earth." Apparently, neither of the brothers-in-law with business connections in Louisville would help him get work, not even a clerical job on a riverboat.

He eked out a living doing black and white portrait sketches, teaching drawing and painting, and was briefly employed in Cincinnati as taxidermist and artist at the Western Museum, until that, too, folded; it was another casualty of the depression. In 1820, Audubon at last took the bit in his teeth and leapt into the life that had been waiting for him—the empty niche with his name on it. "Ever since a Boy I have had an astonishing desire to see Much of the World and particularly to Acquire a true Knowledge of the Birds of North America . . . and having a tolerably Large Number of Drawings that have been generally admired, I concluded that perhaps I could Not do better than to Travel, and finish My collection." On the first leg of this lifetime journey, he worked his way down the Mississippi as huntsman and provider of game for the crew of a keel boat. One of his art students went with him—Joseph Mason, who at age thirteen was already a first-rate botanical painter—and served as his apprentice for the next two years.

Audubon was not one to stay by his own fireside. He was a rambler and rover with a longing to see what lay in the next valley, the valley beyond, and beyond that. A million miles of wilderness lay at his feet, and he had taken to frontier life with gusto. He loved the drama of rolling up in a buffalo robe to sleep in the snow. He loved the drama of wearing his clothes to shreds and stomping back to civilization muddy to the knees, with his beard so long it warmed his chest, carrying his rifle in hand, hunting knife at the hip, and a bedroll strapped across his back. He prided himself on being an American woodsman, sometimes giving this as his occupation when signing the register at an inn.

He loved the drama and challenge of finding food in the wilderness—bird, beast, or fish. Audubon would eat almost anything, whether from curiosity or hunger. The horned grebe he found to be fishy, rancid, and fat; the hermit thrush and red-winged blackbird good and delicate; the puffin dark, tough, and fishy; the flicker strongly flavored of ants. The meat of fledgling bald eagles, he reported, tastes like veal. Mason told the story of a day when he and Audubon came upon an Indian eating roasted wasps. They joined the feast, being rather "sharp-set," and found the wasps to be sweeter than honey, "a strange but most agreeable flavor." In Labrador in 1833 he was introduced to charcoal-broiled lobster, another Indian recipe which he found far more flavorful than the white man's boiled lobster. And in the palmy days in England, after a sumptuous dinner party, he longed for the simple fare of the huntsman—wood ibis cooked on the campfire and turtle eggs from the nest.

From 1820 onwards it was catch-as-catch-can. "My Birds, My Beloved Birds of America fill all my time and nearly all my thoughts," and he pursued his travels with pick-up jobs as an itinerant painter, drawing master, dancing master, fencing master. "Unfortunately," said he, "naturalists are obliged to eat and have some sort of garb." For Lucy, it was a series of partings and reunions, pride hurt and pride swallowed, with her inevitable recriminations and distresses. The dream was one thing, reality another, and Lucy was as human as any of us in the face of poverty. "The world is not indulgent," she told him time and time again, but in the end it was Lucy who supported herself and the children. Her education and English background were valuable assets, and she eventually found a safe haven as schoolmistress for the children of plantation families around St. Francisville, Louisiana. Friends of the Audubons during those trying years passed along their memories of Lucy's sharp tongue and the "pen-lashings" she gave her husband in her letters, which would send him into depths of gloom and guilt. Any yet they adored each other. Throughout his life, their reunions would often be an emotional storm of tears and kisses.

Audubon's two jobs as live-in tutor and drawing master, also at St. Francisville, ended badly. At the Oakley Plantation he paid a bit too much attention to his young pupil, Eliza Pirrie, at least in the estimation of Eliza's mother, who was alarmed by the flirtations and flattery offered by a handsome Frenchman to a susceptible fifteen-year-old. Audubon was summarily dismissed. The next run-in was at the Beechwoods Plantation where Audubon, the drawing master, painted a portrait of the Percy girls. Mrs. Percy did not like the coloring he had given their complexions. Too yellow, she said. There were words, tempers flared, and again, Audubon was dismissed. Lucy, also employed at Beechwoods as schoolmistress, stayed on, and a few nights later John James stole back and snuggled into Lucy's bed. A servant alerted the Widow Percy, who burst into the room and ordered Audubon out. That humiliating event rankled for years. To think, he would write to Lucy when he was becoming famous in England, that there were times at Beechwoods where certain people scarcely thought fit to look at him.

He had his own good friends in the neighborhood. Among them was Dr. Nathanial Pope, a hunting buddy, whose wife wrote an admiring memoire.

> Audubon, [said Martha Pope] was one of the handsomest men I ever saw. In person he was tall and slender, his blue eyes were an eagle's in brightness . . . his hair a beautiful chestnut brown, very glossy and curly. His bearing was courteous and refined, simple and unassuming. . . . He kept his drawings in a watertight tin box, which remained in my parlour for months . . . and often our house was filled with visitors who came to see his drawings and paintings, which he would spread out on the floor for inspection, and he never seemed weary of unpacking and explaining them. He was very sociable—being the center of attraction in every circle in which he mingled. . . . After spending short times with his family, he would start out again on his lonely journey in the woods, alone and on foot . . . While he was wandering the forest his noble wife was working in order to assist him in having his pictures engraved. It grieved him exceedingly . . . Every time he returned home he found his wife fading and drooping and he could not help but compare her to a beautiful tobacco plant cut off at the stem and hung up to wither with head hanging down, as he put in his quaint way of using similes.

Poor Lucy. That sort of remark must have set her teeth on edge.

There were also such rousing successes as his dancing classes in Woodville, Mississippi, which brought in a few more dollars to add to his English travel fund.

> I marched to the hall with my violin under my arm, bowed to the company assembled, tuned my violin; played a *cotillon*, and began my

lesson. . . . How I toiled before I could get one graceful step or motion! I broke my bow and nearly my violin in my excitement and impatience! . . . I pushed one here and another there, and all the while singing to myself to assist their movements. . . . After this first lesson was over I was requested to *dance to my own music*, which I did until the whole room came down in thunders of applause in clapping hands and shouting.

Audubon arrived in England in July, 1826, and within two weeks was hailed as a genius, an American original. A whirlwind of acclaim beyond his wildest imaginings. "It is Mr. Audubon here, and Mr. Audubon there," he wrote to Lucy, "and I can only hope they will not make a conceited fool of Mr. Audubon at last." A life mask was made of his face, a phrenologist "read" his skull and compared it to Raphael's, his portrait was painted—hair to the shoulders, rifle in arms, wolfskin coat on his shoulders. This painting, by John Symes, now hangs in the White House Collection, though of all the portraits eventually done of Audubon, it was his least favorite. Said he at the time: "If the head is not a strong resemblance, perhaps the coat may be."

Little more than a year after his arrival in England, the prospectus for *The Birds of America* was published under the patronage of George IV. "The King! My dear Book! . . . His majesty was pleased to call it fine. . . ." And what, Audubon asked, did his brothers-in-law think of him now? What do they say?

What he probably did *not* know, and just as well, was that a sister of Lucy's wrote to an English cousin saying that Mr. Audubon hoped to stop in for a visit—"you will find him pleasant in his manners and I hope much improved in character. . . ." But there had indeed been a change. He was a markedly different man from the rough-and-ready fellow who worked his way down the Mississippi as a huntsman. He was more polished, more self-aware, and in the few intervening years his command of English had improved to an astonishing degree. From his journals and letters we now learn that he was well read, not only in natural history, but in poetry, essays, and novels—Byron, Milton, Dryden, Samuel Johnson, Voltaire, Dickens, Ben Franklin, Sir Walter Scott, Cervantes, Dante, Sterne's *Tristam Shandy*, Goldsmith's *The Vicar of Wakefield*, among others. He loved the theater—*Tartuffe, She Stoops to Conquer*, and *The Beggar's Opera* are some of the plays of which he made particular mention. And he knew his Shakespeare. He was a master at chess, backgammon, and whist. He delighted his English friends with parlor imitations of such American birds as the turkey, the mourning dove, and the barred owl, and gave presents of Indian moccasins which he made out of snakeskin. And yes, he had his hair cut at the urging of his new friends, marking the event in his journal with a black-bordered message of mourning, and then promptly let it grow again. He was also urged to get a new wardrobe, suitable to his position, and found himself once more in silk stockings and pumps, and told Lucy that he had even taken to shaving every morning and sometimes changed his clothes twice a day.

Above all, now that he was in charge of his own life, doing what he wanted to do, he was a dynamo. Nothing was neglected or overlooked as he labored at *The Birds of America*. He was already a painter, now he became a man of business. But as Louis Agassiz Fuertes once said of Audubon, he was "a reed bent by the slightest breath of emotion." He missed Lucy fiercely when they were apart. He had visions of her dead and in her shroud. He fell to the floor in a deep faint at thoughts of the miles between them, and said goodnight to her, out loud, every evening from his bed. He kissed her signature when her letters arrived, wept into his pillow when they didn't. "I am on thorns without news of thee." "It is now three long months since I pressed thee to my bosom." "Oh my Lucy, sweeter to me than all the Riches in the world can ever make me." He sent her presents: a gold watch, kerchiefs, four pairs of spectacles, gloves—"french and also fashionable"—a dozen pairs of stockings "with hopes that they will suit thy dear ankles." When he sold a sporting oil, "Spaniels Surprising English Pheasants," for a hundred guineas, he sent her a set of sterling silver to replace the silver she had forfeited in Henderson.

Yet at the same time, he was, as ever, attracted to pretty women, particularly young ones, and enjoyed flirting with them. He prattled on to Lucy about engaging friendships with the daughters of households in which he was a guest and about his strolls with these lovely companions on country roads, describing the electrifying rustle of a silken gown, the lure of playful curls, dark eyes seen through a veil, rosy cheeks and "well-shaped forms." And then, "Oh My Lucy, what I would give now in my possession for a kiss on the Lips and—"

Despite his new fame the insecurities that plagued him would suddenly come to the fore. He spoke of himself as a man of no education, said that he had never looked into a French or English grammar and had "scarce one of those qualities necessary to render a man able to pass through the throng of the learned." And now, to his astonishment and panic, he was lauded as a man of science by "men of learning." At a dinner meeting of the Antiquarian Society in Edinburgh, toasts were raised to the king, the dukes of Clarence and York, Sir Walter Scott, and many others. Then a toast was raised to Mr. Audubon. "The perspiration poured from me. I thought I would faint." He rose and managed a brief, gracious reply, though undone by stage fright, his hand too now wet with perspiration, which he also felt running down his legs. William Lizars, seeing his anxiety, poured him a glass of wine and said, "Bravo! Take this." But it had happened before, and it would happen again: *"Miserable stupidity that will never leave me!"*

At another party, when Audubon had entered the dining room with his hostess on his arm, he noticed that the other men had lingered behind. Audubon was instantly convinced that they had hung back to make comments about him, and he blushed. But when his moods turned, he was cocky and confident and full of no end of high spirits, and in letters to family and friends at home sent kisses to everyone, "thousands of kisses on the wing." "Kiss all the dear ones for me." And he basked in the attention of strangers. He wrote of hurrying down a street, his locks "flowing freely" from under his hat, "and every Lady that I met looked at them and then at Me." In a chance encounter with a pretty maid in a public garden, she praised his curly locks and called him The Handsome Stranger. At an exhibition of his paintings, he noticed the eyes of the ladies searching his face and "the undulations" of his chestnut hair.

All told, there would be three more trips to England, and Lucy finally took the risk of giving up her school in Louisiana and traveling with him. Otherwise, when he wasn't drumming up subscriptions for the engravings, his time spent in America was mainly in pursuit of new species of birds. Though he covered almost every corner of the eastern half of North America, it was a lifelong regret of his that he had never crossed the Rockies, never gone to the northwest and Ft. Vancouver, never gone to Mexico. He began to worry about old age when still in his early forties. Time was running out. He must work harder and faster than ever. Yet there seemed to be no limit to his endurance. A day's round in all its exhausting detail was written up by Dr. Benjamin Strobel, who met Audubon at Key West in 1832. First he spoke of Audubon's engaging manner and French *savoir-faire* which made him such an agreeable companion. "It is impossible to associate with him without catching some portion of his spirit. . . ."

With that Dr. Strobel rolls into his day with Audubon, which began at 2:30 A.M. They journeyed by boat and on foot, scrabbling over the roots of mangroves, slogging through bogs, trudging the sandbanks of the mainland. By 8 A.M. it was intensely hot, and mosquitoes and sandflies were biting. "One of our party gave out about this time and took to a boat. Most gladly would I have followed his lead," said Strobel, "but was deterred by pride." A couple of hours later he threw in the towel, went home by horseback, and fell back into bed, while Audubon and the remaining stalwarts made their way to Key West by boat. And this, said Strobel, was an everyday affair, with Mr. Audubon, "this surprising man," spending the afternoons painting those birds he had found in the morning's jaunt. Strobel was impressed by Audubon's "unquenchable ardor in pursuit of science, and his amiable deportment as a gentleman."

At about this time Audubon met the man who would be his dearest and closest friend, the Reverend John Bachman, a Lutheran minister in Charleston, South Carolina. He was an amateur naturalist whose particular field was zoology, and an enthusiastic huntsman. He was of inestimable assistance to Audubon, not only in collecting birds but in the scientific research. A workroom-laboratory was established at Bachman's house for the study of specimens, for dissections and corroborative observations, in which John Bachman's sister-in-law, Miss Maria Martin took part. She was their devoted colleague and contributed insect and plant drawings for a number of Audubon's paintings. "Our sweetheart," Audubon called her.

The two men revelled in each other's company. The bond between them was further strengthened by the marriage of Audubon's sons to Bachman's eldest daughters, their joy in their grandchildren, and their grief at the loss of both young wives, who died of tuberculosis. Bachman was the mastermind behind the *Viviparous Quadrupeds of North America*—the zoological authority, writer and editor of contributions to the text taken from Audubon's journals. In the last years before Audubon's death, when he was no longer able to work, Bachman completed the project with John Woodhouse Audubon as the artist. It was Bachman who identified the black-footed ferret as a new species never before described or pictured. They had been sent a single specimen collected in North Dakota and shipped east with a stuffing of *Artemisia* as a preservative. For almost a quarter century this was the only specimen known to science, and it was even rumored that Audubon and Bachman had faked a new mammal to promote their book.

Bachman and Miss Martin were also helpful in identifying the plants that Audubon chose for his backgrounds. Though he had an artist's eye for forms and colors that complemented his birds, he otherwise had only a minimal interest in North American flora, which seems a rather surprising blindspot for a man with such an inquisitive turn of mind. He knew a few plants and trees by name, of course, but it is clear from his journals that botany did not really interest him: "Many pretty flowers in bloom," or, "Saw a purple flower today." Nary a description or sketch in the margin. As he himself said, "I wish I were a better botanist." In a letter to Bachman from England: "How you will laugh when you have read that yesterday, I was offered the Presidency of a Botanical Society in London! . . . after this what am I next to expect."

Their friendship was not without its conflicts. The Audubon-Bachman correspondence lays bare another family secret—Audubon's weakness for alcohol. Bachman had chided his friend for years about his excessive drinking, and Audubon would write letters of reassurance. One, for example, sent from the Gulf of Mexico: "There is no grog aboard of the Campbell!!! what do you say to that?" Entries in his journals and occasional letters also gave Audubon away when he had been drinking: the prose became overwrought, maudlin, vituperative, or bawdy as the mood might have struck him, and the handwriting uncontrolled, with sloppy scrawls and heavy dashes drawn across the page as thoughts were abandoned in mid-stream. The ties with Bachman almost came to an end in 1840 when Audubon had been in Charleston for a lengthy visit and "the worse for drink" almost every afternoon. "Unfit for conversation," wrote Bachman to Victor Audubon, "garrulous, dictatorial and profane. . . . I wished the infernal whiskey jug at the bottom of the sea." Bachman advised Victor, "whenever you think it is seasonable & proper," to show the letter to his father. Evidently Bachman's anger and concern were effective. Their friendship was renewed, as close as ever, and Audubon seemed to have got a grip on himself, drinking only in moderation—to his family's relief. On one trip away from home, he reassured Lucy: "Would you believe that I have not drank a drop of anything but water since I left the Steamship Massachusetts on my way to Boston. I am growing thin as a snake."

One addiction shared by both men was snuff. "I will tell you *entre nous*," wrote Audubon to Bachman early in their friendship, "snuffing is a most dirty business, I abhore it as much as I do Grog." But in spite of New Year's resolutions—away with snuff, goodbye forever—Audubon was never able to conquer the habit.

Audubon's fame continued to grow, at home and abroad. He was a celebrity, reports of his latest doings appeared in the press, and he himself sent travel notes and essays to friends who were journalists. The public could not get enough of Mr. Audubon—the great, the wonderful Mr. Audubon, as he merrily spoke of himself, though he had anxious moments when he wondered if he really deserved all this attention. There were, however, critics and journalists in America who began asking questions, in print. Just who was he and where did he come from? Why was he so ambiguous about his background? A Louisville paper, for one, said that Mr. Audubon had given the impression of being a native of Kentucky, but now it seemed this was not so: "Possible he was misinformed on the subject of his nativity."

John Neal, a Boston critic and the editor of *The New England Galaxy*, after a tribute to Mr. Audubon's "magnificent work," proceeded to lace into him. "Why this careful and studious concealment of two facts—so simple in themselves? . . . Nobody knows to this day where Mr. Audubon the ornithologist was born, or whether he was ever born at all. Just so it is with his age—not a word on the subject." Neal wound up his diatribe with the conclusion that Audubon was one of those extraordinary men who are born nowhere, but are erected—like a public monument. Audubon's private comment on this attack reflected his new-found assurance. He was above back-biting: "I really care not a fig. . . ."

The expeditions continued, Audubon throwing himself into his work with his usual energy and passion, but the specter of old age loomed large. "So much travelling, exposure, and fatigue do I undergo that the Machine me thinks is wearing out." He compared himself to two drawings he had done in his youth at Mill Grove, "one the Otter, the other a Mink . . . both quite rubbed and soiled like ourselves having suffered somewhat from the hand of time." He itemized the loss of his teeth, dyspepsia that made it hard to breathe, the times when he missed his footing and fell. There were the trials of his business trips from town to town, drumming up subscribers for *Birds of America*, and the difficulties of collecting overdue payments. (Daniel Webster and John Jacob Astor, among others, were particularly tardy in paying up.) But Audubon still kept his sense of humor. A typical, wry entry comes from Salem, Massachusetts, where he canvassed the town. "I called on a Miss Stisby—seven or eight seasons beyond her teens, and very wealthy. . . . Although she had the eyes of a gazelle, and capital teeth, I soon discovered she would be of no help to me; when I mentioned subscriptions, it seemed to fall on her ears, not with cadence of the Wood Thrush or Mocking Bird . . . but as a shower-bath in cold January. . . . At last I bowed, she curtesied, and so the interview ended."

However, in Richmond, Virginia, where Audubon had tea one afternoon at a seminary for young ladies, his charm and winning ways did not go for naught. On his departure, the young ladies asked that he kiss them goodbye, and Mr. Audubon obliged.

By 1840, he had three works to peddle: the "large work," as the family called it; the "small work," which was a seven-volume octavo edition; and the forthcoming *Quadrupeds*. He wrote from Baltimore that the amount of attention he received was "bewildering . . . the very streets resound with my name, and I feel quite alarmed and queer as I trudge along." He spoke of headaches, attacks of cholera morbus, feet swollen from pounding the pavements, homesickness, and bad dreams. And once more, when there was no mail from the family: "What in the name of God can be the matter at home?" On a selling trip to the north, when the Albany steamer passed the Audubon's new country house on the Hudson River, handkerchiefs were waved from the shore and his sons came out in their sailboat to bid him godspeed, and as the steamer pulled away upstream and the sailboat faded in the distance, Audubon bent his head and wept.

On his last expedition, up the Missouri to the Dakotas, he was fifty-eight. His horse was an aged mount called Old Peter, and the younger men kept riding circles around him and urging Old Peter on. One of Audubon's last interviews was given in St. Louis that summer and appeared in the Buffalo *Courier*. He was described as having hair white with age and somewhat thin, gray whiskers, and a robust constitution even though his frame was not stout. Audubon told the reporter he had not taken a particle of medicine for twenty years, was impervious to fatigue, could walk thirty-five miles a day with ease, and endure all climates. His principal food was then sea biscuits and molasses, since he had by that time lost all his teeth, "from which he suffers and is obliged to boil his meat to rags. He says he will live to a hundred years with temperate habits, regularity, and attention to diet."

He came home to stay in October and within a few years slipped away into senility. In 1848 John Bachman wrote: "The old Gentleman has just gone to bed after having eaten his eleventh meal, handed his [snuff] box all round, kissed all the Ladies. . . . His is indeed a most melancholy case. . . . Imagine to yourself a crabbed, restless, uncontrollable child, worrying and bothering everyone and you have not a tythe of a description of this poor old man. . . . I turn away from the subject with a feeling of sadness."

Audubon died in 1851 at the age of sixty-five, though the family let it be known that he was well into his seventies. He is buried in Trinity Churchyard at Broadway and 155th Street in New York City.

Saving The Pieces

8

> In this year, 1922, the lovers of outdoor America for the first time began seriously to realize that we have been so busy as to be blind. Now the truth comes home.... There is no longer any wilderness. Betrayed by its guardians, forgotten by its friends, the old America is gone forever. Never again shall we have more than fragments. If even these be dear, then surely it is time to call a halt. Can any human agency work the great miracle of giving the ages a part of the America that was ours? I do not know. I dare not predict.
>
> —Emerson Hough

During a political campaign in 1923, I followed Governor Gifford Pinchot through a crowd in a Pennsylvania town and managed to touch the hem of his garment. To my family, as to many citizens, Pinchot was the saint of conservation, but historians have since revealed the politician beneath the white robe. Even during the Teddy Roosevelt administrations, there were those on the inside track who thought that Pinchot could not see beyond the end of the lumber pile.

In contrast, Audubon's reputation was not founded on the presumption that he was a conservationist, but over the years he has come to embody the very spirit of that cause. Unquestionably the Audubon Society can take most of the credit for Audubon's present status as a symbol of environmentalism. Has this group, so to speak, dragged Audubon kicking and screaming into that field? Was John James Audubon really a conservationist at heart during his lifetime?

Audubon left us such a profuse written record of his thoughts and feelings that it should not be difficult to judge the degree to which he can justly be considered a conservationist in attitudes and actions. First, however, it is well to call to mind the kind of world in which he lived; this, too, can be visualized from the naturalist's writings. More accurately, we can approach that but hardly really believe it, conditioned as we are by our own experiences in our time.

What, for example, are we to make of this: On the Maine coast, Audubon secured forty lobsters one afternoon "simply [he wrote] by striking them in shallow water with a gaff-hook."

> Whilst at Indian Key [Florida] I observed an immense quantity of beautiful tree snails, of a pyramidal or shortly conical form, some pure white, others curiously marked with spiral lines of bright red, yellow, and black. They were crawling vigorously on every branch of each bush where there was not a nest of the White Ibis.

He saw Great White Herons in *flocks*, sometimes of more than a hundred, on their *feeding* grounds. On Sandy Key he saw White Ibis nests on every bush, cactus, or tree; he thought there might be as many as ten thousand active Ibis nests per acre. In 1832, Alexander Wilson saw a flock of Passenger Pigeons that he estimated contained at least 2,230,270,000 birds! The living world as it was in Audubon's and Wilson's time is really inconceivable to moderns, but we can understand why conservation was not then a burning issue in the public mind.

Hunting and fishing are pursuits which have convinced many, but far from all, of their devotees of the need for conservation. Some of the strongest protectors of wildlife, paradoxically, are those whose hobby is to chase and reduce the quarry to possession. The chase may be more satisfying than its outcome, so that hunting and fishing are often mainly excuses for getting out to enjoy the out-of-doors. Not only physically but also psychologically, the development of an individual is thought to recapitulate in many respects the history of the species. Aldo Leopold pointed out that the hunter of today is the cave-man reborn. Many, if not most, wildlife conservationists represent, or have passed through and gone beyond, the hunting-fishing stage. Certain it is that hunting was not only an essential part of Audubon's stock-in-trade as a naturalist and artist, but also that he enjoyed it as a sport for many years.

Leopold, as a young federal forester in Albuquerque, was a dedicated duck hunter along the Rio Grande and the irrigation-drainage ditches. The founder of the first Audubon Society, George Bird Grinnell, was a hunter and editor of a sportsmen's magazine. William T. Hornaday, the most fanatical of wild-game protectionists, admitted that he had been a mighty killer in his youth. Theodore Roosevelt and Dr. C. Hart Merriam were hunters as well as noted mammalogists. Collecting specimens was as necessary for that science as for ornithology or geology. Stalking and killing the still plentiful game was a way of getting to know and respect animal life.

The forester knows and respects trees, encouraging nature to produce more, so that more can be cut down and cut up. All of us depend upon photosynthesis for food also—if even the strictest vegetarian is to remain alive, many living things must die for him. The 4-H child or his parents on the farm who have assisted at the birth of calves and cared for them as they grew to maturity do not have to hate the animals to lead them to slaughter. Who cares more deeply for a living, color-spangled brook trout, the city-dweller who has loved no bright mountain streams or the veteran fly-fisherman who pits his skill against the wary old king of the crystal pool? The primeval Indian hunter became one with the quarry in spirit, took its name and totem as his own, knew that its flesh would become his flesh, and worshipped the animal's spirit. "For each man kills the thing he loves. . . ." John Muir ran a sawmill in Yosemite Valley!

It is fortunate, considering present population numbers, that birdwatching and outdoor photography, walking and jogging, have tended to supplant hunting and fishing as field sports. These non-consumptive activities do not erode away the base that makes them possible, except sometimes through overcrowding at certain favored places. They are well suited to a time when increasing urban populations take to the country for recreation.

Some modern readers of Audubon and of books about him are shocked at the numbers of birds and other animals he brought down. During the anti-plume campaign at the start of this century, a defender of the millinery-feather trade hit a sensitive nerve of the bird-protectionists: "Audubon, patron saint, one might say, of American naturalists, gloried in the sport of shooting." Happily for Audubon himself, there were as yet no Audubon wardens lurking in the cove near the rookeries of Florida wading birds.

> As we approached the next island, I saw twenty or thirty pairs of Herons, some of which were pure white, others of a light blue color, but so much larger than the [Little] Blue Heron . . . that I asked the pilot what they were, when he answered, "the very fellows I want to shew you, and you may soon see them close enough, as you and I will shoot a few by way of amusement." Before half an hour had elapsed, more than a dozen were lying at my feet. . . . Well, the white immature birds were the very same as the individual to which, as the representative of a new species, the name of Peale's Egret had been given [by Charles Bonaparte].

This species was the Reddish Egret or Purple Heron, now a relatively rare member of its group.

Audubon's "unsatisfactory" record of the Greenshank (previously discussed, in chapter 2) in North America was based on three birds he shot on Sandy Key, thinking that they were "Tell-tale Godwits." His casual attitude at this time (1832) may be gleaned from his writing, "They had been shot merely because they offered a tempting opportunity, being all close together, and it is not often that one can kill three Tell-tales at once." This was during the season when birds normally had nests with young; fortunately all three were males, though he did not know this until they were already dead.

At the same place the previous month (April), Audubon and his crew had collected a "small haycock" of shot birds, and utilized a few of them to make skins. He sometimes came near to apologizing for the overkill perpetrated in Florida; once he termed it "murder." But the modern reader would feel better if Audubon had tried to restrain his bloodthirsty guide.

In our time, when even professional ornithologists are reluctant to kill birds, we tend to forget how little was known about bird life in Audubon's day. Admitting that he then enjoyed the sport aspect of collecting, we still should remember that a naturalist in that period really needed a good series of skins of a species he was working on, for such series could not be found in museums as they can today. Were the dozen individuals of Reddish Egret, not a rare bird then as it is now, too high a price for learning that an accepted species was merely the juvenile stage of another species?

A number of specimens were required for judging the variability caused by age, sex, and individual differences in species about which very little was known. Such information enabled him to avoid errors in his art. He must have felt the inexorability of putting a bird down on paper for posterity. Perhaps someone pointed out to him that three of the eagle portraits he painted showed an incorrect number of feathers in the outspread tails.

Once he examined more than a hundred of each sex of the White Ibis, and ascertained that the male has five black-tipped primaries, but the female only four, except sometimes in very old females. That sort of variation is not easy to establish the first time it is suspected. The naturalist in Audubon demanded accuracy as much as the artist called for drama. By 1831, he had become quite accurate.

Probably it touched Audubon's sense of fair play when in 1821 he saw hunting parties from New Orleans calling down Golden Plovers to a full day of slaughter during which he estimated that at least 144,000 birds were killed. Perusal of his Florida writings reveals some glimmerings of an attitude that birds are creatures with an inherent right to be spared unnecessary destruction, but it seems to have been what he saw going on along the eastern coast of Canada the following summer, 1833, which opened his eyes to man's inhumanity toward nature. The increased sensitivity detectable in his writings from that time on is best brought out by quotation rather than paraphrase or extrapolation. Since most of the criticism of Audubon has been that he does not measure up as a conservationist, it is only fair to let him speak for himself in the matter.

Seeing the bloody ruthlessness of sealers and whalers and the merciless greed of the commercial collectors of seafowl eggs for human food hardened Audubon's attitude against cruel and wasteful exploitation. It angered him that the eggers would take every bird that they possibly could from the rock islands for the feathers and meat, then clean out every last egg.

> So constant and persevering are their depredations that ducks, guillemots, puffins, gulls, etc., which, according to the accounts of a few settlers I saw in the country, were exceedingly abundant twenty years ago, have abandoned their ancient breeding places. . . . Nature having been exhausted and the season nearly spent, thousands of these birds left the country without having accomplished the purpose for which

they had visited it. This war of extermination cannot last many years more.

The captain stated in the ship's log that he had no idea of the extent of these operations. Four eggers from Halifax took 40,000 eggs, which they sold at twenty-five cents per dozen. Twenty other ships were so engaged. "In less than half a century these wonderful nurseries," predicted Audubon, "will be entirely destroyed, unless some kind government will interfere to stop the shameful destruction." Upon finding a cabin abandoned by sealers, he worte, "The Seals are all caught, and the sealers have nought to do here now-a-days."

This sort of heartfelt feeling of loss and foreboding for loved birds and beasts was a new note in Audubon's writing. Shocking observations had come to expression, and in the pessimistic vein which, too often justifiably, typifies conservation literature. He deplored the unethical aspects of the eggers' greed, as much as mourning the loss of the practical economic and other benefits to man that were being stolen from future generations.

> We talked of the enormous destruction of everything here [Labrador coast]; the aborigenes themselves melting away before the encroachments of white men. . . . For as the Deer, the Caribou and all other game is killed for the dollar which its skin brings in, the Indian must search in vain over the devastated country for that on which he is accustomed to feed, till, worn out by the sorrow, despair and want, he either goes far from his early haunts to others, which in time will be similarly invaded, or he lies on the rocky seashore and dies. We are often told rum kills the Indian; I think not; it is oftener the want of food, the loss of hope as he loses sight of all that was once abundant, before the white man intruded on his land and killed off the wild quadrupeds and birds. . . . Nature herself seems perishing.

Audubon's developing new appreciation of wild creatures first becomes prominent in his Labrador journal. "All—all is wonderfully grand, wild—and terrific. And yet how beautiful it is now, when one sees the wild bee, moving from one flower to another in search of food. . . . The little Ring Plover rearing its delicate and tender young." This is the delicate and tender attitude which the older, more sensitive and philosophical Audubon was growing into. "About a dozen common Crossbills," he confided, "And as many Redpolls, came and perched on the topyards, but I would not have them shot, and none was caught." And again this sympathy for wildlings: "I watched the Ring Plover for some time; the parents were so intent on saving their young. . . . We left them and their young to the care of the Creator. I would not have shot one of the old ones, or taken one of their young for any consideration and I was glad my young men were as forebearing." How much this sounds like Theodore Roosevelt at Pine Knot, Virginia, in 1907, watching alone the last wild flock of Passenger Pigeons known, and writing afterward that "nothing could have persuaded me" to shoot one to validate this most dramatic bird sight-record of the twentieth century.

It is in Audubon's journal of his Missouri River Expedition in 1843 that his expressions of compassion and outrage are most insistent. He confessed, for instance, "I started a Woodcock, and caught one of the young, and am now sorry for this evil deed." He had come a long way from the collector at Sandy Key who had constructed a "small haycock" of the carcasses of egrets, spoonbills, ibises, and pelicans.

Aboard the steamer on the Missouri, there was a good deal of promiscuous target practice at the expense of birds and animals along the shore, but Audubon and his assistants did not take part. He tells of several instances involving wild geese. "The Geese were shot at, notwithstanding my remonstrances on account of the young, but fortunately all escaped." It is clearly necessary for him and his young men to collect in order to fulfill the trip's objectives, but he enforced suitable restraint. When his taxidermist, John Bell, shot a Canada Goose as it ran along on the shore and the boat's captain would not stop for it to be picked up, Audubon wrote, "I was sorry to see the poor bird dead, uselessly."

The naturalist learned much about the fur trade by staying at the fort of one company and often visiting that of a rival firm. He had summarized his observations about this business on the Canadian coast, and saw no reason to change his conclusions for it in our Midwest: "Fur animals are scarce, . . . but every year diminishes their numbers. The Fur Company may be called the exterminating medium of these wild and almost uninhabited climes, where cupidity and the love of gold can alone induce man to reside for a while. Where can I go now, and visit Nature undisturbed?"

In recounting one deer hunt, Audubon told how one shipmate called the does to the slaughter with a "bleating whistle." He termed this "a cruel, deceitful, and unsportsmanlike method, of which I can never avail myself, and which I try to discountenance."

The plight of the bison touched him most deeply. Although its population still seemed high in 1843, he saw the handwriting on the wall. Buffalo was in great and continuing demand for feeding the steamboat party and the fur people. Audubon had this comment about men shooting a young swimming bull from the steamboat: "The poor thing was killed by a rifle bullet. I was sorry, for we did not stop for it, and its happy life was needlessly ended." This was not the sort of attitude that was embraced by his companions in the business community; it was definitely subversive of contemporary American values.

The naturalist went aboard some commercial buffalo-boats on the Missouri near the mouth of the Dakota or Jacques River. "They had ten thousand Buffalo robes on the four boats; the men live entirely on Buffalo meat and pemmican." That day, he saw three white wolves. Wolves habitually scavenged the carcasses which the white hunters let go to waste very largely. Audubon relates how hunters from the steamboat killed four bison.

> Only a few pieces from a young bull, and its tongue, were brought on board, most of the men being too lazy, or too far off, to cut out even the tongues of the others; and thus it is that thousands multiplied by thousands of Buffaloes are murdered in senseless play, and their enormous carcasses are suffered to be the prey of the Wolf, the Raven, and the Buzzard. . . . What a terrible destruction of life [on another hunt], as it were for nothing, or next to it, as the tongues only were brought in, and the flesh of these fine animals was left to the beasts and birds of prey, or to rot on the spots where they fell. The prairies are literally covered with the skulls of the victims, and the roads the Buffalo make in crossing the prairie have all the appearance of heavy wagon tracks.

The evolving conservationist did not feel constrained to keep his unusual opinions to himself, for he noted, "My remonstrances about useless slaughter have not been wholly unheeded." Although Audubon's friend Harris nearly lost his life during a stampede-type bison hunt, Audubon's thoughts were for the animal victims. "Thus these poor animals which two hours before were tranquilly feeding are now dead; short work this."

Audubon's writing from the Missouri country does not glamorize the West, which was then still the young Old West, nor romanticize the red man or the hunters, trappers, or fur traders. He called George Catlin's book "humbug" for doing so. Audubon's "remonstrances" (a voice crying for the wilderness) had no effect in his time on a scale of any consequence. Later on, a few states passed laws to regulate hunting of the bison, but they were not enforced. The Plains Indians lived on the bison as their almost sole direct natural resource—from its highly efficient utilization they derived food, clothing, and shelter. General Phil Sheridan and Grant's Secretary of the Interior officially advocated exterminating the bison for the effect that would have on the Indians, and a Congressional bill that would have helped conserve the bison was killed by Grant's pocket veto. In the unequal contest between the bison and the commercial hunters, Audubon was on the side of the bison.

> One can hardly conceive how it happens, notwithstanding these many deaths and the immense numbers that are murdered almost daily . . . besides the hosts that are drowned in the freshets, and the hundreds of young who die in early spring, so many yet are to be found. Daily we see so many that we hardly notice them more than the cattle in the pastures about our homes. But this cannot last; even now there is a perceptible difference in the size of the herds, and before many years the Buffalo, like the Great Auk, will have disappeared; surely this should not be permitted.

From the obviously vast land areas that would have to have been set aside for such a purpose, this comes close, by implication, to being a suggestion for national parks. But the very first such proposal had already been made publicly in 1832, by professional painter and amateur Indian George Catlin, in a newspaper article. Forty years before the first national park, Yellowstone, was established, Catlin lobbied in Washington for a great park in the Great Plains. This is how he put it in his two-volume work *North American Indians*:

> And what a splendid contemplation too, when one (who has travelled these realms, and can duly appreciate them, imagines them as they *might* in future be seen (by some great protecting policy of government) preserved in their pristine beauty and wildness, in a *magnificent park*, where the world could see for ages to come, the native Indian in his classic attire, galloping his wild horse, with sinewy bow, and shield and lance, amid the fleeting herds of elks and buffaloes. What a beautiful and thrilling specimen for America to preserve and hold up to the view of refined citizens and the world, in future ages! A *nation's Park*, containing man and beast, in all the wild and freshness of their nature's beauty.
>
> I would ask no other monument to my memory, nor any other enrolment of my name among the famous dead, than the reputation of having been the founder of such an institution.

This is far more explicit than Audubon's remarks, and in 1843 Audubon was probably quite unaware of Catlin's proposal and lobbying efforts in Congress. Both writers, however, saw that preserving the bison herds in any significant numbers would depend on such vast tracts of land that only a "kind" government could possibly accomplish it. Even the total acreage that is now preserved privately in Nature Conservancy properties and Audubon sanctuaries would be quite inadequate.

Audubon, in discussing the fate of Passenger Pigeons, seemed to understand that the key to saving a species is to save its habitat. Not until the Nature Conservancy became effective in the nineteen forties was any private or public agency specializing in saving smaller pieces—unique or unusual habitats. John Muir is well known for having been one of the moving forces in the establishment of many of our major natural parks, but hardly known at all for another important conservation concept which, unlike the idea of national parks, originated with him. As a very young man, he tried to persuade his brother to sell him two small pieces of the family farm, to enable John to preserve a bog and meadow he loved. It was not his chief motive to protect any particular endangered species, but to save these little ecosystems for their intrinsic value in their entirety. Muir later founded the Sierra Club, one of our strong preservation groups. More than three decades after his vain effort to keep the cows and plows out of his cherished sites, this bearded prophet told the story to those attending a Sierra Club meeting, and stressed the importance of saving small natural areas. He was still far ahead of his time, for that club meeting was in 1898!

It is evident from the thoughts expressed by Audubon, the man who symbolizes more than any other individual the idea of conservation for many millions of us, that he exhibited the usual symptoms we see today in those who have an environmental turn of mind. As he grew older he showed a progressive loss of interest in killing animals for sport, along with increasing feelings of kinship for wild creatures and of responsibility for preventing senseless destruction of them. Increasingly, ethical beliefs were perceived as applicable also to the natural world. He developed the so-called doom-saying skepticism which many regard as typical of his modern disciples, and for the same reason—he could see what was happening outdoors. Again, this attitude was leavened in Audubon by the optimistic hope that one's "remonstrances" might have some effect, in the long run, and his certainly have. From a viewpoint very close to that of a "game-hog," he had come very slowly to these perceptions during a period when he and Catlin were practically the only ones to have seen things that way and to have left a record of it. In Audubon's case, this may be taken to illustrate a familiar axiom, which may be paraphrased as "It takes a former thief, ofttimes, to recognize thievery."

A Bird on the Hat

9

> For several years past the National Association of Audubon Societies has been employing guards to protect the few remaining breeding colonies [of egrets] as far as they are known. These nesting places are distributed from the coastal region of North Carolina southward to the Florida Keys, but it is debatable whether the species can be saved, although without the efforts of the Audubon Society the bird would probably have disappeared entirely by this time.
>
> —T. Gilbert Pearson, 1917

After his Florida trip, Audubon wrote of the American Egret, now called the Great Egret: "The long plumes of this bird being in request for ornamental purposes, they are shot in great numbers while sitting on their eggs, or soon after the appearance of their young." However, he did not seem to deplore this; the egret populations were not being seriously threatened during his lifetime, and in 1832 Audubon had not yet become preservation-minded. It was the threat to the plume birds that prompted the founding of the Audubon groups which soon banded together as the

National Association of Audubon Societies and finally evolved into the National Audubon Society. Thwarting extermination and re-establishing populations of the beautiful waders was the first Audubon success and perhaps their most spectacular conservation triumph up to the present.

Fifty or more species of wild birds were being substantially taken for the millinery trade, largely in the subtropics and tropics of both the New and Old Worlds. "Aigrette" was the term given the long, silky feathers which herons and egrets assume for the breeding season, especially. An "osprey" was a tuft of (usually) those feathers or of some from birds-of-paradise worn on military headgear or on ladies' hats and gowns. Killing adult birds on the nesting grounds condemned their young to death by starvation. By 1875 the feather traffic had become so destructive that scientists recognized it as a severe threat and feared it would exterminate the principal species involved. "Murderous millinery" included, besides plumes, the wings of seabirds and others, heads of owls, and entire stuffed skins of birds from hummingbirds to gulls. Preservationists urged the use of pretty ribbons, artificial flowers, and feathers from domesticated ostriches. A male wag recommended that ladies should "kill two birds with one stone" by decorating themselves with the carcasses of rats, mice, and other obvious pests instead of useful birds. Opposition to the feather trade became the main stimulus that put into motion the events which led to the creation of our Fish and Wildlife Service with its many sanctuaries and respected programs of biological research.

Much more effective than scientific or economic arguments were publicity and photographs depicting the cruelty of collecting and killing wild birds or, worse, failing to kill them quickly, for their feathers. Despite counter-propaganda from the feather merchants, it became clear that getting the plumes nearly always entailed slaughtering the birds.

In 1886, the year that Dr. George Bird Grinnell proposed the formation of the Audubon Society, *Science* printed a 16-page supplement about the plume industry, which included a model law for bird protection, but by 1891 only five states had passed laws satisfactory to the American Ornithologists Union. Even in those states, enforcement was weak or nonexistent. The Audubon people realized the necessity of direct action, and soon hired their own wardens, set up their wildlife sanctuaries, and stepped up their educational work. For many years to come, leaflets with color pictures of birds were prepared by the thousands for schoolteachers to pass along to their pupils, and the name Audubon became entrenched in the public consciousness. It was its eventual (relative) success in the fight against fashion that gave the Audubon movement its first impetus toward its present importance in the general environmental movement.

A Florida boy of eighteen, T. Gilbert Pearson, who later led the national Audubon group, was deeply affected in 1891 by coming upon the site of a millinery massacre at an inland hammock.

> Upon approaching, the screams of young birds reached our ears. The cause of this soon became apparent by the buzzing of green flies and the heaps of dead herons festering in the sun, with the back of each bird raw and bleeding. . . . Young herons had been left by scores in the nests to perish from exposure and starvation.

Theodore Roosevelt established the first federal bird sanctuary early in 1903, by executive order. It protected the rookeries on Pelican Island in the Indian River east of Orlando, Florida. During his administration, fifty-one federal sanctuaries were established, distributed in seventeen states, Puerto Rico, Hawaii, and Alaska. (The present wildlife refuge system has areas in every state; there are more than four hundred refuges and they comprise several million acres.) In 1899, TR had endorsed the Audubon effort against the plume hunters, calling destruction of a species a loss as severe as though the Catskills were removed, or *all* the works of some great writer had perished.

Reformers are usually assailed by cries of "hypocrisy." The Audubon group was not exempt, the plume interests attacking the cruelty argument by pointing out that the upper classes, who led the battle for protection, did not oppose sport hunting or the wearing of furs, nor were they vegetarians. They claimed also that stopping the importation of heron feathers from India would make many a poor family there even more desperate. Ornithologists countered with convincing denials of the humane claims of the feather trade, and often proved that commercial plumes were the real thing when the trade claimed they were fakes, not taken from any birds. Some professional bird scholars reported their statistical bird-watching on feminine hats encountered during field trips through the streets of large cities. More emotional outcries compared plume traffic with the slave trade, while commercial spokesmen ridiculed the bleeding-heart sentimentality of the opponents of legitimate business enterprise.

What really turned the tide of general public opinion against plume hunting was man's inhumanity to man—the ruthless murders of two Audubon wardens. Guy M. Bradley lived in Flamingo, Florida, in a house at the west end of what is now the campground area there. Like many of his neighbors, he was a plume hunter in season, and knew the region thoroughly. He was, it is said, as "tough as a red mangrove," but he respected the new law against plume hunting, unlike many of the shady characters who haunted and hunted southwest Florida. When the Audubon people in 1902 offered him $35 a month to serve as warden through the Monroe County sheriff's office, which had no funds to enforce such a state law, Bradley accepted the job. It was an impossible assignment—his territory was the present Everglades park, the Florida Keys, some of the Big Cypress Swamp, and the Ten Thousand Islands, and he was up against lawless hunters like murderer-at-large John Ashley, and Ed Watson, and Fred Whitley. (The last-named used to row out on a lake during storms to blaspheme God, shaking his fist at the sky in challenge to retaliate. Finally, Whitley was killed out there by a bolt of lightning.)

A New York plumer cruised up and down the southwest coast of Florida with several taxidermists in a boat, which served as the mother ship for many of the resident plume hunters in the region. As the birds' numbers declined, one George Cuthbert searched the southern Everglades for a big rookery where he could make one last killing. He found it in 1889 on an unknown island in a large lake east of Flamingo. From one day's slaughter there he made $1,800, and used it to buy half of Marco Island. Again in 1904 someone decimated Cuthbert Rookery, and Frank Chapman, ornithologist of the American Museum of Natural History, was prevented from visiting it when Guy Bradley assured him that it had already been shot out.

One of Bradley's neighbors at Flamingo, Walter Smith, was at loggerheads with the conscientious warden, for Smith's sons were known plume hunters. Bradley, who was then thirty-five, heard shooting at Oyster Key (the Bird Key) three miles west of Flamingo and went to investigate. He found Smith's boat, aground at low tide; in it were the plumers, literally red-handed. Bradley attempted to board in order to arrest the sons, but Smith shot him in the chest. Bradley fell back in his boat, apparently without having fired a shot, and his body drifted in the boat for a day before it was discovered.

Smith was jailed briefly on a homicide charge, released on $5,000 bail, but never convicted. Bradley's widow did not favor punishment for the husband of her best friend, and local opinion was then on the side of the plume hunters rather than that of the wardens and the "furriners" who supported them. Bradley's family was helped by means of a fund set up by national Audubon headquarters. Bradley's grave at East Cape suffered devastation by a hurricane and cannot be located; its bronze plaque was later found and may be seen in the NPS visitor center at Flamingo. A new memorial provided by the Tropical Audubon Society was dedicated at Flamingo on March 30, 1975.

Another Audubon warden, Columbus McLeod, was killed near Charlotte Harbor, Florida, and other wardens were assaulted or threatened. The martyrdoms to the conservation cause shocked the general public. However, the impression that Bradley's death brought about an early solution is in error, for the new laws (outlined below) proved difficult to enforce with the inadequate funds the states and federal government allowed. It was illogical that enforcement was left largely to a private citizens' group. When Guy's brother Louis guided Frank Chapman, A. C. Bent, and Louis Agassiz Fuertes to Cuthbert Rookery in 1908, Chapman recommended strict protection, but estimated that this would require two wardens for four months each year to adequately insure it, at just that one rookery of the many that needed guarding.

The Lacey Act of 1900 was the first official blow against the industry in America. It made the Department of Agriculture responsible for bird protection, and prohibited interstate traffic in birds killed in violation of state laws, but failed to prohibit imports of foreign bird skins for millinery. The shock of the Florida murders helped induce New York state, where the trade in this country was concentrated, to pass Pearson's bill in 1910, but this could not prevent Florida feather hunters from selling to foreign buyers, who shipped the plumes back into New York. A federal tariff provision was adopted in 1913 after dramatic confrontations in Congress in which Pearson led the preservationist forces. The tariff law was improved by amendment in 1922. A comparable battle had been proceeding in the United Kingdom; the British Plumage Act went into effect in 1922.

The manufacture of the offending hats was concentrated in Paris, London, and New York. French customs records, for instance, revealed that 50,000 tons of plumage entered France between 1890 and 1929. America substantially reduced its plumage trade first, England considerably later.

During Theodore Roosevelt's presidency, covering most of the first decade of the new century, general appreciation of nature and opposition to the feather trade stimulated each other in a mutual feedback relationship. This was the first great era of conservation, and its like was not to be seen again until the 1960s.

The Audubon people did not single-handedly bring about the reduction of plume hunting in this country and the world. *Youths Companion* and *Saint Nicholas* magazines had preached bird study and protection for scores of years. Audubon's art and writing had been important in arousing interest in bird life, and other popular literary and artistic naturalists helped keep it alive later. Edward Bok's *Ladies Home Journal* frequently condemned plume hunting and the styles that made it possible. Plumed hats became inconvenient as the automobile gained acceptance. World War I brought on simplification of hats and other wearing apparel. The British royal family and President Woodrow Wilson helped directly and indirectly. Wilson's two daughters performed in a public anti-plume play, one in the role of "Ornia, the bird spirit."

The aigrette war never ended completely. Pearson testified in 1930 before a U.S. Senate committee that egret hunters posing as Audubon wardens were watching rookeries until the birds attained prime plumage and then shooting them out. Robert Allen, director of all the Audubon sanctuaries, reported thus in 1934:

> The success of our sanctuary work does not mean that the desired end has been accomplished. The job is far from done. Florida, as always, presents a constant problem, and although the Association has been able to maintain a year-round warden in the most critical regions, with three men on duty during the rookery season, Herons, Egrets, and Ibises are still being killed in certain areas. . . . The plume trade is not dead and the lives of our south Florida wardens are still threatened by the emissaries of that trade, and by those who kill Ibises for food.

Cuban fishermen would go up the Shark River at the end of the mackerel season, kill and salt down thousands of birds for sale in Havana. A rookery was found destroyed in 1937. Thereafter, one decade passed before the establishment of Everglades National Park, certainly a crucial step in the protection of the great wading birds. Park status was much better than ineffective wildlife preserve status, but still did not end the menace of human greed. Overburning, hauling away truckloads of plants by orchid thieves, active deer-poaching, and commercial alligator-hunting were prevalent long after 1947, and are said to still go on to a limited extent. But the direct damage to wildlife has been supplanted by a probably more threatening indirect disaster, as shown in the last section of this chapter.

New generations arise, unfamiliar with the triumphs and tragedies of their predecessors. The plume trade still raises its ugly hats from time to time, and Audubon's New York office remains alert to illegal activities.

The plumage laws in New York state were still being amended as late as 1947, and opponents were finding legal loopholes for several years after that.

Exploitation of wild birds changes form but continues. Against NAS advice, the Interior Department recently legalized the commercialization of birds of prey for falconry. Unscrupulous falconers have been stealing eggs and chicks from nests and selling the birds as bred in captivity. Duck Hawks brought them $2,000 apiece, and Gyrfalcons shipped abroad have sold for $50,000. Half of the birds taken from the wild have died during handling. In mid-1984, federal and state wildlife agents concluded a three-year investigation by arresting many leaders of falconry organizations, charging that more than 500 raptors had been taken illegally. The only practical solution to the "laundering" of wild birds to pass them off as captives is to put a complete stop to the sale of all birds of prey.

The historic expansion of conservation issues, from particular species like plume birds or localized issues, to encompass entire ecosystems, and the parallel change in conservation groups like Audubon, are epitomized in the story of Everglades National Park.

The attraction which brings most visitors to Everglades National Park is the aggregation of spectacular subtropical wading birds. The finest birding that Audubon found in his life was within what is now this park, particularly at Sandy Key near the present park headquarters at Flamingo. He made a special excursion to Sandy Key on his cruise southward to Key West, and again on his northward return trip. This is a part of the distinctive human history of the Everglades which, together with the past and continuing splendor of its natural history, would seem to justify as much protection today and tomorrow as the best ecological analyses determine is desirable.

The fifteen species of herons, ibises, and storks that nest in Everglades Park are at or near the top of the food chain, and are good "indicator species" for investigators to use in monitoring possible trouble in the environment, now that direct hunting by man is negligible. National Park Service and Audubon Society have protected their rookeries and promoted public appreciation. They have also sponsored periodic counts of the bird populations.

The reports indicated that 129,000 wading birds nested in southern Florida in 1974-75. The most common ones were White Ibis (56,000) and Cattle Egret (33,300). One thousand Roseate Spoonbills nested in Florida Bay. Of the 8,700 Wood Storks nesting in southern Florida, only 2,600 nested in the park. "Population levels of the medium-sized egrets and herons were surprisingly low," Kushlan and White stated. "When the environment was in its natural state, most of the southern Florida wading bird population nested [in the Park]. . . . The shift of nesting birds out of the park suggests that the southern Everglades no longer provides conditions adequate for large scale nesting and . . . that the natural ecological system is not functioning in the southern Everglades."

Plume hunting had practically ceased by 1920, enabling the populations of the birds involved to reach a peak about a decade later. But, as Robertson and Kuchlan reported in 1974, "Progressive degradation of the southern Florida environment has led to a second period of population decline from the 1930's to the present."

Recent testing of birds and their environments for pesticides has failed to find significant concentrations. Brown pelicans are very sensitive to pesticides and were once exterminated from that cause along the Louisiana coast. Now they are abundant along the mainland shore of the park. We must seek other cause or causes.

The first conservation effort in the Everglades had a single straightforward aim: stop the slaughter of birds for their plumes. Had that effort failed, plume birds would now be gone and the ecosystem thus changed directly and indirectly, but what remained would still have justified park status. Today the threat is a much more complex one; it challenges the entire Everglades ecosystem in a direct way. Whether and how it is to be met will reveal where society really stands on the environment issue when it comes to the crunch.

Much of the water on which the Everglades depends seeps and trickles south from Florida's largest lake, Okeechobee, and from Big Cypress Swamp. Practically all of Florida from Fort Myers and Palm Beach southward was originally a biological paradise of swamp and marsh. A swamp is tree-covered; a marsh is dominated by herbs like sawgrass, reeds, and cattails. Everglades is the only national park that does not control its own water supply. Nature cannot fulfill her contract for delivery. Man intercepts water for other uses on its course down the peninsula, or water flow is blocked by highways, or drained away for subdivisions, some of which never materialized with houses. Under natural conditions, a few casual streams lazed seaward. Today, the thousands of canals cut by developers and the Engineer Corps into the tissue of south Florida cause a continual hemorrhage from the severed capillaries. The lifeblood of the Everglades is dissipated into the surrounding sea. The lowered water table permits replacement of underground freshwater by saltwater. Thus, of the limited freshwater, much of the small portion that does not evaporate or transpire away from irrigation use or go for direct domestic uses is diverted unnecessarily from its natural function of supporting the Everglades water-cycle. Drought damage to wildlife, vegetation, and soil intensifies as the frequency and severity of dry periods go far beyond the normal alternation between seasonal moisture extremes to which the living forms gradually adapted over the millennia.

Broadly stated, it is the development of "real estate" which is mercilessly advancing upon Everglades National Park. As development accelerates the man-made desiccation, the organic soil oxidizes in the hot sun and disappears. The alligator holes, normally refuges from ordinary droughts, are lost together with their diverse, concentrated inhabitants. The marl-muck areas crack, burn, settle, and solidify. Now we can understand the plaint uttered years ago by Joseph Wood Krutch, that when a man destroys a work of art we call him a vandal, but when a man destroys a work of nature we call him a developer.

The destiny of the park in the Everglades, which is unlike any other of our national parks, is inseparable from that of southern Florida as a whole. Carry the existing direction of change some way further toward its logical conclusion—a salt desert—and southern Florida will become incapable of supporting any kind of terrestrial animal life except people and vultures, nor will it long remain suitable or attractive to either of those kinds of animals.

The British ecologist Elton long ago pointed out three reasons for our maintaining the diversity of Nature: "Because it is a right relation between man and living things, because it gives opportunities for richer experience, and because it tends to promote ecological stability—ecological resistance to invaders and to explosions in native populations." The combination of these reasons provides a wise principle of co-existence between man and Nature, one that we disregard or flout at our hazard.

To point out the end result on the assumption of certain trends going to their logical conclusion is not to predict that this will necessarily happen. That would be the logic of the rash environmental publicist who allegedly predicted a few years ago that within a few months we would all vanish in a puff of blue smoke. (The specific color was not explained.) Few trends ever fully proceed to their "logical conclusions" because of the unimaginable intricacy of potential counter trends mitigating the harmful effect. Social and economic feedback mechanisms can enter into the situation, as well as natural ones. The more evident the bad consequences become, the more effectively may the negative feedbacks operate to counter them.

That point does not justify complacency or procrastination. The feedback of political responsibility by decision makers is usually lacking in conservation matters because they are out of office by the time the effects of decisions are apparent, so that they seldom suffer the consequences of bad decisions in a direct, personal way.

A harmful change often begins slowly and without attracting notice, then builds in geometric progression, doubling and redoubling with progressively shorter doubling-times as the change overwhelms all opposing feedbacks or trends. As Paul Sears commented, "The highest function of science is to give us an understanding of consequences." The bad consequences may not become generally understood until a particular doubling finally makes the disaster glaringly obvious, as though it had all happened quite suddenly. That stage, for Everglades National Park, was reached in the 1950s. The "remedial steps" that have been taken since then have merely slowed the operation of the factors of degradation. Unlike most of the national parks, whose problem has been financial (rather than physical) thirst, mere appropriation of more funds for use *within* Everglades Park cannot deflect the threat from the north due basically to the increase of population and development, and spreading agriculture and industry. Remedies attempted for the park have been overwhelmed by that juggernaut. There are far fewer plume birds in the park today than there were when Guy Bradley was killed in their defense in 1905!

During some recent years the park, especially its deer population, has suffered from excess rather than deficiency of water. The park cannot even choose whether to succumb to thirst or drowning, for its fate is in the hands of political figures and water control engineers outside the park, and its welfare is not a major priority with them. The entire national park system suffered from benign neglect for the first half or more of the 1970s, and from malign neglect in the early 1980s with respect to the natural features which justified making these areas into parks in the first place.

It now appears that the tide may have started to turn. Led by Governor Bob Graham, Florida has committed itself to restore and preserve drained and damaged wetlands, with federal and local help. Portions of the new program are already under way. The general goal is to make the Everglades of the year 2000 look more like the Everglades of the year 1900 than the Everglades of today. "We will attempt in the next seventeen years to heal the damage inflicted over the past century," Graham declared in 1983.

The plan calls for reestablishing the natural characteristics of the Kissimmee River, once a gently meandering stream ninety miles long. The Everglades Park boundaries would be expanded by acquiring adjacent lands which are in the same biome, such as the 50,000-acre Aerojet properties in the East Everglades, and "reclaiming" to their original condition the 95-square-mile Rotenberger and Holey Land tracts.

Highways would be modified so that the natural southward flow of water would be less inhibited than it is now. Deer herds would be managed so as to avoid "mercy killings" and the drowning of deer during periods of high water. Ways would be sought to prevent the extinction of the endangered Florida panther. "The mistakes of a hundred years will be expensive to correct," Governor Graham stated, "but whatever the price, the price of inaction is higher still. . . . Ultimately, our ability to support human life on the South Coast of the Florida peninsula depends on the health and well-being of the Everglades."

In His Name

10

His long raven locks hung curling over his shoulders, yet unshorn from the wilderness.... His fine-featured face bespoke a sort of wild independence; and then such an eye, keen as that of a falcon! His foreign accent and broken English speech ... removed him still further out of the commonplace circle of this everyday world of ours, and his whole demeanor—it might be with us partly imagination—was colored to our thought by a character of conscious freedom and dignity, which he had habitually acquired in his long and lonely wandering among the woods, where he had lived in the uncompanioned love and delight of nature, and in the studious observation of all the ways of her winged children.

—National Portrait Gallery

Ornitheology is a popular faith, whereas ornithology is one of the biological sciences. The communicants of Ornitheology, including the present writer, revere John James Audubon as the original prophet. His beatification occurred well before the 1862 publication of the book *National Portrait Gallery*, from which the above liturgical paragraph is quoted.

Originally, the doctrine essentially limited itself to the amateur study, appreciation, and conservation of the world of birds, but the dogmas grew increasingly catholic over the years. Today, the attitudes and activities apply to the natural world as a whole—in leafing through a modern ornitheological journal one is likely to find more on general environmentalism than on birds. This broadening of emphasis reflects the maturation, discernible in both individuals and organizations, from an absorption with a narrower salvation to a vital socio-political modernism. The present doctrine is that the avocational souls of nature lovers cannot be saved unless they support missions both foreign and domestic. Thus, a laity of deep convictions supports a dedicated professional priesthood.

There are, of course, other philosophical and empirical approaches besides Ornitheology which lead to an individual's birth into the environmental faith. We may note how the various denominations are related, and how their beliefs and works differ, by exploring the parallelism with groups more commonly accepted as being religious. Most of the latter organizations are old-line churches, but some are efflorescences of more recent origin.

The National Parks Association, the Conservation Foundation, and the America the Beautiful Fund appear analogous to the high-church Episcopalians. In both emotional and intellectual aspects, the ritual and preachments are moving and effective. That the priestly class is high-minded and well-educated, while it meets the needs of the membership, tends to limit mass participation. There is a minimum of ecumenism with the newly born Moral Majority groups.

The Wilderness Society, Environmental Defense Fund, and Resources for the Future also draw support from the "upper class," a term not referring here to monetary criteria primarily. The leadership and membership are high-toned intellectuals, the Resources group having economists and the Defense crowd having scientists as their archbishops. The Wilderness Society also concentrates on the scientific side of the C. P. Snow fence. All environmental groups show an interest in survival. Therefore, they necessarily proselytize to some degree, but this does not seem to be an overwhelming concern with these three sects. What religious group could this description match except the Unitarian Church?

Like the Quaker Church, the leadership of the firmly established World Wildlife Fund and the International Union for the Conservation of Nature and Natural Resources is intellectual and active as well as pious, and the thoughtful, dedicated supporters rate above the average in this world's assets. All three of the denominations are internationally oriented and charitable toward the Third World, but not overly proselytizing at home or abroad.

The National Audubon Society, the founder and most orthodox promoter of Ornitheology, is the long-established Presbyterian Church of environmentalism. Both groups consist of business-like, solidly respectable citizens, who are aggressive without being "far out." The pastors and elders are known for rational and persuasive discourse, exceptionally appealing in its presentation. The flock is substantial in both numbers and worldly goods.

The Izaak Walton League and the National Wildlife Federation together count for a large fraction of all North American conservationists, and retain close spiritual affinity to the original old-time religion preached by Theodore Roosevelt from the "bully pulpit" of the White House. A good many members of both denominations attained grace through an early or present interest in hunting and fishing rather than from Ornitheology. This orientation provides a needed balance in the overall conservation community. The name Izaak Walton misleadingly suggests a group made up principally of anglers, yet many in this and the Federation are simply outdoors men and women who hold strong conservation convictions. Many are politically conservative; they wonder how the meaning of the term "conservative" became distorted into *opposition* to conservation! Their relative conservatism by no means inhibits their aggressive activism in conservation causes, nor belies a strong emotional element in applying the tenets of their faith locally and nationally. The League and Federation, thus, go in more for rousing revival services and camp meetings than for profound philosophical sermonizing. The comparison that is inevitably suggested is that with the Baptist Church, especially the Southern Baptists.

The Friends of the Earth appeals to many young people and has spread practically world-wide. In many respects it resembles Methodism. For the converts, faith rests upon deep emotional underpinning, and is applied aggressively and vigorously toward a broad range of concerns in society. Its "John Wesley" is the founder David Brower. This Arch-Friend is regarded by exploiting types as the Arch-Fiend. Doubtless his followers feel a sympathy for pantheism not paralleled among the United Methodists, for founder Brower is affectionately known as the Arch-Druid.

The venerable Sierra Club, founded by John Muir, is the parent group to Friends of the Earth. The two are not essentially different.

The American Forestry Association, like the Church of the Latter Day

Saints, is conservative, close-knit, tightly hierarchical, with uniform and deep indoctrination in the membership. Each of these well-organized and unified sects is single-minded, and closely related to business interests, hence is highly practical in dealing with worldly matters. Both are long and firmly established institutions serving valuable purposes in our culture. Most conservation organizations join forces ecumenically in addressing issues, but this is less true of the Pinchot-following Forestry group. As more oriented toward a particular interest in the conservation field, it is more self-contained and independent.

We now come to the neo-fundamentalist "true life-style believers," the peripheral, outward-bound groups only some members of which consider themselves environmentalists. We have the health food addicts, the organic farming adherents, solar energy proponents, and resources recycling workers. I don't intend to imply that this is necessarily the lunatic fringe (in Theodore Roosevelt's phrase) of conservation, for to a degree and in part, their insights *may* foreshadow the future of all of us. At least in their 190-proof fervor, I detect resemblance to the Moral Majority and similar true believers.

The television-viewing public is *conscious of* flailingly activist cults out of all proportion to their membership and accomplishments. Earth First! is allegedly willing to countenance sabotage actions. Greenpeace consists of gutsy mariners, not in the mainstream, who set their courses for serious confrontations with Soviet whaling leviathans. These activities remind us of ceremonial rattlesnake-handling by the devout of certain churches in the southern mountains.

Let us conclude this sociological analysis by noting the back-to-nature communes and the survivalist fortifications. These outposts on the tattered fringes are more isolationist than environmentalist. Their homologues in religion seem to be such nuisance "churches" as the Moonies, Hare Krishna, and certain opportunist cults created for income-tax purposes. The first two of these religions seem at least as serious about their beliefs as any others are; in America they have a legal right to any dogma whether or not the rest of us consider it heretical or worse.

All the conservation-environmental groups and their religious counterparts contribute in their own ways to the diversity of our prevailing sociopolitical and religio-philosophical ecosystems.

The National Audubon Society stands at the heart of historical and current Ornitheology, in both its avocational and environmental-campaign aspects. This historic and effective institution grew originally out of the American Ornithologists Union members' unofficial determination to stop the slaughter of plume birds for the millinery trade. Thus, the popular Audubon movement was an activist offshoot of a group of scientists, just as many years later the scientists' Ecological Society of America gave rise to an activist splinter-group, the Ecologists Union, which was soon to change its name to The Nature Conservancy.

The AOU members Frank M. Chapman, William Dutcher, and artist Abbott Thayer enlisted Dr. George Bird Grinnell as their public relations outlet through his *Forest and Stream* magazine. Thus, Grinnell is given credit for founding the first Audubon Society.

As a child, Grinnell was a pupil of Lucy Audubon's at the school she ran in New York after her husband's death, and a playmate of the Audubon boys, Victor G. and John Woodhouse Audubon. Lucy aroused in her small pupil a lifelong interest in the world of nature. He was the scion of a wealthy family. As a young man, he went along as a naturalist with General George Custer to the Black Hills in 1874, and the next year accompanied another Army expedition into the new Yellowstone Park. Grinnell took his Ph.D. in zoology at Yale University. Although he made his living as editor and owner of *Forest and Stream*, he managed to visit the Cheyenne tribe in the West every year for forty years, and wrote on anthropology both popularly and technically. In 1899 he served as the anthropologist on the private Alaskan expedition of financier Edward Harriman, of which Gov. W. Averell Harriman is the only survivor today. Grinnell instigated the establishment of our Glacier National Park, and its Grinnell Mountain and Grinnell Glacier commemorate this. As one of Theodore Roosevelt's cronies in the Boone and Crockett Club, he was in the forefront of the burgeoning conservation movement, and used his magazine to save the bison, protect the Florida plume birds, and, in 1886, to found the Audubon Society, which he named to honor Audubon, and his own friends in the naturalist's family.

In Dr. Grinnell's editorial in the February 11, 1886, issue of his *Forest and Stream*, he wrote, "We propose the formation of an association for the protection of wild birds and their eggs, which shall be called the Audubon Society." If it now seems curious that eggs were specifically mentioned, it was because of the swarms of egg collecting hobbyists or "oologists" then prevalent.

An *Audubon Magazine* was launched in 1887, selling for six cents a copy, but folded after two years. *Bird Lore* was founded, owned, and edited for the Audubon movement by Frank M. Chapman; it first appeared in February, 1899. Its first number discussed the anti-plume campaign, and listed fifteen Audubon Societies. *Bird Lore* was succeeded by *Audubon Magazine*, which later shortened its name to *Audubon*.

Before discussing the National Audubon Society, a subject so complicated that I can do little more than outline it here, I should point out that some Audubon societies pre-date the national body and were never absorbed into it as chapters. Probably the Massachusetts group is the best-known of these. The Indiana Audubon Society was founded in 1889, separate from the other organizations then and now, and lacks any affiliation with the national Society or its local chapters, except for holding some meetings jointly at its 600-acre Mary Gray Bird Sanctuary. Besides holding meetings, the Indiana society issues its two journals to members, sponsors a Big Day in May, and conducts many field trips.

That the Audubon name is not the exclusive property of the NAS is also illustrated by two historical-educational institutions. Audubon House at Key West, a popular tourist attraction, is owned by the Mitchell Wolfson Family Foundation of Miami. The Audubon Wildlife Sanctuary, near Valley Forge a bit north of Philadelphia, features the old Mill Grove home of young Audubon, one of the few authentic Audubon shrines which is open to the public. It is owned and operated, with a fine Audubon museum, by Montgomery County.

Except for the Buddhists, Lutherans and Christians in general, the Audubon Society now seems to be the largest group of any kind named officially for an individual person. It has about 500,000 members. The Izaak Walton League has a tenth as many. There is only one continuing group commemorating a U.S. President, the Theodore Roosevelt Association chartered by Congress in 1920; it has only a few thousand members. The organization honoring the name of another oldtime naturalist, the John Burroughs Memorial Association, has still fewer members.

The present National Audubon Society and its precursor groups have not consisted of "long-haired men and short-haired women." As environmentalists go, this is a thoroughly mainstream group of centrists. Its membership represents a fairly high average with respect to family income. The society's efforts are not just educational, "on paper" ones, for over a broad practical spectrum it is highly activist on a well-thought-out conceptual base, as though its motto were "Be sure you're right, then go ahead." During its long and complex history, toward which the merest bow can be made herein (see chapter 9), from opposing the plume-bird killers to lashing back against the present backlash, the Audubon Society has been a leading group in the conservation-environmental movement. Through the decades of search for rational solutions to crunching socio-political controversies, while opposed by many who consider environmental safeguards un-American, it has not lost sight of its more specific mission—to stimulate, guide, and perpetuate popular interest in bird life and its protection. For example, on one day each year, it marshals about 34,000 serious birders throughout the country to collect data during the Christmas Bird Count.

In 1968, Elvis J. Stahr resigned from the presidency of Indiana University in order to assume leadership of the National Audubon Society, succeeding Carl W. Buchheister. In 1979 Russell W. Peterson took up the reins. He had previously served as the chairman of the top official body in its field in this nation, the Council on Environmental Quality. He had headed the research and development branch of the Du Pont Company, and the congressional office of Technology Assessment. Peterson has also been governor of Delaware, and a member of the presidential commission to study Three Mile Island. As a noted environmentalist with an impeccable record in technological developments also, he brought to the Audubon job the best of both worlds. He has announced that he will retire from this position by mid-1985.

A major aim of his presidency is to mobilize American citizens to hold the hard-won conservation advances made by Theodore Roosevelt and the long line of like-minded workers after him. These gains are currently threatened by the ideology "If you can't dig it up or cut it down, it doesn't serve any value at all." To work effectively toward the Audubon objective, a society president need not be able to identify an immature female Bay-breasted Warbler during fall migration (although the membership includes some "*rara aves*" who are quite capable of that feat).

The annual budget of the society is something over $21 million. Its office of development brings in about $12 million each year. Merely to keep its membership constant, the society must recruit 125,000 new members annually. There is a 75 percent renewal rate across the board, but, of those who have remained members for four years, 95 percent continue on. The society enjoyed a ten-fold growth in membership from 1965 through 1982. There are eleven categories of membership. Dues for the Individual class are $30, with $9.50 going to the appropriate chapter, and for the Student class, $18, with the chapter receiving $5.50. The shares received by the chapters form their major source of funds for their activities. The present dues schedule does not represent a real increase in dues since 1968, only an adjustment for inflation.

During the recent economic recession, the NAS threw dignity (or stuffiness) to the winds, and adopted the proven sweepstakes technique for attracting new members and raising supplemental funds from old ones. The contest was called "Earthstakes." It offered some highly original prizes—a trip for two in a hot-air balloon, a "wilderness" experience in New York's Central Park, a "baby elephant" folio of Audubon *Birds*. If the patron saint is now spinning in his grave, some medium should explain to him that the economics of environmental groups is now as precarious as his own once was in Kentucky. The traveling salesman J. J. Audubon had adjusted his methods to the economic realities and social mores of his time. Few of those who support the Audubon cause, or merely wish it well, are likely to object to the use of current marketing ploys, as long as the society's spirit remains conformable with the potential motto "*Semper Aves*," and not with "*Caveat Emptor.*"

The ten regional offices and four satellite offices employ forty-one people, including twenty-seven professional staff people. In addition, there are six persons in the Regional Activities staff of the New York office.

Two-thirds of the national members belong also to an Audubon chapter at the more local level; there are 480 such chapters, forming the connection between the national society and grass-roots conservation issues. They hold meetings, very often with excellent programs, prepare and distribute newsletters, conduct field trips and bird censuses, carry out nature and environmental education of broad scope, and help to keep governmental conservation officials honest. Each regional office has two or more full-time, professional conservationists who aid and coordinate the work of chapters in their region, supervise the Audubon nature centers, testify before legislatures and courts, and advise the chapters on administrative, educational, scientific, and legal matters.

The national office functions through the efforts of 125 employees of all ranks, carrying out a far-flung and varied program. One vital facet, long a tradition of the society, is running a system of wildlife sanctuaries: there are now seventy-five. The forty-five wardens both protect birds and their habitats and assist visitors to enjoy them.

Audubon operates five Environmental Education Centers, where twenty professionals and many volunteers work year-round. The first to be established was the one at Aullwood, near Dayton, Ohio, which is the best-known of the five. From each center, extension work penetrates throughout the whole Audubon region in which the center is located, to assist chapters in their educational programs.

Six research scientists work out of the national office. With many specialists assisting as consultants, they concentrate on endangered species: Atlantic Puffin, California Condor, Bald Eagle, Whooping Crane, the Florida kites, eastern timber wolf, black-footed ferret, and alligator. Broader issues, such as land, water, and energy uses, are explored with the collaboration of expert advisors. Three other professionals devote full time to human population stabilization by largely educational (rather than clinical) work through the United Nations.

Forming an Office of Government Relations, nine professionals and four support people work, from a Capitol Hill headquarters, with legislators and federal agencies. They cooperate with other environmental groups, and litigate when all else fails. For instance, an Audubon lobbyist headed the coalition of twenty-five organizations which frustrated the Reagan Administration's efforts to have Congress turn its back on the present Endangered Species Act. Audubon worked for nine years, also in concert with other groups, in the Alaska Coalition. The reasonable settlement of the Alaska public lands issue, reached in 1980 after protracted compromise with resource-users, is already being seriously challenged by those with their own designs on lands and resources belonging to all of us. NAS does not take on every environmental issue; it was one of two major groups remaining neutral on Senate confirmation of William Clark as Secretary of the Interior.

Like all the private groups of environmentalists that I know of, Audubon does not consider the environment as a Republican-Democratic issue. It will impartially and cheerfully assist or condemn either party. Naturally, the party in power tends to be the one under the most intense scrutiny. Audubon's criticism of the environmental policies and practices that began in 1980, while more complete than that of *Science*, the impartial journal of the American Association for the Advancement of Science, is actually no more hard-hitting.

After plenty of time had elapsed for the performance of the Reagan administration on environmental questions to be judged fairly, Audubon joined nine other non-partisan groups of private citizens in publishing a 144-page book analyzing the situation. Considering that about half of the people who support the nine organizations must be Republican in their politics, the book furnished a remarkable illustration of the candor and courage of Audubon and the other groups' leadership.

They present what they term an "indictment" of 220 documented charges of negligence and neglect in pollution-control, energy-leasing and the overall energy problem, water resources, federal public lands and their (our) resources, regulatory "reform," the Council on Environmental Quality, and the international environment. A third of the book, signed by fourteen different groups, alleges that the present administration's energy plan is a "major power failure." As a result of it, the groups claim, our energy problems can only deepen and become more intractable, and they urge support of reliable and economic sources of energy. The book then analyzes a federal budget submitted for Congressional approval, and suggests alternative proposals which they say would reduce the total outlay by $8.5 billion, restore an adequate and balanced program for protecting the natural environment and public health, and serve as a guide to wise management of our nation's resources. However, these environmentalists *supported* presidential proposals for user-fees for government-built ports and waterways, and for requiring the nuclear-power industry to pay waste management costs, instead of continuing to enjoy tax breaks and subsidies. By making essential changes on the revenue side, the book asserts, we could well afford the level of environmental protection we really need. In general, the Administration budget was found to "reorder national priorities away from conservation and protection of the environment toward support for a few resource-extractive industries, and a continued trend toward spending for economically dubious and environmentally damaging development at the expense of less costly, more benign alternatives." Finally, these citizens' organizations offered a "Citizen's Guide to Action: What To Do If You're Outraged."

The national office has established four educational summer camps that provide intensive, college-credit courses combined with enjoyable natural history experiences that enhance the students' feeling for the necessity of conservation. The four "ecology camps" are open to persons over the age of 18. The one with the most modern accommodations (meaning, I suppose, least like a camp) is near Greenwich, Connecticut, thirty-five miles from New York City. The sessions there (only) are geared to different backgrounds and degrees of interest, and only one-week sessions are offered. The emphasis is on field ecology, and the cost of a session is $375. The first Audubon camp was started in 1936; it is in the Todd Wildlife Refuge on Hog Island off the Maine coast. (In its second summer, I served there as an instructor.) Within easy access of this camp is the Rachel Carson Salt Pond Preserve, Popham Beach, and the sea-bird islands and rocks farther offshore. It offers a special ten-day session in late June for youngsters of 10 through 14; this costs $370. Each two-week session for adult leaders is priced at $620 at the three camps where they are offered. The camp near Spooner, Wisconsin, is the only one offering both one-week and two-week sessions. It is in the northern canoe country. Trail Ranch Lake is the only western camp; it is four miles from Dubois, Wyoming, at 7,500 feet in a valley in the Wind River Range among 13,000-foot peaks. Campers choose among a broad range of outdoor subjects according to their own academic level, interests, and physical condition. All the camps provide interesting talks, films, and special guest lectures for the evenings. They also leave time open for recreation. Two one-week workshops are held at two of the camps after the last regular session. Another educational vehicle, in more than one way, is the mobile Audubon Ark. Navigated by a naturalist, it carries the story about endangered species to 85,000 people annually at shopping centers, libraries, and schools, with many additional persons reached through local media in the towns visited.

The Field Seminars, introduced in 1979, have grown to ten specialized programs with small groups of adult students in some of the beauty spots of North America. In the West, Audubon offers nature photography in Wyoming, a natural history backpacking excursion in the same state, a winter ecology ski-tour in the Yellowstone, and limnology in the Flathead Lake area of Montana. Desert exploration is pursued in the nation's largest state park, the Anza Borrego of California. An environmental policy seminar is held at a campus of Colorado State University in the Rockies. On the forest and canoe trails of Minnesota are the Northwoods Winter ski camp, and a Boundary Waters canoe trip northward into Canada.

One southern attraction is a Nature Photography seminar in Ding Darling National Wildlife Refuge on Sanibel Island off Fort Myers, Florida, combined with the society's most famed refuge, Corkscrew Swamp, inland. Finally, there is a field ornithology seminar in an area of west-central Mexico where more than 500 species of birds occur. Incidentally, the Colima Warbler, extremely rare and localized where I have seen it, in Big Bend National Park, shares its specific common name with the city in Mexico where this Audubon seminar makes its headquarters. All the seminars go on for eight days. The Mexican one is the most expensive at $790; the others range from $360 to $650.

An Audubon Expedition Institute offers school-year, one semester, or summer travel-study programs in the United States and Canada for high school and college students to examine natural and social issues on the ground where they are relevant. These appeal to youth by means of shared adventures in wilderness backpacking, biking, canoe trips, terrain appreciation, community history, and ecology. The locales of these accredited expeditions are New England, Down East Maine, Eastern Newfoundland, Western Newfoundland to Southern Labrador, the Pacific Northwest, and the American Southwest. These are peripatetic Audubon Nature Camps for those of tender years with tough feet and musculature. Also under this program is a special Teacher Training Workshop.

The society licenses three travel agencies to manage Audubon Explorations, which provide a choice of tours here and abroad led by highly qualified naturalists. A frequent destination is that biological treasure-trove, the Galapagos Archipelago.

A current series of radio "shorts" about groups of birds is financed by a grant from the society. In its Wildlife Film Program, Audubon sponsors 550 film showings annually in at least a hundred cities, each narrated in person by one of twenty free-lance photographic naturalists. This puts to good use the phenomenal improvement in wildlife photography in recent years.

Collaboration between the NAS and Ted Turner, the environmentalist who heads Superstation WTBS, produced the TV series *The World of Audubon,* hosted by Cliff Robertson. Starting in autumn 1984, each of the five hour-long shows will be aired four times. Nature and the work of the modern NAS are featured. (John James Audubon is the subject of a series prepared by the BBC that will be released in this country in 1985 on the Public Broadcasting System by WNET-TV, New York.)

The Audubon publication program is extensive and effective. This concentrates on periodicals, reports, monographs, promotional releases, and booklets. While most of the Audubon Society's publications are written in popular style, some result from technical research of scientists on the national staff.

In July of 1984, the NAS brought out an updated version of its national energy plan, along with specific legislative proposals. (The Society will send a summary free on request.) The plan is designed to " . . . bolster the economy by providing large reductions in energy cost, strengthen national security by relieving our dependence on foreign oil, and protect the natural environment from the intolerable damage [from ever-increasing use] of fossil fuels."

The superb magazine *Audubon* with its outstanding illustrations is too familiar to require description here. Production quality places it at one extreme among environmental journals, opposite the deliberately modest format of the pulp, newspaper-like *Not Man Apart* through which the Friends of the Earth group makes the point of life-style reduction. The appeal of *Audubon* is to a more affluent (on average), significantly less "activist," clientele, and it does economize by issuing only six numbers annually. Its superlative visual product represents outdoor photography at its finest. Its cartoons (like the "April Fool" issues of *Not Man Apart*) help to counter the calumny that environmentalists are humorless. In its textual contents, often the most thoroughgoing source of information on current controversies and issues, an inbred tendency is sometimes detectable, perhaps resulting from the fact that the journal's own large staff does so much of the writing. On controversial issues the writers, while not pretending to complete impartiality as do many journalists, often make an effort to present views opposed to their own. But since the general, non-environmental magazines often present inadequate or unbalanced stories on such issues (see *Time Magazine*'s early coverage of Rachel Carson), such organs as *Audubon* hardly seem bound to use their limited resources in making a case for their opponents, on whose side the money, power, and political clout commonly reside already.

Most *Audubon* subscribers are not dedicated bird hobbyists and hence do not take the second most important NAS journal, *American Birds*, which also appears six times annually, printing both monochrome and color figures. It is not for coffee-table ornithologists or general environmentalists, but specifically intended for amateur and professional students of bird science. It runs informative articles on birds and prints a large volume of detailed records, from the twenty-six Audubon regions of North America, on the Christmas Bird Count, Breeding Bird Census, Spring Migration, etc. There are also book reviews and reproductions of the leading entries in an annual bird-photography salon. This could have been the principal publication of the NAS if the group had not become involved with environmentalism. It stands between the popular *Audubon* and such highly technical journals, usually lacking color figures, as *The Auk* and the *Wilson Bulletin*, which are sponsored by strictly scientific bodies.

The quarterly *Audubon Action* goes to all society members; it is much more environmentally than ornithologically oriented, being the organ for various announcements and calls to action, the president's annual report, and issues which may be regional in scope, fast-breaking, or relatively minor. It represents the "working papers" sent out to members.

The *Audubon Leader* is a twice-per-month environmental newsletter, more "in-house" than the other society periodicals. Its aim is to guide and stimulate the official family of employees and other workers, especially the volunteer staffs of the many chapter newsletters; thus information and ideas trickle down like the passage of energy through a natural food-chain. Look for nothing here about a bird species unless it is the subject of current controversy, legislation, experimental programs, or last rites.

While the Sierra Club and Friends of the Earth have their own book publishing programs, the NAS has not copyrighted a book series since *The Audubon Nature Encyclopedia* in the early 1960s. The NAS has "sponsored" many books by licensing publishers to use its name, with all costs borne by the licensee. Everything, including the marketing, must be approved by the national office. Such arrangements yield much-needed funds to support Audubon's many conservation priorities. Some recent volumes and series are jointly sponsored by the NAS and the National Wildlife Federation.

In the century and three-quarters since John James Audubon started working toward his gigantic double-elephant folio volumes of *Birds of America*, the work has never been reprinted in the original size. The NAS is now engaged in that task; a limited edition is expected to be ready by the bicentennial of Audubon's birth. No expense is being spared and the utmost pains are being taken to produce the most perfect verisimilitude which modern technology and old-fashioned meticulous care can provide. The publisher is Abbeville Press. Approximately 1,500 copies are now expected, at a price of about $6,000 each. This facsimile edition should appeal to collectors and investors.

The NAS has licensed many field guides; no one of them is *the* Audubon bird guide, for such does not exist. The first fieldbook of birds was copyrighted in 1906 by artist-naturalist Chester A. Reed. As a Boy Scout, I carried the 1916 reprint, which I still have. It seldom particularly emphasizes field marks, although the principle of recognition marks was introduced by Ernest Thompson Seton to professionals in an 1897 paper in *The Auk,* and to amateur birders in *Bird Lore* in 1901. Youthful readers saw the idea applied to identification of ducks in his 1911 book *Two Little Savages*. Reed kept his bird guides small by having the water birds in a separate book. The guides proved so successful during the surge of interest in outdoor things in the first decade of this century that Reed published handbooks to other groups also. He kept them all small enough to be carried handily, thus justifying the term "manual." My copy of Reed's guide weighs five and a half ounces and fits into a shirt pocket. In contrast, a recent "field guide" weighs 12.5 times as much, comes in three volumes, and will scarcely fit into anything smaller than a briefcase!

In addition to the ways of contributing to and benefiting from the NAS as outlined above, one may buy material objects, other than books, of interest and beauty from firms licensed by the society. This constitutes part of what one fellow-member calls "the Audubon industry." Other non-profit conservation groups sell directly to their constituents such things as art notepaper, woodsy artifacts, T-shirts, and other "gifts." The National Wildlife Federation, Center for Environmental Education, Save-the-Dunes Council, and Sigurd Olson Environmental Institute come to mind. The NAS has done rather little of this directly, but has an extensive system of renting its name and the use of its flying white egret symbol. The latter has been available for more than three decades.

Fine arts objects, like plates, porcelain figurines, and statuettes, often of extraordinary delicacy and appeal, are among the products of private industry which provide one way of assisting the NAS. The society also places its cachet of excellence on the "Audible Audubon" series of sound recordings of songbirds and other creatures, from the sound laboratory of the Cornell Laboratory of Ornithology. On the same cards as the plastic record are text descriptions of the species and a color print. The California firm which produces and markets the series also includes an ingenious miniature player for the record-cards. It is readily possible to carry the bird records into the field and play them back to the bird species involved.

The seventy-five wildlife sanctuaries of the National Audubon Society deserve discussion beyond that given them above in connection with functions of the national office, for this system is a historic and very practical application of the group's long-standing commitment to protecting birds. (The figure mentioned does not include the many bird refuges owned and managed independently by local Audubon chapters, nor by separate groups also named for Audubon the ornithologist.)

A sanctuary should be literally sacrosanct, and not, as many federal and state "refuges" hypocritically are, public shooting grounds in season. Neither should hunting or poaching be permitted in the old-line national parks and monuments, and preferably not in anything else called a "park" in our country. In the lower Forty-eight, the non-hunting policy has applied in the national parks and monuments under the National Park Service. In Alaska, that agency administers vast land areas, and subsistence hunting by Native Americans (Indians and Eskimos) is properly allowed there, and sport hunting is permitted to whites in often-adjacent lands termed "preserves" in Alaska. Happily, hunting is prohibited in the Audubon lands—they are true sanctuaries year-round. They are either owned outright by the NAS or leased; Audubon wardens patrol them and are responsible for intelligent management of the vegetation and wildlife. Until recently, we have not realized how important it is to have such lands independent of political control at the federal or state level.

The smallest Audubon refuge is the twelve-acre area surrounding the grave of Theodore Roosevelt at Oyster Bay on Long Island, New York. The largest is the 26,000-acre Rainey Wildlife Sanctuary in Louisiana, where the eight miles of ocean frontage, the bayous, and brackish marshlands harbor flocks of wintering waterfowl. The society's ecologists determined that the refuge's purpose would not be compromised by oil drilling, and an arrangement for this was negotiated with the Continental Oil Company.

One refuge for winter protection of the painfully recovering population of Whooping Cranes is the 200-acre Robert Porter Allen Sanctuary in Texas, named in memory of an outstanding bird scientist who served in the society's research branch. Another Whooping Crane sanctuary is the 5,720 Audubon acres on Matagorda Island, close to the famed Aransas National Wildlife Refuge.

Pine Island Sanctuary comprises 3,600 acres of freshwater marsh and two miles of ocean shore and dunes in North Carolina. The state university system carries on research on the ecology of bird populations and the plant communities that support them.

The much-visited Corkscrew Swamp Sanctuary in inland Florida covers about 11,000 acres. Strollers along its celebrated boardwalk may be lucky enough to see wild otters, as I was. Here in an excellent large stand of undisturbed bald cypress is the only colony now remaining of a spectacular endangered species, the Wood Stork, which is the only American stork. A 6,500-acre sanctuary north of Lake Okeechobee preserves areas of the Kissimmee Prairie with its Sandhill Cranes, Burrowing Owls, and Caracaras. The Big Pine Sanctuary of 200 acres is leased gratis to the federal government for protection of the miniature key deer.

The San Francisco Bay Sanctuaries total 1,800 acres of salt marsh where nesting and migrating shorebirds and waterfowl are protected. South of Los Angeles, about 4,000 acres are included within the Starr Ranch Audubon Sanctuary. Mountain lions still roam the dry terrain there. The Northeast Audubon Center near Sharon, Connecticut, is set within 526 acres of mixed forest.

It may be necessary to keep certain sanctuaries closed to public visitation when the plant or animal life is too vulnerable to damage from human disturbance, which means that the public is discouraged from coming to a few units of the Audubon system. Others, normally open, may limit or prohibit visiting under special circumstances. Many, however, are always open to the interested public, and some actively encourage visitors by maintaining museums and educational programs. Arrangements for visits should be made in advance; in some it is necessary for the warden to meet visitors by boat. No picnicking or camping is permitted at Audubon sanctuaries.

The true sanctuaries for wild things, where they may find protection from people the year around, are few in number worldwide. But where are the earth's people themselves to find sanctuary in the event of nuclear holocaust? Today, this international issue, which probably most of us scarcely consider an environmental one, is recognized in *Audubon*'s editorial columns as being the conservation issue to end all conservation issues, for it is all-encompassing.

After the "dogs of war" were let slip for World War II, only three megatons of explosive power were released throughout the entire course of those hostilities. At the start of 1984, however, the world's stockpiles of missiles, disregarding conventional weapons this time, total 15,000 megatons. Who can assert that the readied destructive force of 5,000 World War IIs is no concern of life-cherishing societies like Audubon? Incontrovertible scientific conclusions supported by over five hundred research physicists, climatologists, chemists, biologists and physicians as this book goes to press prove that a mere fraction of the available megatonnage would destroy the survivable atmosphere, suddenly bringing on a "nuclear winter night" of some years' duration and lethal to the higher life forms on our planet. One aspect of it alone, the opaque shroud filling the sky, would be infinitely worse in its effects on organisms than the non-radioactive shroud thrown up sixty-five million years ago by the impact of a comet-head or asteroid—the probable cause of extinction of another stupid earthly population, the dinosaurs.

From this overview of its work and structure, it is obvious that the NAS does not limit itself to answering the question "What kind of bird is that?" While most similar groups concentrate on a few methods to advance their environmental aims, this society uses amazingly imaginative and diverse ways to do its essential work and obtain its financial support for that. One can appreciate its strength of spirit and enjoy the fellowship of kindred outdoors people only by being one of the half-million enthusiastic members who stand behind the able and dedicated officers and staff, in the difficult effort to establish a just and lasting peace between economics and ecology.

After one century of existence under one name or another, meeting one urgent environmental problem after another, this remarkable group, able to look back on an honorable history of achievement, is now required to challenge a resurgence of the plume-hunter mentality, and to dare contradict highly placed political figures who tell it like it isn't. Like other such organizations of private citizens doing what they believe in, the society cannot be chary of either receiving or dispensing pointed criticisms.

In the aggregate, all environmental and consumer groups organized on a non-profit basis in the United States muster about five million actual members at a given time. But the professional spokespersons represent also many millions of "closet environmentalists" who have the same convictions, as the public opinion polls consistently reveal. Also, both members and sympathizers speak out individually to make their views heard in the councils of government at all levels, knowing that this is needed for countering powerful opposing pressures. Surely the conservationist Audubon who emerged during his Labrador and upper Missouri trips would have approved.

Although the "struggle for existence" of a residue of the Nature we have known goes on in the meetings and writings of environmentalists, in the media, legislative halls, refuges, parks, and forests, the controversies and the resulting civic arrangements do not add up to an ultimate objective. This chapter started in a mood of illustrative levity, but we soon found in one society of naturalists, as we would in others, the deep commitment to firmly held beliefs, and the action in support of them, characteristic of religious people. Beyond these traits lies also a communion with the natural world where, as Bryant wrote at age seventeen, "The groves were God's first temples." Where we gather together in meadows or woods, or in some rare and relict wilderness, we form the most sentient part of a vast congregation. We join there the regular members of the same wide community of faith—birds and other animals, trees, wildflowers—representing denominations more or less different from ours but united in the organic wholeness we now recognize in the life of the planetary ecosystem. Those who can perceive and feel this new-found integration are among the blessed, for they enjoy a privilege in our time not accorded to the great Audubon in his era. Thus, not a few nature lovers of the present day experience, besides the learning, enjoyment, and appreciation in the wild, a species of worship.

Where to Look for Audubon

11

> One taste of the old times sets all to rights.
>
> —Robert Browning

During the Kentucky years, when Audubon was in reality the American woodsman of his later reputation, he spent much of his time in a stretch of hardwood forest between Henderson and the mouth of Green Creek a few miles up the Ohio. Today some of that woods is part of Audubon State Park, and one can hike through a piece of timberland which he especially cherished. The beeches, white oaks, sugar maples, and tulip trees, some of which were doubtless seedlings or saplings when he strode among them, have brought me closer to the living Audubon than has the excellent collection of Auduboniana on display indoors, for no building in the park knew his step or the sound of his voice.

Throughout the later years of his Kentucky stay, when Audubon was oppressed by financial worries, he took from this forest not only the consolation and hope he always found in nature, but also the practical boon of wild game and fish upon which the Audubons, his partner Rozier, and their clerk Pope often depended for sustenance. The artist found there, also, many birds to paint for his growing portfolio.

Audubon also saw in these woods two species now gone completely and forever—Carolina Parakeets and Passenger Pigeons. He often saw long, strung-out flocks of the little parrots passing overhead, their ragged lines like signatures in the sky. Because the native parakeets became rare long before wild pigeons did, there is remarkably little scientific knowledge about them. They were most common in the South, but Audubon reported the species from as far north as the mouth of the Maumee River near Toledo. Dates of the "last sighting" of them range as late as 1920, but the 1904 sighting by Frank Chapman is the one considered authentic. Many early settlers regarded the flocks of voracious birds as the worst enemy of crops and orchards. However, they made easy pickings because the surviving birds during a shooting affray would not fly off, but hover with ear-splitting screeches over their fallen comrades. They were beautiful birds—their bright plumage suggested the tropics—but their appeal was to the eye and not to the ear. One day Audubon with a few shots secured a basketful, and used the least damaged birds for painting. A juvenile specimen he depicted as all green became a subject of some controversy.

Apparently no ornithologist ever saw the Carolina Parakeet at its nest, but amateur reports had them nesting in hollow trees. Roosting for the night took place in great hollow trees; the noisy flocks of birds hung to the inside of the tree by their feet and beaks. The presence of such old, standing trees mark one difference, important to animal life, between the woods of Audubon's time and those of today. One of the contributing factors to the extinction of parakeets must have been the preemption of the dwindling supply of hollow trees by the non-native honey bees, which spread rapidly after they were introduced from Europe in colonial times.

Passenger Pigeons are reputed to have been the most abundant bird in the world, and Audubon took particular interest in this extraordinary species. It was easy to watch the flocks as they crossed the Ohio River toward this Kentucky forest. On one occasion Audubon was riding his fine horse Barro, near Hardinsburg, when he saw wild pigeons overhead, flying toward the southeast, in larger numbers than he had ever seen before. Watching from a hilltop, he marked down one dot for each passing flock. Nearly all the flocks were very large. After twenty-one minutes, when he had wearied of this, he had recorded 160 flocks of this one species. As he rode farther eastward, the sky was filled with pigeons and the noonday light was obscured as if by an eclipse. While waiting for dinner at Young's Inn, a building that still stands where Salt River joins the Ohio, he watched immense legions going by, their front reaching far beyond the Ohio on the west and the beech forests directly east of him. As he rode into Louisville, fifty-five miles from Hardinsburg, the migrating pigeons were still passing over in undiminished numbers. If Audubon had met a stranger on the road who had told him that in less than a century there would not be one passenger pigeon left on earth, I wonder what he would have answered!

The woods along the Green River in and near the present park contained huge trees favored by the pigeons for overnight roosting. Audubon reported one pigeon roost there which was forty miles long and averaged three miles wide. A large camp had been pitched at the woods' edge, and men with horses, wagons, and guns waited there for two weeks before the main body of migrant pigeons arrived. Two farmers had driven more than three hundred hogs the seventy miles from Russelville to fatten on the slaughtered birds.

The main flock arrived one evening after sunset. Audubon heard, while the birds were still distant, a sound like that of a great gale of wind passing through the rigging of a close-reefed ship. He was much surprised by the strong gust of wind created by the flock when it reached the roosting area. The noise of wings and of breaking boughs kept him from hearing the guns going off all around him, or the shouts of the men at his side. Pigeons alighted everywhere one above another; they formed solid masses on every branch and stick. It was a scene of unimaginable uproar and confusion—a magnificent, terrifying sight in the brilliance of bonfires all around. The roar was heard more than three miles away from the edge of the roost, and continued throughout the entire night.

"Most people believe," wrote Audubon, "that great numbers of wild pigeons will always be with us, but a few think that such shooting will eventually decimate them. I cannot agree with either opinion. Murderous as the slaughter is, nothing but the gradual diminution of our forests can accomplish their decrease."

The northern edge of Pennsylvania's Valley Forge State Park adjoins the lower loop of a reversed "S" section of the Schuylkill River north of Philadelphia. Into the curve of the upper loop, from the north and east, broad Perkiomen Creek flows along the western edge of the 130-acre Mill Grove property. The latter is outstanding as both an outdoor and indoor shrine to John James Audubon. Audubon's father owned the sturdy farmhouse, now a fine museum, for seventeen years, but he never lived in it. John James had the run of the valley and rolling hills. There he became a volunteer but dedicated apprentice to Nature herself.

Mill Grove was his first home in America, and is the only real home of his which is still standing. He lived there for nearly three years at a time of his life when most lads of his age were establishing themselves in a profession or business.

The farmhouse was built in 1762 by James Morgan, who later sold it to John Penn. A military officer, Augustine Prevost, purchased the property from Penn and in 1789 sold it to Captain Jean Audubon, who in turn sold it to Francis DaCosta, his business agent, in 1806. Seven years later it was bought by Samuel Weatherill of Philadelphia, and remained in Weatherill hands until 1951, when Montgomery County purchased it and developed an Audubon museum and wildlife sanctuary there. The site is included in the National Register of Historic Places.

The New York Historical Society has an old painting entitled "Mill Grove Farm: Perkiomen Creek, Pennsylvania." It was done in 1820 by Thomas Birch (1779-1851) in oil on wood panel, while the Weatherills owned the estate. When Audubon returned to Mill Grove in 1825 for a nostalgic visit, the place then surely looked essentially like the painting, which shows the stone barn that was built in about 1820. The house is a double structure, with the smaller part on the creek side. The barn, for horses and carriages, is very nearly as high on the hillside and east of the house. The hilltop, above and beyond the house, barn, and smokehouse, is densely wooded in the painting, as is the facing hilltop across the open vale below those buildings. Mill Grove took its name from the large mill, which stood at the east end of a low stone dam that impounded a sizable pool. In the painting a man is rowing a skiff on the pool, and a fisherman is wading below the dam. Water is flowing over the full length of the dam, as it does over the (or at least "a") dam there today. Near the mill and some rods farther from Perkiomen Creek was a white house, presumably the miller's, with a picket fence and a shed. A visitor is shown talking with the occupant. A rail fence parallels the creek bank from near the dam to a large cattle barn which, with three other substantial stone buildings set close together, form a row on the slope ending with the smokehouse near the home. A long retaining wall of rounded stones ran along the contour below the house and between it and all other major structures except the horse barn. The stone wall is still there, but all the buildings shown below it in the painting are now gone.

Conspicuous in the painting is a crude wooden aqueduct, probably of hollow logs, supported by A-shaped log trestles. It stretched from a spring (still flowing today except during droughts) in the woods behind the house, past the springhouse (attached to the smaller house unit), and obliquely downslope to the mill. It carried clean springwater for cooling and drinking, important practical considerations, but it jarringly detracts from the aesthetics of the painted scene.

Six miles of trails run through the 130-acre tract, where more than four hundred species of flowering plants and one hundred and seventy-five kinds of birds have been officially recorded. Feeding stations and nesting boxes help augment the variety of bird life, and suitable native species of shrubs and trees have been planted for its food and cover. In spring the flowering orchard trees and meadows call for nothing more to fulfill their agelong function than the voices of the children who come in bevies to catch the spirit of the youthful naturalist in his most cherished of all places.

The director of this institution is Edward W. Graham, in whose office hangs a black-white copy of the famed Joseph Inman portrait of 1833, which Audubon called his favorite likeness. The old house contains many fascinating pieces of Auduboniana. Prominent on its interior walls are mural paintings done in 1954 by George M. Harding which portray scenes of bird life in a southern swamp, a western prairie, and the bird-nesting rocks of the St. Lawrence River. Other museums, most notably the one at Audubon State Park in Kentucky, also contain fine relics of the naturalist and his time, but in no other existing building does one sense that he is so near, particularly in the topmost floor. The attic has three dormer windows facing upslope, and two overlooking the Perkiomen valley. It has been restored to portray the use to which John James actually put part of it—as a studio and taxidermy work area. Rooms on the floors below are crammed with Audubon artwork, mounted specimens, and memorabilia, with the rooms furnished in the style of the early 1800s. Two pieces of furniture owned by Audubon are there; they came from Minniesland, the only house he owned after leaving Mill Grove in 1806. This museum owns a bound set of *Birds of America*, one volume of which is always on display. On the walls are forty framed prints of Audubon's birds and eight of his "Quadrupeds." At Mill Grove a visitor can rest a hand on the antique wood of window sills and door frames that knew the young naturalist's touch, or stand silent for a while in one of Audubon's attic workrooms, listening.

Out of doors at and around Mill Grove, with neighbor boys and alone, John James became familiar with the wild inhabitants of the stream, flood plains, meadows and wooded hills. He also worked with business agent

DaCosta to develop the lead mine on the property; its site near the house is marked today. DaCosta did not find in his young associate much promise as a potential estate manager, but he did detect the lad's major strength. Once, he was comparing a specimen of Great Blue Heron, which John James had shot on the stream bank and wired to stand up as a model, with the nearly completed painting of it. He then looked John James straight in the eye and told him that he must keep up with and improve his painting of birds and that he would become a great naturalist and artist. The youth took the advice and prediction seriously, especially since he and DaCosta did not get along well.

Young Audubon excelled in all the outdoor sports available to him, for in these ways he spent much of his time. He hunted and fished with young Tom Bakewell and the boy's father William. Speed skating was done on the ice of a smooth stretch of the Perkiomen. Once he skated full tilt past Tom with a rifle, sending a ball through the crown of a hat that Tom had thrown as high as he could into the air. Farther upstream, where John James and some friends had been hunting ducks one cold day, he fell through a hole in the ice. He was swept along under it for "thirty or forty yards," but found another opening and crawled out through it, nearly done for. Years later he wrote that this was the greatest peril he had ever encountered.

In Audubon's time at Mill Grove, there was a dim, shallow cavern along the outer edge of the floodplain; quarrying has since destroyed it. There, on a ledge on the far wall, a pair of Phoebes returned each year to raise a family in their soft bulky nest. John James had gentled the parent birds and used them so much as models for his drawing practice that they would alight on his head and shoulders in greeting. He particularly admired the lay of their feathers. The young birds, too, readily took to him, and he marked their legs with short "silver threads" before they left the nest, to learn whether they would return the following spring. Some did; one built a nest about a mile upstream from Mill Grove.

Young Audubon's experience with this bird family, so different from his usual work with dead specimens, convinced him that he must develop far more skill in depicting birds as in life. The little cavern meant even more to him after he brought Lucy Bakewell to see his pet birds, and as the lovers stood among the ferns at the entrance, he obtained her promise to become his wife as soon as he could afford to support her.

Within easy walking distance of Mill Grove was the Bakewell estate, Lucy's girlhood home. The Audubons returned there from Henderson in 1812 to visit his in-laws. One day John James and young William Bakewell ranged afield with a gun. "We kept going on without shooting at anything, so great was our admiration of every bird that presented itself to our view." William went up a tree to bring back an egg from a large nest. Finding a parent bird on the eggs, the boy brought it down, at Audubon's suggestion, in a handkerchief. This female bird proved to be a species new to Audubon, a Broad-winged Hawk. Making no attempt to escape, she rested in Audubon's hand during the walk back to the house; there she posed trustingly on a stick fastened to a table. "I passed my hand over it to smooth the feathers by gentle pressure." The hawk permitted Audubon to measure its bill and other parts as he worked on the painting, which became Plate 91 of *Birds of America*. Lucy kept her husband company while he painted—both were deeply moved that a wild hawk would behave thus. It almost seemed that this individual was able to look beyond the daily hazard and violence of its brief lifetime to an immortality in a realm being created by this man. After Audubon completed the portrait ". . . without the bird ever once moving," he released the confiding Broad-wing through a window and it flew toward its nest on powerful wings without a cry.

Although Key West is the westernmost of the consecutive keys of Florida, the fact was not the reason it was so named. Finding the island littered with bones from an Indian massacre, the early Spaniards named it "Cayo Hueso," which means "Bone Key." Later, Englishmen slurred the pronunciation into "Key West." The Spanish governor of Florida granted the island to Juan Pablo Salas in 1815, and Salas sold it in 1821 for $2,000 to John W. Simonton of Mobile.

When Audubon headed for Key West in 1832, he was in his prime professionally and already famous enough to have federal government ships assigned for his use. On the way to Key West and back, the visits he made to Indian Key were highly useful as well as happy ones.

The motorist driving toward or away from Key West on the Overseas Highway may see Indian Key without stopping the car, if he is satisfied with a glimpse of it over nearly a mile of water. Looking east from the south end of the causeway linking Upper and Lower Matecumbe Keys, or from the Indian Key Fill picnic area at mile marker 79, one can see this small, otherwise isolated key. It is an elongated key of about ten acres, covered with mangroves and other woody plants and from a distance looks (even through binoculars) utterly wild and as if it had always been so, yet it was once the only settlement of whites on the Florida Keys, and even long after Key West was founded, still surpassed it in importance.

The Spanish called it Matanzas, or Place of Murder, after four hundred Frenchmen who had been shipwrecked were rounded up on this key by Caloosa Indians and slaughtered. The only traces of human habitation remaining there today are low ruins of the foundations of old warehouses, trading store, mechanical shops, residences, rock cisterns, and gun emplacements. To go ashore on Indian Key is prohibited. The island is the property of the state and has been held in limbo for some years, although there are plans to someday make the entire key into a historical park, rebuilding the docks and the buildings as they were in the days when Audubon visited the island.

Because of its associations with Audubon and its fascinating human history (in which conquistadors, hostile Caloosa and later Seminole Indians, buccaneers, smugglers, salvagers, and scientists all figure), the place has a high potential for becoming an exceptional state park.

When Audubon first stepped ashore there, he was pleased with the settlement—an outpost of southern civilization—with its sun-drenched streets and shady walks under beautiful trees. The birds he noted were almost all new to him; he was satisfied that he had found the right area for painting the Florida waders. He was enraptured by the "gorgeous flowers, the singular and beautiful plants, the luxuriant trees."

The leading citizen, Jacob Hausman, was the entrepreneur behind most of the culture. He operated the Tropical Hotel; his store and Indian trading post did $30,000 in trade annually. He estimated the value of what he had built on Indian Key at more than $200,000. The government had a customs station there, and a modest naval base at nearby Tea Table Key, and an Army post at Cape Florida. The show of force was expected to discourage Indian attacks on the Indian Key establishments, federal and private, during the long period of the Seminole uprisings.

Six years after Audubon's visit to this key, Dr. Henry Perrine, a well-known horticulturist and medical man, came from New York with his wife, two teen-age daughters, and a twelve-year-old son to settle there. One of his plantations of economic plants was set up on Indian Key; some exotic *Agave* specimens he planted there are said to be still living. At 2 A.M. on August 7, 1840, a war party of Seminoles stole ashore and set fire to the buildings. They massacred seven persons; one of them was Dr. Perrine. His family barely escaped the slaughter; the Hausmans also escaped alive, but were ruined financially by the fires. Thus ended the first white settlement on the Florida Keys.

In a fascinating paper in *Daedalus* on "The Ecology of Imagination in Childhood," psychologist Edith Cobb argued that the *natural* environment exerts a powerful force in the development of human intellect and emotion. Among the manifestations of these traits which one might expect, intuitively rather than from scientific evidence, to weaken or disappear in the technology-dominated world of the future is the "sense of place" which people generally feel today. The world of earth-bound nature surely is extremely important for stimulating appreciation of the most familiar and cherished spots of one's youth.

Are young humans and animals "imprinted" on the terrain in which they are reared, as well as upon their living environment of parents or surrogate parents? Is some conceptual "territoriality" established in our youth for our specific, immediate surroundings with which we are most familiar? If so, how does it compare with the well-known territorialism in birds and mammals, applying to a considerably larger area than the home (nest) itself? How does it originate? I am unaware whether psychologists who study their own species are addressing such questions, or are leaving them to the animal behaviorists and the poets.

Part of my rapport with John James may come from the fact that each of us lived in seven towns before reaching the age of twenty-one. A series of moves in childhood and youth is not a bad way for a naturalist to get his start. Because his work in maturity is likely to call for extensive travels, it would seem best not to become too attached to any one spot.

Audubon experienced several distinct natural biomes before he reached manhood. One wonders whether any of them "imprinted" a strong "sense of place" upon the child or youth. Mill Grove had been lost to him after his brief and happy time there. In Kentucky, he could not even hold ownership of the soil in which he and Lucy had buried their two small daughters. He long remained bitter about his treatment in Henderson, Louisville, several places in Louisiana, and perhaps Cincinnati. He was fifty-seven before he settled down in the Minniesland home on the Hudson, no trace of which is seen today.

Probably Audubon felt more deeply about his father's home in France, where he enjoyed great freedom to explore the out-of-doors, than he did about any of his homes in America. But I sense that what he came to cherish most was not a town or a house or anything else made by man—that where he felt most at home was in the woods of America.

Epilogue

Doubtless many of those who were privileged to meet John James Audubon envied him. He was a handsome man, who carried himself with pride and confidence (although it is clear from his letters that he had moments of despair and self-doubt). He had charm and versatility and the courage to develop his talents and follow his inclinations, and he persevered to make a reality and a success of what many people had dismissed as an idler's dream. Roamers and lovers of solitude must have coveted what they saw as his independence and freedom to explore the wildlands. Surely many a family man would have wished for himself what seemed to be this man's lack of domestic cares. Those of a sociable bent must have envied his attractiveness to women, his social graces, and his lionization in the drawing rooms of two continents.

In boyhood, I too should have liked to have been John James Audubon. But just to have been Audubon the naturalist and woodsman would have been quite sufficient. For he had the great good fortune to travel through vast parts of the American wilderness when it was still intact. What he experienced no one now alive and no one to come can ever see again.

I still wish that I had been privileged to stroll awestruck in the virgin timber, among the crowded, massive columns of ancient white pine, red oak, "sugar," and yellow poplar before they were felled, rolled into ravines, and burned. I should also have cherished knowing the emotion of standing in the clamorous, confused shade where branches were crashing down under the weight of multitudinous Passenger Pigeons attempting to roost for the night, their crops filled with ripe fruits, fat acorns, and the angular nutlets from the interlacing gray twigs in the beech foliage. Or to have watched the irresistible tidewaters sweep across the soapy flats and dendritic channels of Florida Bay, forcing the myriads of winged waders up the beach of remote Sandy Key toward my hiding place in the mangrove thicket. Along the coast of Labrador, I would have been enthralled by the sporting seals and by the whistling calls and complex flight performances of the Eskimo Curlews, as those disciplined aerialists sought the beds of black crowberries on the tundra.

What outdoors-lover would not have relished the taste of Indian pemmican and steamed maize at a village of the now-extinct Mandan people? Who would not have enjoyed galloping his horse over the flower-jewelled infinity of plains grassland where the rule of the bison was challenged by man alone? Oh, to have known, as Audubon knew, not only the land but also the giants who were matched with and against it—George Rogers Clark, his brother William Clark, Daniel Boone—and the pioneer naturalists Rafinesque, Nuttall, Wilson, Townsend, and Bonaparte, whose idea of conquering the wilderness was to understand it!

Science and technology have done wonders for us in the two centuries just past. Audubon scarcely benefited from these, but at least he did not suffer from the trade-offs which they seem to have necessitated—the commercialism and materialism that overwhelm us from childhood on, and the domination of our later years by absorption with luxurious comfort, health care, and longevity. Audubon at maturity burned the candle at both ends, and it made a lovely light. Would he have had a better and happier life from knowing the fact that the smoke of his campfire contained carcinogens, or that his hearty breakfast of Ibis eggs on Sandy Key was rich in cholesterol?

One hears that there are a few otherwise normal individuals who would, if it were possible, trade back all the changes wrought during the past century and a half if this would bring them what the natural world has lost since then. These deviates are obviously neo-Luddites. How many of us really feel bereft of a simple, natural freedom because, in our travels through the countryside, we must not drink from streams and lakes as Audubon did? Be that as it may, it would be a delightful surprise in mid-June to come over the crest of a ridge and see, in the broad valley below, a distant lake where there should be none, then, on close approach, to find that the bright blue is an uninterrupted sea of meadowland, thick-spread with wild iris. Or else to walk along the edge of a genuine lake earlier in spring, following for miles the high-heaped, dark windrows, bordering the storm-beach, of trillions upon trillions of delicate dead mayflies washed ashore after their frantic day of adult existence, a lesson not so much in death's importunity as in the incredible profusion of life.

Very well, I admit that such things may now be seen only in books and journals on the history of natural history, or may be done only in nostalgic dreams and dim recollections. But is it quite unreasonable to expect at least that one should retain the right, a right of human-kind through time immemorial, when traveling in the cloudless dark, to look up to bright stars, unpolluted by extraneous light or unnatural haze, and be assured that one is truly a part of this universe?

All right, I guess you may add my name to the list of those still jealous of John James Audubon for his famous love affair with his young continent in the New World.

Biochronology

1785	Jean Jacques Audubon born at Les Cayes, Santo Domingo (now Haiti) on April 26. His mother, Jeanne Rabin, died six months later.
1791	Voyaged with a half-sister to Nantes, France, to live at the permanent home of his father, Jean, a sea captain, and Jean's wife, Anne.
1803	At eighteen, came alone to the United States to learn to manage his father's Mill Grove farm at what is now the village of Audubon, near Norristown, Pennsylvania.
1805-06	Went home to France for a short time, then returned to Mill Grove. Worked as a clerk in New York City.
1807	Formed business partnership with J. Ferdinand Rozier.
1808	Married to Lucy Bakewell, daughter of William Bakewell of Fatland Ford estate near Mill Grove.
1809	Victor Gifford Audubon born in Louisville.
1809-19	Merchant, mainly at Henderson, Kentucky. Son John Woodhouse Audubon born in 1812. Audubon severed connection with Rozier in 1910; suffered business failure.
1820	Employed as a taxidermist at a private museum in Cincinnati. Took on J. R. Mason as pupil and assistant in painting flowers in the bird pieces. Moved to the South.
1821	Taught and tutored in Louisiana. Made portraits on commission and painted birds during his wanderings.
1824	Returned to the Northeast; for the first time, an art piece of his was published. Continued bird painting.
1825	At loose ends except for bird study and painting, and some teaching where Lucy was employed as a teacher in Louisiana.
1826-28	Toured Scotland and England to obtain subscriptions to his *Birds of America* double-elephant folio production, engraved first by Lizars in Edinburgh, later by the Havells (father and son) in London.
1829	Painted birds in the eastern United States, assisted by George Lehman for plants and backgrounds.

1830	Took Lucy to England, and started *Ornithological Biography*.
1831	Returned with Lucy to the United States.
1832	Federal ships made available to him. Bird collecting and painting expedition to Florida; his most important sites were the St. John's River, Indian Key, Sandy Key, and Key West.
1833	Summer cruise to Labrador and the Canadian coast.
1834-35	Worked in England to publish volumes of *Birds of America* and *Ornithological Biography*; traveled to obtain subscriptions there.
1836	Back in the United States.
1837-38	Traveled by sea to the Gulf coast and Texas. Followed that with his last trip abroad.
1839	Returned to the United States; lived with family in New York City. Completed *Ornithological Biography* in five volumes.
1840	Started work on *Viviparous Quadrupeds of North America*.
1842	The Audubon family moved to their Minniesland property, on the Hudson River at what is now West 155th Street and Riverside Drive in New York.
1843	Spent the summer on expedition with assistants and Edward Harris to the Upper Missouri River region, by steamboat.
1847	Audubon, whose health had been failing, was lapsing into mental incompetence.
1848	*Quadrupeds,* in three volumes, finished by collaborator and friend John Bachman.
1851	Died at home on January 27, age 65.

In 1874 Lucy Bakewell Audubon died in Shelbyville, Kentucky, at age 86. In 1886 the first Audubon Society was founded by Lucy's old pupil George Bird Grinnell, editor of *Forest and Stream*.

The Contributors

MARY DURANT, former editor at American Heritage Publishing Company, is a novelist, biographer, and natural historian. Her magazine pieces have appeared in *Audubon, Country Journal,* and the *New York Times.* Now in paperback is her wildflower dictionary, *Who Named the Daisy? Who named the Rose?,* and she is co-author with her husband, Michael Harwood, of *On the Road with John James Audubon.*

MICHAEL HARWOOD, journalist and natural historian, is the author or co-author of eight books, including *On the Road with John James Audubon* (Dodd, Mead), which he wrote with his wife, Mary Durant. He has published many articles in the *New York Times Magazine, Audubon, Smithsonian, Harper's,* and other publications. Born in Boston, he is a graduate of the Putney School and Harvard College. He and his wife live in northwestern Connecticut.

FRANK LEVERING was born and brought up, the youngest of six children, on the family orchard in Virginia's Blue Ridge Mountains. He was a football player, poet, and playwright at Wesleyan University in Connecticut, was graduated in 1974, and received his master's degree at Harvard. Levering spent one full summer climbing in Mount Rainier National Park, another getting to know Alaska, and has traveled in Europe. He now works as a Hollywood screenwriter (*Parasite, The Eureka Kid, Heart's Desire*), and is married to journalist and author Wanda Urbanska.

ALTON A. LINDSEY is Emeritus Professor of Ecology at Purdue University. He was graduated from Allegheny College, served as the vertebrate zoologist with Admiral Richard E. Byrd in Antarctica in 1933-35, and worked as a ranger-naturalist for four summers in two western national parks. His doctorate is from Cornell University in botany and zoology. His research has included Arctic tundra vegetation, and that of deserts, coasts, mountains, and midwestern forests. He has written eight books, most recently his memoirs *Naturalist On Watch.* A new genus of midwestern animal, and fifteen antarctic islands, were named for him, and he received the Eminent Ecologist Award for 1976 from the Ecological Society of America. He and his wife, Elizabeth, have two children.

ROBERT AARON PETTY was born in Crawfordsville in 1961 and grew up in rural Indiana. He earned his Bachelor of Fine Arts degree from Washington University in St. Louis in 1984, where he received several scholarships and awards. He is the son of Dr. Robert Owen Petty and Ann Marie Petty. Currently he works as a free-lance artist, and teaches art and outdoor skills at the Storm King School in the Hudson Highlands of New York State.

ROBERT OWEN PETTY was born in Indianapolis in 1933. He is Professor of Biology at Wabash College. In addition to publishing scientific papers on ecology, Dr. Petty has been a frequent contributor to publications of the National Geographic Society, including the books *Wilderness USA* and *Our Continent*. He authored the text of the book *Deciduous Forest*. With his wife Anne Marie, he has contributed chapters and essays to various publications, including portions of *North American Wildlife* for Reader's Digest. Dr. Petty is a published poet and has been the recipient of awards for wildlife conservation. He resides with his family in rural Montgomery County near Crawfordsville, Indiana.

SCOTT RUSSELL SANDERS was born in Tennessee, on the Mississippi River, grew up in the Ohio Valley, and spent part of his childhood in Louisiana. He attended Brown University, and earned a Ph.D. from Cambridge University. His books of fiction include *Wilderness Plots* (1983), about the settlement of the Ohio Valley; *Fetching the Dead* (1984), a collection of stories; and, most recently, a biographical novel about Audubon. Sanders teaches literature at Indiana University, in Bloomington, where he lives with his wife and two children.

Index

Accidents, 76
Accomplishments, minor cultural, 107–8
Accuracy in bird depiction, 28, 118–19. *See also* Bird art; Proportioning
Allen, R. P., 130, 151
Amateur, Audubon as, 32–33, 44
Anthropomorphism, 60–61, 99
Audubon, Anne (stepmother), 101
Audubon, Jean (father), 100, 102, 158
Audubon, John James: birth, ix, 39, 52, 100–1; childhood in France, 2; education, 2, 39, 101, 102, 104; physical appearance, 6, 102, 107, 109, 114; death, 13, 114; biographical myths, 101, 102, 104; youth at Mill Grove, 102; aging, 75, 113–14
Audubon, John Woodhouse (son), 12, 13
Audubon, Lucy: girlhood home, 2; marriage, 2; work, 4; earnings, 10; in England, 12, 110; role in publishing, 30; background, 102; dowry lost, 105; chidings, 106; at Phoebe cavern, 160
Audubon magazine, 147–48
Audubon, Maria R., 11, 50–52
Audubon (PA town), 16, 157–61
Audubon Society, National: name and name changes, 116, 126; activity in 1917, 125; origin (Grinnell), 126; reports on Florida waders, 131–32; analogy to religious group, 138–54; founding, 140; mission, 141–42; finances, 142–43, 149; methods, publications, and facilities, 143–52
Audubon State Park, Kentucky, 16, 155
Audubon, Victor G. (son), 12, 13
Authenticity problem: mentioned, 8, 20, 35, 44, 45, 63, 97, 100

Bachman, John: meeting, 13; collaborator, 22, 29, 111; comment on Audubon in age, 114

Banding, bird, 27, 160
Bankruptcy, 105
Barro (horse), 85–87, 156
Bear, black, 29, 71–72, 88–89, 91
Beechwoods Plantation, 107
Birds: association with plants in paintings, 25–27; banding, 27, 160; Common Greenshank, 28; Townsend's Bunting, 28; behavior, 33–34; Chimney Swift, 33–34; Great White Heron, 116; Broadwinged Hawk, 161. *See also* Passenger Pigeon, Herons, and other specific bird names
Birds of America: start of work, 5; distribution, 7, 14; size of folio, 7, 42; subscriptions, 8–9, 113; completion, 12; costs, 14; descriptions, 14–15, 43; present locations, 16; modern reprint, 147; Mill Grove set, 16. *See also* Copper plates, Portfolio, Lizars, Havells, Mason, and Promotion
Bison (buffalo), 91, 95, 121–23
Boone, Daniel, mentioned, 20, 55, 63, 67, 73, 90
Botany, 27, 112. *See also* Plants, Birds
Bradley, Guy, martyred warden, 128–29. *See also* McLeod

Camps, Audubon Society, 145–46
Catlin, George, 122, 123, 124
Chapman, Frank M., 128, 129, 140, 141, 156
Character. *See* Temperament, Values
Chimney Swift, 33–34
Chronicles, American, 62–63, 68, 70–71, 79, 90, 92–94
Cincinnati, Western Museum, job at, 5
Clark, George Rogers, mentioned, 67, 71, 166
Clark, William (of Lewis and Clark Expedition), mentioned, 37, 67, 166

172

Index 173

Collecting specimens, need for, 117–19
Conservation: Audubon as symbol of, xi, 116, 124; literature, 19, 120; attitude toward, 57, 119–22 *passim;* relation to hunting, 116–17; Audubon's influence on, 129; analogy in religious groups, 137
Cooper, James Fenimore, 62, 93
Copper plates of bird engravings, 7, 15
Cranes, Whooping, refuge, 151
Critics of Audubon, mentioned, 44–45, 46, 47, 53, 58, 59, 113
Cuvier, Frederic and Georges, 31–32

Darwin, Charles, 21, 59
Development, Florida Everglades terrain, 132–33
Disasters, natural: logjam released, 84; flood, 84, 94; earthquake of 1811, 75, 86, 93; fire, 88; Florida hurricane, 93; general, 93–94
Distinctions: name commemoration, ix; learned societies, 8, 15; recognized by royalty, 9, 108
Diversity, natural, 133

Eccentrics: Jarvis, J. W., 81. *See also* Rafinesque
Ecology, 19–20, 23–24, 26
Edinburgh, 7, 110
Egg collecting from seabirds, 119–20
Egrets. *See* Herons
Endangered species, 121, 144
Environmental conditions, early, 116, 118
Environmental movement, mentioned, 123, 127, 129, 131, 133, 137, 142, 144, 153
Episodes in *Ornithological Biography:* aims, 11, 22, 43, 62; credibility, 20–22, 45; evaluation as literature and history, 61–63; content, 74
European reception, 7, 9, 108, 110
Everglades National Park, 128, 131–35
Everglades, reclamation of, 134–35
Expeditions and journeys: Alleghenies crossed, 3; Florida, 11; Texas, 12; Labrador and Newfoundland, 11, 119–21; Missouri River, upper, 13, 75, 114, 121–23; winter flatboat trip, 70; trips summary, 75
Exploitation, animal. *See* Persecution

Fatland Ford, Bakewell estate, 2, 160
Feather trade, millinery: defense of, 127; opposition to, 127–30 *passim;* Lacey Act, 129. *See also* Audubon Society, Bradley, Herons, McLeod
Ferret, black-footed, new mammal, 111

Fieldbooks and their expansion, 149
Fire, forest, 87–88
Fires, 163. *See also* Woodcraft
Fishing lore, 93
Floods, 23, 94
Folkways. *See* Chronicles, Episodes
Food habits, birds, 33
Foods. *See* Woodcraft
Fries, W. H., 14–16
Frontier lore. *See* Chronicles, Episodes
Fuertes, Louis Agassiz, x, 109
Fur trade, condemnation of, 121

Geological descriptions, 23
Golden Plover slaughter, 119
Grinnell, George Bird, 140, mentioned, 117, 126
Guns, 73, 99

Harris, Edward, 91, 122
Havells, father and son, engravers, 9, 26, 42
Hawk, Broad-winged, posing alive, 160–61
Henderson, Kentucky, 4, 103, 155. *See also* Audubon State Park
Herons (Egrets): Great White Heron, 116; Reddish Egret, 118; Great Egret, 125; persecuted for plumes, 127–30 *passim*
Honors. *See* distinctions
Humor, 69–70, 80–82. *See* also Tall tales
Hunter, Audubon as, 58, 71–73, 93, 98, 117–18
Hunting: black bear, 90–91; swan, 91; defense of, 116–17; Golden Plover kill, 119; Wild pigeon kill, 156–57; prohibited in parks and refuges, 156–57. *See also* Bison, Hunter
Hurricane, fictitious, 21, 93
Hyperbole, 83–84. *See* Tall tales

Ibis, White, 116, 119
Indian Key, Florida, 161–63
Indians, mentioned, 57, 65, 70, 90–91, 98, 106, 120

Jokes, practical, 35, 80–81
Journals, original Audubon, 51–54; changes by editor M. R. Audubon, 50–51; writing analyzed, 54–58

Key West, Florida, 161–62

Labrador, 11, 119–21, 166
Language skills and limitations, 97
Lehman, G., 25
Leopold, Aldo, mentioned, 20, 117
Letters, 52–54
Literature: nature, 64; influence of con-

Literature—Cont.
 temporary authors, 55, 65. See also Naturalists, literary
Lizars, W. H., engraver, 7–8, 9, 110
Logjam, Maine stream, 84
London, stay in, 8–9, 12
Louisiana, 5, 106–7
Louisville, Kentucky, 2–4, 156–57

MacGillivray, W., 11, 38, 50–51
McLeod, Columbus, warden martyred, 129. See Bradley, Guy
Mammal (ferret), new species, 111
Mammals. See Viviparous Quadrupeds
Martin, Maria, 25, 111
Martyrs in anti-plume fight. See Bradley, McLeod
Mason, Joseph, 5, 73, 105
Mill Grove: arrival at, 1803, 2; woods experience, 67; history of house, 158; condition in 1820, 158; life at, 160–61
Minniesland home, New York, 13, 15, 75, 163
Mission, Audubon's, 5, 74, 77. See also Birds of America, Ornithological Biography, Viviparous Quadrupeds
Mother, Jeanne Rabin, 101
Muir, John, 124, 138
Museums about Audubon: Mill Grove house, 15, 141, 158–59; Audubon State Park, Kentucky, 16, 155
Music, 71, 107–8

National Audubon Society. See Audubon Society
National Park idea, 123
National Park Service, 134, 151
Natural area idea, Muir's, 124
Naturalist, definition and types, 18–19
Naturalists: literary, 19, 25, 64, 133; scientific, 19–20; associations with, 30; preceding Audubon, 63–64
Nature Conservancy, 123, 124, 140
New Orleans, 5, 104
Nolte, V., 80, 104
Nuclear winter night, 152
Nuttall's dogwood, named by Audubon, 27
Nuttall, Thomas, 12, 22, 27
Ornithological Biography: initiation, 10; progress, 12; MacGillivray's help, 38, 49; description, 59–61, 74–75
Ornithology: status, 32; contributions by Audubon, 30, 46–47

Parakeet, Carolina, 156
Passenger Pigeon. See Pigeon, Passenger
Pearson, T. Gilbert, 127, 129
Persecution, of birds and mammals. See Egg collecting, Feather trade, Golden Plover, Hunting
Personality. See Temperament, Appearance
Peterson, Russell W., 142
Philadelphia, 2, 4, 22, 86, 157
Phoebes, tame, drawn, banded, 27, 160
Pigeons, Passenger, 156–57, mentioned, 116, 121, 124
Pirate story, Episodes, 87
Place, sense of, 163–64
Plants in bird plates, 25–27
Plume trade and its opposition. See Feather trade
Portfolio, bird drawings: displayed to Wilson, 3; loss of, 4, 5
Portrait, painting of, 105
Portraits of Audubon, 73, 108, 137, 159
Promotion methods for Birds, 6–7, 16
Publications of National Audubon Society, 147–49

Rabin(e), Jeanne (mother), 101
Rafinesque, C. S., 35, 80, 81
Refuges, wildlife, 150, 151–52. See also Wildlife sanctuaries
Religion, 69, 137
Roosevelt, Theodore, mentioned, 19, 115, 117, 121, 127, 129, 139, 151
Royal patronage, 9, 108
Rozier, Ferdinand, 3, 70, 103

Sandy Key, Everglades Park, 118, 121, 131
Scott, Sir Walter, 6, 62
Self-portrayal, 79, 108
Seton, Ernest Thompson, originated field mark use, 149
Slaves, 89, 98, 105
Societies, learned, 8, 9, 15, 73, 110
Squatters along the Mississippi, 92
Stories, importance of, 94. See also Chronicles, Tall tales
Strobel, Dr. Benjamin, 110–11
Style, literary, 55, 62–63, 65, 83, 85
Subscriptions. See Birds of America
Swan hunt, 91, 98

Tall tales, 70–71, 79, 84–87
Taxidermy, mentioned, 5, 24, 43, 74, 105, 159
Techniques, pioneer, 79, 92
Temperament and character, 51, 52–53, 55, 56, 65, 68–69, 87, 92, 94, 97, 107. See also Authenticity; Joker
Territoriality in humans, 163

Values, intangible, 68, 88, 93–94, 95
Viviparous Quadrupeds work, 13, 29–30

Wildlife sanctuaries, Audubon Society, 16; system summary, 150–52; hunting prohibited, 151
Wilson, Alexander: meeting with, 3–4; use of his book, 37, 41; Passenger Pigeon estimate, 116
Winter camp, 72

Woodcraft: foods, 57, 106; fires, 70, 72; tools, 72; love of woods, 96–97, 106. *See also* Chronicles, Guns, Hunter
Woodsman, American: in Europe, xi, 6, 8, 55–56, 61, 74; symbol, xi, 67–77 *passim*
Writer, Audubon as, 48–65 *passim*, 67, 79. *See also* Chronicles, Tall tales